Victoria Talwar is the leading authority on the development of lying and deception in children. I'm a huge fan of her work. *The Truth About Lying: Teaching Honesty to Children at Every Age and Stage* is especially for parents, but I recommend it to anyone interested in the topic.

Talwar is a renowned researcher of children's deception, and this book will enhance her reputation among scholars and, what's more important, explain the nuances of lying to a lay audience. It is chock full of evidence-based insights for parents and children. There is nothing quite like it, and both parents and students will benefit immensely from reading it.

the truth about lying

the truth about lying

teaching honesty to children at every age and stage

victoria talwar, phd

 AMERICAN PSYCHOLOGICAL ASSOCIATION

Published by
APA LifeTools
750 First Street, NE
Washington, DC 20002
https://www.apa.org

Order Department
https://www.apa.org/pubs/books
order@apa.org

In the U.K., Europe, Africa, and the Middle East, copies may be ordered from
Eurospan
https://www.eurospanbookstore.com/apa
info@eurospangroup.com

Typeset in Avenir by Circle Graphics, Inc., Reisterstown, MD

Printer: Gasch Printing, Odenton, MD
Cover Designer: Mark Karis

Library of Congress Cataloging-in-Publication Data

Names: Talwar, Victoria, 1974- author.
Title: The truth about lying : teaching honesty to children at every age
    and stage / by Victoria Talwar.
Description: Washington, DC : American Psychological Association, [2022] |
    Includes bibliographical references.
Identifiers: LCCN 2021059074 (print) | LCCN 2021059075 (ebook) |
    ISBN 9781433836213 (paperback) | ISBN 9781433840272 (ebook)
Subjects: LCSH: Honesty. | Truthfulness and falsehood in children. |
    Parenting. | BISAC: FAMILY & RELATIONSHIPS / Parenting / General |
    PSYCHOLOGY / Developmental / Child
Classification: LCC BF723.H7 T35 2022 (print) | LCC BF723.H7 (ebook) |
    DDC 179/.9--dc23/eng/20211217
LC record available at https://lccn.loc.gov/2021059074
LC ebook record available at https://lccn.loc.gov/2021059075

https://doi.org/10.1037/0000300-000

Printed in the United States of America

10 9 8 7 6 5 4 3 2 1

Contents

the truth about lying

Introduction: We *Can* Teach Honesty to Children

Truthfulness is the foundation of our lives. On it rests our relations with others and our trust and security in those around us, in our community, in our institutions, and in our ability to organize, function, and govern our society. Without it as a foundation, we have no firm basis to build our relationships or institutions. Does this sound overblown to you?

Let's do a thought experiment together. Imagine there is a fire in your office tower. One of your colleagues is the designated fire warden for your floor, and they are giving you directions. You follow their directions; there is no time to lose, and you trust your colleague to guide you. You get to the ground floor, and firefighters are rushing in through the doors. They, too, give you directions. Again, you follow those directions and get to safety. You trust that they are trying to communicate information and directions to help you. You trust they are giving you truthful, accurate guidance—that they are trying to help you, not deliberately mislead you. You may not have time to think this consciously; you just react with the assumption that you can trust what they are saying. In this case, this assumption helps you move quickly and protect your life.

Because honesty is a foundation for relationships and institutions, we want our children to be honest. We have relationships of trust that we build with our children. When children lie, we can feel indignant, upset, frustrated, angry, or even betrayed. These are natural feelings when we discover someone has lied to us. However, with our children, these feelings can be even more acute and are mixed with concern: Why is my child lying to me? What does this mean about my child, about our relationship? What should I do to stop this behavior? This book aims to answer these questions for parents and adults who care for children.

If we want children to grow up to be truthful and caring adults, we have to teach them. Children acquire behaviors, abilities, and knowledge through education. We teach children many things: how to cross safely at street corners, how to do multiplication, how to write an essay. We must also actively teach them to be helpful, actively engaged adults who exemplify qualities of character we feel are vital to their positive growth and to our world. Expecting children to notice these lessons on their own is neglecting and leaving to chance the very behaviors and qualities that make a difference to their success.

If you value honesty and want your children to be truthful, you must talk to them about it, teach them what it looks like in different situations, and help them to develop their own understanding and value of this quality. You must discuss different situations and how you can practice honesty. Given the temptation to lie that we all can face, the complexities of our social interactions, and our desire to act with concern for others as well as our own interests, children need help to navigate how to be truthful and honest in different situations as they grow and encounter new social contexts and new friends, and as their own self-identity develops.

We *can* teach children to be honest. As a psychological scientist, I have spent years studying children's lying and truth-telling. Based on my studies and those of other researchers, we know what works and what doesn't. In this book, I present practical, proven ways to foster children's truthfulness from early childhood to the late teens, when children are transitioning to adulthood. This includes both proactive approaches, such as talking to children about honesty and modeling it for them, as well as how to respond when lying does occur (as it inevitably will!). I have written this book primarily for parents. It is also a valuable resource for teachers, counselors, youth group leaders, and others who work with children.

Because my recommendations are based on psychological studies, I also describe some of the most interesting experiments that are relevant to my recommendations. Readers who are more academically minded may wish to read the original studies, so I provide citations where they are relevant. However, the book remains solidly geared toward parents and those who work with children, so the emphasis is on practical recommendations that you can use to foster honesty in children.

When there is specific advice for different ages or research findings that are about a specific developmental stage, I refer to the specific ages of the children involved or refer to the developmental stages depicted in the figure. When speaking in general terms that apply to your children across ages (whether 7 or 14 years of age) or referring to the relationship between parent and their offspring, I use the term "child."

The first three chapters of the book, which collectively make up Part I—What You Need to Know About Children's Lies— provide essential background information. To teach children effectively to be honest, you must first have a broader perspective about how common (or uncommon) lying is in adults. As Chapter 1 explains, most adults are honest most of the time, but even adults who are honest almost all the time will tell an occasional lie. Knowing this will hopefully help you develop a wise and compassionate stance toward children while teaching them to be honest.

Ages and Stages

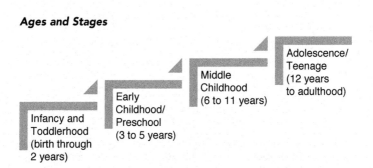

Infancy and Toddlerhood (birth through 2 years)

Early Childhood/ Preschool (3 to 5 years)

Middle Childhood (6 to 11 years)

Adolescence/ Teenage (12 years to adulthood)

Chapter 2 examines how children develop the ability to tell lies and what influences their decisions to tell the truth or lie. Very young children do not initially tell lies. This ability is one that actually emerges as their verbal and cognitive skills become increasingly sophisticated. By understanding how lying emerges and develops, you can know what typical behavior in children is at different ages.

Chapter 3 examines what motivates people to lie. Understanding motivations helps us to see the underlying conditions that make lying desirable over and above any concern for and value of truthfulness. If we know why a child lies, we can address the underlying motivation and create conditions that promote truthfulness.

Part II—Teaching Honesty to Children—is the heart of the book in which I share practical strategies to promote honesty in children. Because many parents are primarily concerned with what to do when a child lies, we begin there. Chapters 4 and 5 explain how to respond to lies in a way that develops truthfulness and other positive qualities in children. The goal is to remain calm, respond to the underlying motivation, and focus on teaching the child rather than making them suffer.

Reactive strategies are necessary, but we also need proactive strategies. Chapters 6 through 10 present proactive strategies for teaching honesty to children. These strategies include talking to children about honesty (Chapter 6), acknowledging when children tell the truth (Chapter 7), modeling truthfulness (Chapter 8), encouraging open communication with children (Chapter 9), and building a foundation for moral character (Chapter 10).

Although most lies that children tell are clearly undesirable and can be handled using the strategies in Chapters 4 and 5, there are some gray areas, which Part III—The Gray Zone—addresses. For example, depending on the situation, it may be appropriate or inappropriate to tell secrets or to tattle. Chapter 11 explores these issues. In addition, while telling lies is a normal part of child development (even if we do not like it!), sometimes lies can be a sign of other underlying problems.

This is especially true when lies are chronic or compulsive. Chapter 12 considers when lying may be a serious problem behavior and how it may be related to different childhood disorders as well as risky and antisocial behavior in teenagers.

The book closes with remarks on how teaching children honesty is a process and how to manage our expectations. There is no one "fix" or one perfect approach. And perfection is not attainable. However, as is discussed throughout the book, we can teach children to be honest, and, with care and compassion, we can create bonds of trust within our relationships in which truthfulness is valued, practiced, and nurtured.

PART I

What You Need to Know About Children's Lies

1

Keeping Things in Perspective: Adult Behavior

It is easy to get upset when your child lies. After all, honesty is an essential value for society to function, and when your child lies to you, it can feel like a personal affront. But to foster honesty, it is best to avoid overreacting. In Chapters 4 and 5, I explain the most effective ways to respond to a lie. For now, I want to present a broader perspective that will (hopefully) help you keep calm when your child inevitably lies to you. Essentially, I want you to remember that even in adulthood, everyone lies, but *most* people are honest *most* of the time.

Understanding adult behavior is important. It helps us reflect on our own behavior, it helps us reflect on the behavior of adults around us and whom children are observing, and it also helps us think about how we wish our children to grow and what type of adults they will be.

In this chapter, I briefly talk about what *is* lying, how common it is, and why adults tell lies despite the importance of telling the truth. I also discuss our general abilities to detect lies. This provides a context to understanding children's behavior as well as developing a compassionate and consistent response to children's behavior. If we wish to raise children to be honest, we need to think about adult behavior that children observe. But first, let us widen the lens a little to look at deception in general.

INTENTIONAL DECEPTION

Deception is a common phenomenon in nature. Animals from insects to primates use various means, such as camouflage and mimicry, to gain a survival advantage over predators, prey, and even members of the same species. However, camouflage and mimicry rely on physical deceptions and do not require any cognitive sophistication or intentional misinformation. *Lying*, on the other hand, is an act of deception in which there is a verbal statement made with the intention of creating a false belief in another. Lying is fundamentally tied to language. While other physical acts of deception might also be intentional, such as pointing an individual in the opposite direction from one's store of food, it is difficult to determine whether deception seen in animals is intentional in nature. Nonetheless, notable cases of tactical deception have been observed in nonhuman primates (e.g., Byrne & Whiten, 1992; Jolly, 1996; Whiten & Byrne, 1988), and it has been suggested that such cases are intentional in nature.

So, while there may be some instances of deception in animals, intentional deception may be less common and is more commonly displayed by humans. Furthermore, the language requirement makes lying almost exclusively human territory. Lying is an act that is possibly as old as human language. It is a complex behavior, and although the term "lying" could be used to refer to simply stating something untrue, lies actually involve multiple elements. One way to define lying is as a statement that is deliberate and is intended to deceive. Saying something that is untrue is not necessarily lying; it is possible for a speaker to make an honest mistake, believing their inaccurate information. For instance, you are asked by your neighbor when the outdoor pool opens. You have always known the pool to open at 11 a.m. and tell your neighbor this information. However, you are mistaken. The local pool has changed its hours of operation and is now only open at noon. When you told your neighbor the false statement that it was open at 11 a.m., you were not intentionally trying to deceive them;

rather, you were stating what you believed to be true. You made an honest mistake.

When the speaker's statement is false, but the person does not intend to deceive, this would still not be categorized as a lie. When we use metaphors, hyperbole, sarcasm, or tell jokes, we are not intending to deceive, and we typically do not consider these statements as lies. If it is raining outside on a gray, cold day and I remark, "What a beautiful day!" others will understand my sarcastic remark to mean that I think it is the opposite of what I am saying. I also make that statement with the intention that others will know I think that it is not a beautiful day. We usually denote such statements by our tone and facial expressions that help alert listeners to the speaker's intention (e.g., I am saying it is beautiful weather because I want to highlight my belief that the weather is the complete opposite). Lying is when we make statements in which we intend the other to believe the false assertion. We want the others to believe something we do not think is true, and we want them to think that we believe it.

LITTLE LIES, BIG LIES, AND PROLIFIC LIARS

How common is lying in general? Research with adults suggests that acts of dishonesty like lying and cheating are not uncommon. Telling lies is a not an unusual occurrence in adult life. We do not like liars, and we do not like to be lied to, yet we occasionally resort to this strategy to get what we want, to avoid what we do not want, to be polite, or to sometimes help another.

For instance, in one study, the researchers found people commonly cheat—but only a little bit (Mazar et al., 2008). In that study, adults were given 20 matrix number tasks to solve and then self-report how many they got wrong. The task was difficult, and on running the experiment and checking people's answers, the researchers knew that, on average, people could solve only four of the tasks. However, when people could self-report how many tasks they had solved correctly, the researchers found that the majority of people inflated their score. By how much? On average, people reported they had solved two more matrices than they actually had solved. Notably, they only cheated a little. When the researchers increased the incentive by increasing the amount of money participants could win per solved matrix, they did not see a jump in people's false claims. People still only cheated a little. The researchers suggested that people cheat a little to increase the benefits to themselves but not too much so that they maintain their self-concept as being essentially honest. So, we may cheat a little to benefit ourselves just up to the limit that we can tolerate it without making us uncomfortable about ourselves. We like to preserve our feelings about our essential honesty and decency.

It appears that in general, most people are truthful most of the time. For instance, to track adults' daily lie-telling, researchers asked adults from a wide section of society to keep diaries of their lies for a week (DePaulo et al., 1996; DePaulo & Kashy, 1998). When examining these diaries, they found that, on average, Americans lie once or twice per day. Most of these lies are what researchers term *low-stakes lies*, that is, lies that have little serious consequences, such as feigning to your friend that you like the muffins they made and brought into work to share. Most of the lies people told on a regular basis were small lies in the course of their daily interactions. Participants most commonly told lies about themselves—how they felt, or what they thought, or about their actions, such as their whereabouts. They reported that they felt the lies they told were not serious and were generally not planned in advance, and they did not feel high levels of distress after telling them and were unlikely to ruminate about them. Nevertheless, participants also described the interactions in which they told no lies as more intimate and pleasant that the interactions during which they lied.

These researchers also found that lying frequency was higher among women, among younger people, and during interactions between women. However, other studies (e.g., Serota & Levine,

2015; Serota et al., 2010) have found that men reported telling more lies overall. A consistent finding in the research, though, is that younger adults tell more lies than older people and that with maturity, honesty increases.

Following up on this research, other researchers surveyed a cross-section of the U.S. adult population. They found evidence that most people are honest most of the time. A national survey asked 1,000 American adults to report the number of lies they told over a 24-hour period. Of the participants, 60% reported telling no lies at all. However, a small subset of people told frequent lies, and a few prolific liars told the most lies (Serota et al., 2010). These researchers found that approximately 5% of people accounted for more than 50% of all the lies told in their sample!

| *Most people are honest most of the time.*

In another study involving a large sample from the United Kingdom, the findings were similar: Most people were honest most of the time with a small subset of people being prolific liars (Serota & Levine, 2015). The researchers found that prolific liars tell not only "little lies" per day—on average, six lies per day—but they also tell more "big lies" per day. *Big lies* are lies having more serious consequences, such as lies to your partner about where and with whom you have been. The U.K. study found that although most people did not tell big lies on a daily basis—the average was close to zero—prolific liars reported telling between two and three big lies per day.

While most people consider lying to protect another person's feelings as more acceptable than other lies, prolific liars are less concerned about hurting other's feelings (Serota & Levine, 2015). They are more likely to think that lying overall is acceptable, including lying to keep a secret or lying to a child about something the child cannot have. However, prolific liars do not lie with impunity. They are more likely to report being dumped by their partners or being fired for telling lies.

The researchers reported that at work, prolific liars are 4 times more likely than the rest of the population to have been reprimanded for lying and almost 9 times more likely to have been fired for their dishonest behavior. For a small number of people, dishonesty permeates their lives from their work to their personal relationships. However, for most people, although they report telling more lies when they were younger, as they mature, they are less likely to resort to lying and more likely to become more honest in their communications.

All this research confirms an important fact: Most people grow up to be honest most of the time. So, when your preschooler starts flexing their mental and social skills trying to tell a fib, you can keep that in mind. They are unlikely to develop into a consummate liar and fraudster. Although children lie at a higher rate than adults do, they usually grow into honest adults because parents, educators, and others who work with children teach and socialize children to abandon lying as a frequent method of managing their social lives. We have to be prepared to forgive the occasional minor digression as we, too, would hope to be forgiven.

TRUTH DEFAULT THEORY

Based on these empirical research findings, *truth default theory* explains that most of the time we are honest (Levine, 2014). We "default" to honest communication. One of the fundamental assumptions of our conversations is that we are trying to be cooperative and are truthful in our communications.

If we consider all our communications in a day or over a week, we would note that almost all were truthful. Which ones were not? Why were you not truthful on those occasions? What prompted you to deviate from telling the truth? It is worth noting your own lies or instances of dishonesty—not as an exercise in self-flagellation but to learn about what motivates and prompts you to abandon your truth default. We tend to lie only when we see it as unavoidable or most expedient. We choose to tell the truth or to lie based on our interpersonal goals. Most of the time, telling the truth helps us reach that goal.

On certain occasions, we may perceive lying as the faster, easier way to achieve our goals. For instance, a new employee is late to work because they overslept. Their boss asks them why they are late. In an instance, the new employee considers that saying they overslept (the truth) may put them in an unfavorable light with their new boss, so they quickly choose the alternative of lying to present what they believe is a more acceptable reason for being late. The employee tells their boss that there was a traffic jam (a lie). However, at another time, the motivation to lie may not be high and may not override the truth. Imagine a couple of years later, the same employee is late for work, having overslept. This is not a regular habit, and the employee feels established in their job and assured in their coworkers and boss's judgment of them. The boss asks why the employee is late. They respond without hesitation: "I'm sorry. I overslept." We tend to lie only when we feel it is necessary and are justified. It is only when the truth serves as an obstacle to our goals that we may choose to deceive rather than be honest.

In many cases, lying actually requires more cognitive resources than telling the truth. Lying requires more effort. We have to think of the lie, generate a response, and inhibit any behavior that may arouse suspicions or state any information that may contradict the lie. Researchers looking at brain functioning have found that lying is more difficult for the brain to process than telling the truth (Ganis & Keenan, 2009). The act of lying leads to increased activity in various brain regions. It takes the brain longer to formulate a deceptive answer than it does a truthful answer when a person is asked to answer questions at a faster speed. If lying requires effort, we have to be sufficiently motivated to use this strategy. Most of the time, it is easier to default to the truth.

Not only are we truthful most of the time, we also operate on the presumption that the communications of others are truthful. We operate under the assumption that other people are basically honest. This presumption on honesty helps us to communicate and work together. It typically leads to correct belief states because most communication is honest most of the time.

DETECTING LIES

The presumption that most communication is honest also has implications for detecting deception. Because most of our interactions are based on honest communication, we tend to have a truth bias. As truth default theory asserts, we have a natural inclination to believe other people. We usually take other people's communications at face value. This works well for us because, most of the time, people are being truthful. Unless we have some reason to trigger skepticism, we do not usually actively consider the possibility of deceit when others are communicating with us. It is our default state and has an adaptive quality to it. When I say "adaptive," I mean it is something that generally promotes positive, successful functioning in our world. If we did not have this default, we would then scrutinize every interaction, every communication. This would make life difficult and would halt most human interactions. How would coworkers ever get anything done? How would a team ever work together? How would we be able to develop close relationships with friends and family? We would need to devote a lot of time and effort to fact-checking as well as to the scrutiny of others' behavior and motives. We would descend into paranoia and achieve little.

| *We have a natural inclination to believe other people.*

However, when we have some reason to be skeptical and to question the veracity of a statement, our default may be overridden. Overriding this default does not automatically lead to the conclusion that the other person has intentionally lied to us, because we know they may have made a mistake. We are triggered to reexamine the veracity of the statement and consider what the person intended to communicate to us. Sometimes that may lead us to believe the statement is not true, but the other person did not intend to lie. Other times, our suspicions are raised that another is trying to dupe us.

What can trigger us to override this skepticism? It can be some prior knowledge. The person says something we know cannot be true. We can have knowledge that contradicts the lie. For instance, the teenager tells their mother that they were at the library studying at 8 p.m. on Saturday night, but the mother knows the library closes at 6 p.m. on Saturday.

It can also be based on prior experience. For instance, we may have experienced the individual lying, or someone may have told us that the individual is dishonest, which alerts us to scrutinize that individual's statements and behavior. If a person has lied to you in the past, you may be more careful about believing everything they say.

We may be triggered to scrutinize a person's honesty because something in the other person's behavior triggers us to question their intentions or their statement. For instance, they can sound or look nervous, or they may behave in a way that you find suspicious.

However, even when we have some reason to believe that others may be deceitful, we may not always detect it accurately. In psychology experiments in which participants will be shown videos and are told in advance that some people in those videos will tell the truth or lie, accuracy is above chance level—but only just. A robust finding across many studies is that adults accurately detect lies approximately 54% of the time, which is only slightly better than guessing (i.e., slightly better than a 50–50 chance rate; Bond & DePaulo, 2006). We are not that good at detecting others' deceit.

Although nonverbal cues can alert us to someone's deceit, we are not always able to perceive them if those cues are visible. While it may be that careful attention to people's demeanor and nonverbal behaviors may lead to detection, it is not necessarily a reliable method for most partially because we may miss the nonverbal "leaks" that may trigger our detection of falsehood. We may miss them because we are not looking for these leaks and because they can be fleeting.

Furthermore, these nonverbal cues are not always indicative of deceit. The suspicious behaviors may not be reliable indicators of deceit but of just emotion, which may or may not be triggered by dishonest motivations. For instance, common nonverbal cues people associate with deceit include eye contact, fidgeting, and nervousness in the voice. However, not all liars show these nonverbal cues. And truth-tellers can also show these cues given their personal mannerisms or because of stress or nervousness. If you are someone who has never flown on a plane before, you can imagine how you might appear nervous, have darting eye contact, and be restless in an airport as you wait in a security line. These are not necessarily signs that you have something to hide and are a threat; rather, they are signs of your stress levels and nervousness. So people can show these cues for reasons other than being deceitful and have something to hide.

There is no Pinocchio's nose. We have no surefire way to detect all deception or even some deception. There are ways in which experts can, on the basis of probability, believe that someone may indeed be lying. However, there is no foolproof way of detecting lying through nonverbal behaviors.

> *We have no surefire way to detect all deception or even some deception.*

As truth default theory tells us, however, most lies are detected either through comparing what is said to what is or what can be known or thorough solicitation of a confession. As you will see in Chapter 2, this is true with children. Although they can show cues in their demeanor, most of the time, parents become aware of a child's dishonest statements through knowledge about the situation or through the child's inability to give plausible explanations. Younger children in particular are more likely to just confess.

For parents and those working with children, the most important thing to know is that there's no foolproof method of detecting deception, and even so-called experts don't get it right all the time. Even if there were a way for you to learn to be the ultimate deception detector, that would not really help to make children truthful and honest. It would be a reactive way to deal with their behavior and try to make them honest. The "lie detector approach" to teaching honesty means only that children may learn to be truthful if they think you are nearby but not necessarily when they are out engaging with others in the world. Furthermore, that approach can turn you into a paranoid parent who is always scrutinizing their child's behavior lest you miss a fib. This is an unpleasant way to parent and is not conducive to parent health, child health, or the fostering of a strong bond between parent and child.

For healthier and longer lasting results, the way to foster honesty is through teaching children about it and to instill stronger principles and motivations to be honest. This is a more proactive way to create meaningful change. We want methods that teach and instill in children positive behaviors, such as honesty that they exhibit even when we are not around to "see them" and to detect their lies. On a larger scale, if we really want to make our society more honest, it isn't really about creating detectors but, rather, creating citizens for whom truthfulness is so highly valued and so strongly motivated that it becomes an overriding principle of behavior.

CONCLUSION

Adults do tell occasional lies. However, most people grow up to be largely honest and truthful. Reflecting on adult behavior can help us in reacting to children's lies and help us keep the behavior in perspective. It can help us to not overreact and to concentrate on teaching children to be honest and how to deal with different life situations in which dishonesty may be tempting. I discuss this more throughout the book.

Starting by looking at our own behaviors as adults can help us deal with children's lies calmly and with compassion. It is also helpful to understand that children's lie-telling emerges and develops throughout childhood. The next chapter discusses this topic. By understanding how adults behave and also what a typical part of children's development is, we can address and tailor our approach to the specific situation of our child to foster honesty and dissuade the development of lying as a habitual behavior.

2

How Lying Emerges as a Normal Part of Child Development

Lying is an undesirable behavior, and we do not wish children to tell lies. However, it is not the case that because a child tells a lie, they are going to grow up to be a "bad person." Lying is common among adults (see Chapter 1), and, as I outline in this chapter, it also is a normal part of child development. Although undesirable, the ability to lie emerges and develops because of children's developing abilities to understand and interact with the world around them. While the rest of this book addresses how to deal with lying and how to foster honesty, this chapter discusses how children's lie-telling develops as a normal part of children's growing capacities and development. But first, I briefly explain how researchers examine children's lies.

HOW RESEARCHERS STUDY CHILDREN'S LIES

Lying is a difficult behavior to observe and by its very nature is concealed and can be difficult to detect. As a result, observational studies cannot easily capture the behavior, especially if it is successful. Furthermore, researchers need to know the factual truth (e.g., who ate the cookie) to know if a statement (e.g., "No, I didn't eat it") is true or false. In addition, to capture children's everyday abilities to lie successfully (or not), researchers cannot simply instruct children to lie because that does not create a natural situation in which the liar is motivated to create a false belief in the listener's mind. When individuals lie, they typically do so spontaneously without instructions to do so by the lie-recipient. With these requirements in mind, researchers have created experimental paradigms to examine children's spontaneous lie-telling in the laboratory.

One common method used to examine children's spontaneous lie-telling is the *temptation resistance paradigm*. In this paradigm, children have the opportunity to commit a transgression and are later asked about their behavior. For example, preschool children are commonly invited to play a game in which they are instructed not to peek at a forbidden toy when an experimenter momentarily leaves the room. In other versions, older children and adolescents are told not to look at the answers to a quiz. The strictly communicated rule is that there should be no peeking at the answer or the toy. In both cases, some children choose to peek; others do not. On the experimenter's return, the children are asked whether they peeked at the toy or the quiz answers. Here, the children can choose to lie or tell the truth. This situation is usually videotaped using a hidden camera so that children's true peeking behavior can be verified and compared with their responses to the experimenter. This method creates conditions similar to everyday situations children encounter. The children are self-motivated to lie and are not directed on how to behave. The children who do peek can choose to confess or lie about their transgression. Because these studies are controlled experiments, the researchers also can verify whether the child is lying or telling the truth.

Using this paradigm, researchers have examined children's ability to tell lies to conceal their transgression and to avoid punishment. Typically, 80% to 90% of 3- to 5-year-olds cheat in these situations by peeking (Talwar & Crossman, 2011). The temptation to peek is too high, and their self-control abilities are still developing. With age, in middle childhood and adolescence, children are better able to resist the temptation, but still approximately half may peek. As a result, we have learned that children as young as 3 years of age are able to tell lies to conceal their transgressions. For instance, one study found that approximately a third of 3-year-olds who peeked at the forbidden toy denied peeking (Lewis et al., 1989). In studies with my colleagues, we found that only approximately 25% to 29% of children younger than 3 years told a lie in the temptation resistance paradigm (Leduc et al., 2017; Williams et al., 2016). In one of our early studies, we found that 78% of children between 4 and 7 years of age lied about peeking at a toy, whereas only about one third of 3-year-olds lied (Talwar & Lee, 2002a). In subsequent studies, we also found that the majority of children between 7 and 11 years of age lie about such a transgression (Talwar, Gordon, & Lee, 2007). Overall, there is clear evidence that children's lie-telling emerges in the preschool years and rapidly increases with age.

DEVELOPMENT OF LYING

The age pattern in which 3-year-olds and younger are relatively less inclined to lie about their transgression than older children has been observed in children from around the world. Hence, there is convergent evidence suggesting that children start being capable of telling lies in early childhood, and the development of their lie-telling ability appears to emerge from children's normal developing cognitive abilities to understand others and to control their own behaviors, as discussed in the next section.

The Toddler Years: Wish Fulfillment "Lies"

The earliest "lies" that adults may detect in children may not truly be intentional lies; rather, children younger than 3 and 4 years of age may initially tell false statements as "wish fulfillment." At the early start of scientific research on child development, Clara Stern along with her husband, William Stern, conducted observational work on their three children (Stern & Stern,

1999). She took detailed notes of each child's development throughout their childhood. In studying their cumulative data, the researchers noticed that many examples of early lying were what they termed as *pseudo lies*, false statements the children made that were mistaken claims or momentary impulsive utterances. Those pseudo lies reflected what the children "wished" or desired to be rather than intentionally deceptive statements.

For example, one observation of their 3-year-old daughter, Hilde, illustrates such a case. They were standing with their daughter on a hill and looking into the distance. The parents pointed out various sights to the daughter and asked if she could see them. Looking vaguely in the direction they pointed, she always answered yes. They doubted the truthfulness of Hilde's claims and tested her by asking if she could see a fictitious object, and she replied, "Yes." They suggested that in this context, Hilde had no intention to deceive her parents; she *wanted* to see what they were pointing out:

> It was just this wish to realize what we were intending for her that was being expressed in her "yes." It was not a confirmatory "yes I see that" but instead a desirous and expectant "yes, I too would like to see that." (Stern & Stern, 1999, pp. 35–36)

Children's false reports in toddlerhood and at the start of early childhood can be impulsive statements in which their attention while speaking is founded on a desire rather than on a belief. False desire-based responses or "wishful responses" are not necessarily mistakes or lies because the child may be inattentive rather than ignorant of the truth of their statement. These responses are different from when a child has a belief that they falsely represent, which is a lie. In an examination of children's false statements, researchers found that while children younger than 3 years of age could make false statements when asked about desires, when they were asked questions that required them to report their beliefs, they were unable to give false statements above chance until age 3½ years (Ahern et al.,

2011). So, very little children, toddlers, and early preschool-age children may make statements that seem to be false but reflect more what they desire rather than what they believe to be true or false.

Thus, the first "lies" that adults observe in children may actually be desire-based responses rather than fully fledged intentional deceit. However, it may be from these desire-based statements that intentional lies first emerge. By observing others' reactions to their statements, as well as by observing others' deception, children may learn the ability to make false statements to achieve personal goals, such as avoiding getting in trouble or getting something they want. At this level, however, children's lies appear to remain infrequent and tend to be limited to short, simple, verbal answers.

The Preschool Years: Children's Early Lies

The earliest lies children are often observed to tell are those to get out of trouble when they have committed a transgression. Examples include a child's denying taking a toy away from another child or stealing an illicit cookie.

Yet young children's early attempts at deceit are not skilled. Children can often fail to account for evidence that contradicts their lie (e.g., a child claims, "I didn't eat the cookie" when there is chocolate smeared on their face), or they may make subsequent statements that reveal their lie (e.g., later, when mom wonders aloud whether the cookies are stale, the child says, "Oh, no. They taste good").

> *There is clear evidence that children's lie-telling emerges in the preschool years and rapidly increases with age.*

Young children's earliest lies tend to be unsophisticated and are often confined to a one-word response rather than the more sophisticated elaborations of older children and adults.

Through middle childhood, their lie-telling abilities develop, and they become more skilled at avoiding detection.

Middle Childhood: The Ability to Lie Successfully Improves

To be able to lie successfully, a liar must be able to maintain their lie verbally, avoiding inconsistencies between their initial and subsequent false statements. For instance, when lying to deny eating a forbidden cookie, a child has to avoid saying anything that is incongruent with that lie. If the child later comments on how good the cookie tasted, this comment could arouse suspicion. This behavioral control must be exerted not only during the initial lie statement but also throughout all related subsequent conversations about the topic. For example, if an employee has taken time off work with the excuse of being sick with the flu, they later need to avoid talking to colleagues about a shopping expedition or a rigorous tennis practice that took place while the employee was supposedly "sick."

My colleague and I examined children's ability to maintain their lies about their transgression when asked follow-up questions about the identity of the forbidden toy (Talwar & Lee, 2002a). In our study, Canadian children who were told not to peek at a toy would later say that they knew it was the "Barney" dinosaur because "it looked like the shape of Barney" or that it was a "panda" because it was "black and white." Young children under 6 years of age were overwhelmingly likely to reveal incriminating information, like knowing the color of the toy, in subsequent statements after falsely denying having seen the toy. However, approximately half of 6- and 7-year-olds were able to conceal and maintain their lies when answering follow-up questions. Many of the children who concealed would answer that they could not know the identity or color of the toy "because I didn't look!" When adults were asked to judge which children were lying based on transcriptions of the children's verbal reports, they easily detected the younger children who revealed their transgressions verbally, whereas the older children who maintained their lies were indistinguishable from children who told the truth. Older children were better at telling lies that were plausible and harder to detect.

In another study, my colleagues and I saw this age trend continue with children between 7 and 11 years of age: The majority of the 11-year-olds concealed knowledge of the forbidden toy when asked follow-up questions (Talwar, Gordon, & Lee, 2007). In a study with children between 8 and 16 years of age, other researchers found that although only approximately half of children peeked at the answer to a math test with older children less likely to peek, 84% of children who did peek lied (Evans & Lee, 2010).

In these examples, children were telling a lie to conceal a transgression, that is, breaking a rule and cheating. This pattern of increasing their ability to tell lies that are more plausible occurs in other situations as well. In a study investigating whether children will tell a lie to be polite, my colleagues and I found a similar pattern (Talwar, Murphy, & Lee, 2007). Children were given a disappointing gift; they knew there was a toy basket full of gifts that included exciting-looking small toys. The children completed a task, and the researcher, expressing delight at their performance, gave them a wrapped prize from the gift basket. The gift-giver then left to get some materials from other room, leaving the child to unwrap their gift.

When the children unwrapped it, they found a bar of soap—and not just any bar of soap—not a lovely, sweetly scented bar of soap but a bar of pine-scented disinfectant soap! When the gift-giver returned, she asked, "Do you like the gift I gave you?" We found that 68% of the children expressed they did like the soap. However, when the gift-giver asked, "What do you like about it?" it was only the older children who were able to come up with some explanation, such as: "I like the soap because it smells nice." Memorably, one child said, "This is good. We really need soap at home. My dad is always stinky!" Later, when asked by researchers in the absence of the gift-giver if the children liked the gift, the children confessed they would have preferred another gift and were disappointed with the soap. Before the children went home, we made sure they all had a more appealing gift out of the gift basket. In exchange for another gift, the children always returned the soap.

While young children fail to answer plausibly probing questions about their behavior and are more likely to blurt information that will arouse suspicion, as children get older, they become more sophisticated at verbally concealing their lies. Throughout the school years, as children's cognitive and verbal abilities develop, they become more capable of giving plausible answers when questioned and more convincing in their lie-telling. Adults find older children's statements more credible and experience greater difficulty at differentiating between their true and their deceptive statements. The older one becomes, the more likely one is to deceive others convincingly.

Children's tendency to tell lies for prosocial reasons also increases with age. *Prosocial* is a psychological term meaning for the benefit of others. While the earliest lies children tell are generally for self-oriented reasons, even children in early childhood may tell lies for politeness reasons as they learn the social conventions about being polite. In middle childhood, children are more likely to tell a prosocial lie than are preschool children. In a study conducted in China using the disappointing gift paradigm, my colleagues and I found that 40% of 7-year-olds, 50% of 9-year-olds, and 60% of 11-year-olds told a politeness lie (Xu et al., 2010). When asked why they lied, most of the younger lie-tellers reported they were motivated to lie for nonprosocial reasons, such as claiming that the gift-giver would be mad at them if they told the truth. In contrast, the majority of older lie-tellers were motivated to lie for the prosocial reason of avoiding hurting the feelings of the gift-giver.

In another study, my colleagues and I explicitly examined children's motivations for telling politeness lies by varying the cost to self for telling such a lie. Canadian children completed tasks and first received a desirable gift, such as a colorful toy (Popliger et al., 2011). They were then told they had to complete one more task after which they would receive a second gift. The adult who gave the second gift explained that she wanted to give the child a special gift she had made. In this study, there were two conditions: a high-cost and a low-cost condition. In the high-cost condition, children could only keep one gift. After completing the final task, they were asked to hand back their first desirable toy gift to receive their final gift. When presented with the final gift, they discovered it was an undesirable object, such as a pair of knitted socks. In the low-cost condition, children were able to keep the desirable gift in addition to receiving the second undesirable gift.

In both conditions, after being presented with the undesirable gift, children were asked by the gift-giver if they liked the gift. In the high-cost condition, the perceived consequences of lying were high because children believed they would lose the desirable gift they liked. In contrast, if children told the truth, they would not have to keep the undesirable gift. In the low-cost condition, the perceived consequences were low because the children had little to lose by lying and telling the gift-giver they liked the gift.

When children could keep both gifts in the low-cost condition, they readily lied to the gift-giver and told her they liked the gift. However, in the high-cost condition in which they could only keep one gift, children were less inclined to lie politely to the gift-giver. Furthermore, in the high-cost condition, older elementary school children (i.e., 10–12 years of age) were more likely to tell a prosocial lie compared with younger children. Hence, while younger children were more motivated to lie for self-serving motives, such as avoiding negative consequences to themselves, older children were more likely to be concerned about hurting another's feelings and about being polite, even if there were personal costs to self.

In general, altruistic behavior seems to appear increasingly during middle childhood into early adolescence as children both come to require less external reinforcement to engage in such behavior and become more aware of its intrinsically reinforcing nature. Children's prosocial, even altruistic, lying also appears to develop later as their social-cognitive abilities develop.

Indeed, these lies are expected to appear last, developmentally speaking, because they require cognitive perspective-taking skills and empathetic understanding in addition to an appreciation for the intangible benefits of socially appropriate or altruistic behavior, despite the potential cost to the self. As a result, as children grow older, telling these types of lies becomes more common.

Adolescence and Early Adulthood

By adolescence, individuals' ability to tell lies are as good (or as bad) as adults' ability. For teenagers and adults, there are individual differences in their lie-telling ability: Some are better at concealment than others. The reasons for adolescents to lie can change as they become more involved with peers and their own activities. While, in general, young children tend to tell lies about minor misdeeds, as they mature into adolescence, adolescents are more likely to conceal activities and details of their lives that they feel should be private or of which their parents would disapprove.

In particular, adolescents tell lies about friends or activities they consider to be in their personal, private domain. Adolescents and parents often disagree over what are "personal" decisions. For example, an adolescent may lie about being chaperoned at a concert they are going to with their friends; lie about spending time with friends the parents do not approve of; or lie about smoking, drinking, or other prohibited behaviors. As adolescents seek autonomy, they may come into direct conflict with parents' views on what they should be doing or rules of how they should behave. They may also feel that their parents would be disappointed and thus choose to conceal to avoid their parents' disappointment. They may also tell reputational lies, that is, lies to make them appear in a positive light to others, or polite lies as well as lie for others as a way to manage their friendships and social relations with others. For all these reasons, research suggests that on average, teenagers may lie more often than adults may. For instance, one study found that high school students reported telling lies at a rate 75% higher than that of college students and 150% more than that of older adults (Levine et al., 2013). In another study that included participants ranging from 6 to 77 years of age, researchers found that self-reported lying frequency increased throughout childhood, peaked in adolescence, and then steadily decreased during adulthood (Debey et al., 2015).

So by the time teens are transitioning into early adulthood around 18 to 21 years of age, their lying behavior tends to decrease. By this time, many of the struggles of autonomy have declined and youths may not be living at home or under the care of parents anymore. Behaviors that may lead someone to lie, such as risk-taking behavior of youths or experimenting, may have hit their peak in the teenage years and start to decline with the transition to adulthood. Research with adults suggests that dishonest behavior, in general, gradually and steadily declines in adulthood (Ashton & Lee, 2016). Hence, there is some evidence that our lying behaviors in general decline.

COGNITIVE DEVELOPMENT

The ability to tell lies is tied to cognitive development. *Cognitive abilities* are the vital skills and knowledge we develop to be able to do a range of tasks associated with perception, learning, memory, understanding, awareness, reasoning, judgment, intuition, and language. Cognitive abilities encompass how children think, explore, and figure things out. These important foundational abilities are crucial to children's healthy, positive development. As children develop these abilities, they are able to learn, master, and problem-solve many different skills. These abilities can help them communicate with others. In addition to the many positive benefits, as these abilities develop, they also increase the ability for children to lie.

The creation and maintenance of a lie can be a relatively involved task. A successful liar must plan a story and remember it, take into account another individuals' knowledge, construct a false statement that differs from their own true beliefs, and adjust one's demeanor to appear truthful and convincing. Telling such a lie involves complex cognitive functions, which include understanding other people's minds—their thoughts and beliefs as well as being able to understand their perspective—and the ability to regulate and control one's own thoughts and emotions as well as plan and hold in memory the true facts and the false story. Deception can be considered a milestone of cognitive maturity as it emerges once children have developed the cognitive abilities to understand another's mental states and consciously control their own behaviors. Thus, while the development of cognitive abilities is a part of healthy development and facilitates one's competency, it also enables dishonest communication.

We can think of lying as a by-product of children's positive cognitive development.

Understanding Others' Minds

The development of honesty is based on understanding the mental states of other people's minds. This ability, sometimes referred to by psychologists as *theory of mind*, involves the understanding that others have intentions, desires, beliefs, knowledge, and emotions that differ from one's own and that such mental states affect how people act and behave. Once children start to understand that others can have a different perspective of the world than their own, then they understand they can create a *false* belief in another. For instance, if you ask me the location of the nearest pharmacy, and I tell you the wrong location (this could be because I made a genuine mistake or because I intentionally wanted to mislead you), you will have a false belief about the location of the pharmacy. Your belief of where the pharmacy is located differs from reality, but you believe it to be accurate.

By definition, telling a lie requires one to intentionally create a false belief in the mind of another (whereas a mistake is when one unintentionally creates a false belief in another). The child who lies about eating a cookie wishes to instill the false belief in the questioner that the child did not consume the cookie. The teenager who lies to their parent about being at a friend's house when they were actually at a party hopes to instill the false belief in their parent that their child was safely in the home of a known friend. Thus, an important cognitive ability that enables people to lie is having at least rudimentary understanding of theory of mind and the ability to create false beliefs in others. Psychological research suggests that lying is actually a hallmark of the development of theory of mind abilities.

Young children are developing these abilities in the preschool years, and psychological research has found that the emergence of children's early lies is closely associated with their developing theory of mind abilities (Leduc et al., 2017). As children develop a more advanced understanding of theory of mind such that they can reason about complex interactions between mental states, it helps them to gradually become increasingly skilled at maintaining the plausibility of their lies. Children will tell a deliberate lie while ensuring that their subsequent statements do not contradict the initial lie, thereby making their statements difficult to distinguish from statements made by a nonliar. My colleagues and I found that children 7 years of age and older with higher theory of mind scores were more likely to successfully maintain their lies when responding to follow-up questions (Talwar, Gordon, & Lee, 2007; Talwar & Lee, 2008).

While theory of mind abilities initially may help support the emergence and development of lying as children transition into adolescence, children's more advanced theory of mind skills help them to better understand another's perspective, and these skills may make them be less inclined to tell lies. In one study, my colleagues and I found that children who were between 11 and 14 years of age who had more advanced theory of mind skills were more likely to be only occasional liars, and the lies they did tell were more likely for the reason of protecting other's feelings or for politeness (Lavoie, Leduc,

Arruda, et al., 2017). In a recent study, we also found that teenagers with more advance theory of mind skills were more likely to be forthcoming to their parents and friends and less likely to conceal information (Lavoie & Talwar, 2020).

Overall, it seems that theory of mind abilities may support the initial development of lie-telling and concealment in childhood. In the transition to adolescence, though, these same abilities may help children understand the benefits of open communication in their close relationships and lead them to disclose and share information as a way to build and maintain trust with others.

Controlling One's Own Behavior: Executive Functioning

Lying is also related to self-control. To lie, a person has to have the ability to control their natural impulses and regulate their emotions (e.g., fidgeting, to not look nervous or guilty). Lying also draws on cognitive abilities, such as memory skills, planning, and cognitive flexibility (to create plausible lies that can be sustained over time). These abilities fall under the umbrella term *executive functioning*, which refers to a set of higher order psychological processes that serve to monitor and control thought and action. These skills emerge during late infancy and go on to develop throughout childhood. This development is correspondingly associated with improvements in children's deceptive capabilities.

For instance, when choosing to tell a lie, children must have the self-control to conceal the truth (i.e., conceal the transgression or misdeed). The liar must carefully inhibit any verbal or nonverbal behaviors that contradict their false statement while still maintain in their memory the contents of their initial lie and the false information they gave so those remain undetected. A child who has lied about who they were with after school, for example, must inhibit any feelings of worry or fear of their parents' reaction and try to appear unremarkable or unconcerned when they give the false information about who they were with. They then need to remember what they said in that initial lie to make sure they do not later contradict any of those details in anything they say later. If they said they had been with their best friend after school but, later in the conversation, mention that they had not seen their best friend for more than a week, then they have contradicted their lie and are more likely to be detected. Imagine that on that day, there had been a big event at school like a school assembly with presentations about drugs. If the parent now asks the child what their best friend thought of the assembly, the child has to refer to their lie ("I said I was with my best friend this afternoon after school") and infer what the parent would expect them to know ("Mom will expect me to have talked to my best friend about the day and know what my best friend's views were"). The child then must come up with a response that is congruent with their initial lie ("She said it was boring, and I agree" or "We didn't talk about it, actually").

Liars need to think quickly using skills of self-control, memory, and cognitive flexibility to respond and maintain their lie without generating suspicion. Over a number of studies, my colleagues and I found that children who have better performance on executive functioning tasks are more likely to lie and have better lie-telling abilities (e.g., Talwar, Lavoie, et al., 2017; Talwar & Lee, 2008; Williams et al., 2016). However, these same abilities are important for children's healthy positive development. These skills help them acquire new skills, learn, and problem-solve. So, the fact that these skills help children lie does not mean that their development is negative. Indeed, these skills are vital for children's successful functioning. And they are important for their honest communication.

One study with Chinese children between 8 and 12 years of age found that children with better executive functioning skills were less likely to cheat on a game and lie about their performance (Ding et al., 2014). In particular, these children had better self-control. But for those who did decide to cheat and then lie about it, they had the higher executive functioning skill of cognitive flexibility. So having greater executive functioning ability may help children to resist cheating to begin with.

Those who are unable to resist temptation then must draw on executive functioning skills to lie successfully.

Recognizing Why Lying Is Normal

In some ways, we can think of lying as a by-product of children's positive cognitive development. As they develop cognitive abilities to understand others and to control their own behaviors, these abilities give them the skills to deceive. Realizing this can help parents understand that the lies young children tell are part of this normal (and generally positive) development. These same cognitive abilities help children to resist the temptation to cheat and lie. Clearly, just because we have the cognitive abilities to lie does not mean we lie at every opportunity. As research with adults shows, we do not lie very frequently. We generally achieve the principle of honesty in the majority of our communications (see Chapter 1 for further discussion on adult lying). For the times that we choose to lie, motivational social factors influence our choices and our behavior.

SOCIAL CONTEXT

From very young ages, parents, teachers, peers, and others around them socialize children to be honest and truthful in most social contexts. Lying is a morally and socially undesirable behavior that is actively discouraged and judged negatively. Children receive explicit instructions about honesty, they observe others' behavior (both those who are being truthful and those who are lying), they experience the positive and negative consequences of their truth or lie statements, and they learn the social rules of behavior that are accepted and expected in their society.

The main purpose of this book is to talk about how parents can socialize, teach, and model honest behavior. I discuss in greater detail throughout the book how adults can socialize children to be honest. However, here, I briefly address how children can also be taught, implicitly or explicitly, by adults and the culture around them that they should *not* always tell the truth.

How to Tell the Polite Lie

Children are taught to conform to social conventions, which dictate that in some situations, we conceal our immediate reactions and feelings about others to maintain polite and agreeable social interactions. Parents may model, and perhaps even explicitly encourage, lies in some situations as preferable to the truth. For instance, a child may observe their mother politely tell a friend how much she enjoyed her friend's choir recital, even though, privately, the child has heard their mother complain how bored she was. In another case, a parent may instruct the child to say they like an undesirable gift to avoid rudeness and show gratitude. In these cases, deceptive emotional expression is encouraged because children are socialized to hide or mask negative emotions that are deemed unacceptable, a skill that facilitates effective deception.

The Role of Culture

Most cultures have strong dictates about the importance of honesty, a universally desired quality. However, in some situations, we may judge a lie less harshly. It can vary across cultures how different types of lies are considered more acceptable or even desirable than in other cultures. For instance, in Western cultures, many polite people will not tell the truth if they dislike a gift; they will politely express gratitude and pleasure at receiving the gift. What we deem as lies that are more acceptable can vary according to our culture. For example, researchers presented stories to 7-, 9- and 11-year-old Chinese and Canadian children; in those stories, the characters performed a good deed or a bad deed (Lee et al., 1997). When the teacher questioned the story characters, they told either a lie or the truth. All the children rated lying about the bad deed negatively and rated truth-telling about the good deed positively. There were cultural and age differences for the good deed, though. Chinese children rated telling the truth about the good deed less positively than Canadian children. Furthermore, Chinese children rated lying about the good deed more positively than Canadian children. This develops with age: The 7-year-old Chinese children rated lying about a positive deed more negatively, and with age, the children became more positive about lying about the good deed.

The finding that with age, Chinese children were likely to rate lies that downplayed one's good deeds more positively reflected children's increasing awareness of their culture's conventions about modesty and self-effacement in prosocial situations. As children increasingly learn the social rules from being at school and interacting with others, their evaluations become increasingly consistent with cultural norms about modesty (Lee et al., 1997). In another study, Chinese and Canadian children between 7 and 11 years of age were presented with story characters who faced a moral dilemma to lie or tell the truth to help a group but harm an individual, or vice versa. As they got older, Chinese children increasingly rated lies to benefit the collective group more positively than lies told to benefit an individual, whereas Canadian children showed the opposite preference (Fu et al., 2007).

There are other situations in cultures in which someone may say something that for an outsider seems false but may be part of the social conventions of that culture. For instance, my colleagues and I examined children's perceptions of *Taroof*, which is a concept that dictates courteous social interactions within Persian society. For instance, according to the dictates of Taroof, if a host offers a guest something to drink, the guest should politely decline. This is following expected cultural rules of courtesy, and the host knows to persist in asking the guest to have something to drink, and eventually the guest accepts. However, if someone from another culture, such as the United States or Canada, offers their guest something to drink, on hearing a clear refusal, the host will take that refusal at face value and not offer again because they will believe that the guest does not want a drink.

We presented these types of scenarios to Canadian and Persian children between 5 and 11 years of age (Shohoudi Mojdehi et al., 2021). We found that as age increased, Persian children in Iran were less likely to label a false statement made in Taroof politeness situations as a lie compared with Canadian children. As Persian children grew up and learned the social rules of polite interactions, they were more likely to find such statements as acceptable and view them positively. These are examples of social cultural contexts that may influence how we are truthful. These comparisons clearly show that children's evaluations of lies and behavior are influenced by the cultural context in which they are socialized, and, with age, their conceptions and behaviors become more in line with the cultural norms of the society in which they live.

Harsh, Punitive Environment

When children are in environments that do not support their healthy positive development, this can also affect their decisions to tell lies as a way to cope and help them achieve their goals. For instance, how children are disciplined can also influence their lie-telling behavior. My colleague and I found that children who attended a school with a harsh disciplinary code that used physical punishment were more likely to lie than other children were and were better lie-tellers (Talwar & Lee, 2011). Using strict authoritarian discipline had the opposite effect than was intended: It increased the lying and made children better liars. In such environments in which there is strict control and harsh punishment, children learn that lying can be an effective strategy to avoid punishment. Given the high stakes of such lies if found out, they quickly learn to become effective liars to conceal their deception and misdeeds. If they lie successfully, then they can avoid getting into any trouble. Consequently, lying may develop earlier and be relied on more extensively among children from harsh authoritarian

family environments. Other researchers have found that adolescents and adults are more likely to see lying as acceptable
when they view the state as being unjust and tyrannical (Perkins
& Turiel, 2007).

> It can vary across cultures how different types of lies are
> considered more acceptable or even desirable than in
> other cultures.

Wider Social and Cultural Messages

Beyond parents and the family, children also become aware of
others' attitudes and actions in their wider environment, and
these can influence behavior. For instance, when examining
academic cheating, many students have the belief that count-
less fellow students are cheating and that it is a pervasive
behavior (Ghanem & Mozahem, 2019; Jensen et al., 2002). The
belief that others engage in dishonesty and that dishonesty is
common can help an individual to rationalize their behavior
and give them the belief that if they don't lie or cheat, they may
be at a disadvantage. Similarly, with age, youths are more
involved in the world, interacting with others and engaging with
a wider variety of people, both of which have only increased in
the digital age and with the rise of social media. This can lead
youths to see a whole lot of different behaviors, including lying
and misrepresentation. The perceived norms of behavior can
influence a persons' attitude and behavior. If someone believes
that everyone is lying and misrepresenting themselves, they
feel it is okay. If they see prominent people lying or showing
disregard for checking the truth of their statements (i.e., fake
news), it creates a "norm" that such behavior is acceptable.

I recently had a conversation with a father and his almost
grown-up son who is 17 years old. The single father had lately
been considering dating again and had posted on a popular
social media site. He said he had lied about his age because
everyone presented themselves as younger. In this case, his
son took him to task for "being fake" and told him that he

needed to be "genuine" to meet someone really nice. The son gave his father the reminder of the importance of being truthful, which was not lost on the father. This case in which the tables were turned on parent and child illustrates how perceptions of what is "typical" behavior online can influence even adults' behavior.

THE RELATIONSHIP BETWEEN BELIEFS AND ACTION

It is clear that children can receive competing social and cultural messages about lying, which can make it difficult for them to interpret and learn what acceptable behavior is. As they begin to understand what lying is conceptually, they must learn when lie-telling may be socially condoned and when it is wrong morally. They learn these "rules" throughout childhood and as they encounter more and more social contexts. To prevent this normal process from becoming problematic, we need to understand how to create among children the social obligation to tell the truth and remove obstacles to their honesty. Throughout the book, I discuss how adults can do this. To give this discussion context, I briefly outline how children's conceptual and moral understanding of lying develops with age and how it influences their behavior.

Children's Conceptual Understanding of Lies

Children's understanding of what it means to lie develops over time, seemingly from a concrete to an abstract construct. Children as young as 3 years define a statement as a lie solely based on factuality: Incorrect statements made in good faith are called lies, including genuine mistakes (in which the person says something untrue but mistakenly believes it as true) and inaccurate guesses. It is not until ages 6 to 10 years that children consider the speaker's beliefs when characterizing the honesty of their statements. An individual who believed something to be untrue and made a false statement is deemed to have told a lie. Psychological researchers have found that 8- and 11-year-olds are more accurate at identifying lies than 5-year-olds. Furthermore, compared with the older children, younger children are more likely to evaluate lies more negatively if the behavior was punished (Bussey, 1992, 1999).

Indeed, children do not perceive all lies the same. Children as young as 4 years old evaluate polite lies less negatively, believing that polite lies can protect other people's feelings and are sometimes appropriate (Broomfield et al., 2002). By age 7, children evaluate lies based on their effects on others. Overall, children's understanding of lies evolves throughout the preschool and elementary years. Lie definitions might initially be simply rule based (i.e., statements that are incorrect), but the complexity of the concept grows during early childhood to include the speaker's intentions and the impact and social acceptability of the lies.

The Relationship Between Children's Conceptual Understanding and Actual Behavior

How does children's conceptual understanding of lying and its moral implications impact children's behavior? One may be tempted to argue that once a person knows and has internalized that lying is bad, then that behavior falls in line, and the person remains steadfastly honest. Yet, adults tell lies despite knowing that lie-telling is considered morally wrong under most circumstances.

When my colleagues and I initially examined the relation between children's lies to conceal their transgressions and their conceptual and moral understanding of lies, we found no relationship. The majority of children reported that lying to conceal a transgression was bad, could correctly identify a lie, and recommended that others tell the truth. Nevertheless, most of them told lies to conceal their own transgressions (Talwar et al., 2002). Like adults, knowing that lies are bad is not a barrier to telling a lie for one's own self-interest. Perhaps this is not surprising given that adults know what a lie is and can define it but still lie from time to time.

When we examined children's conceptual and moral understanding more extensively, though, we found a stronger relationship between understanding and behavior (Talwar & Lee, 2008). We presented children between 4 and 8 years of age with a range of different situations in which true and false statements were made by story characters, and children were asked to determine if what the character said was the truth or a lie and whether what they said was good or bad. As expected, children's ability to classify correctly lies and other true and false statements (i.e., mistakes) in this study increased with age. In terms of children's moral evaluations, younger children were more likely to attend to factuality and making a promise but were less likely to take the speaker's motivation into consideration compared with older children. However, older children considered the character's intention to deceive when making their evaluations.

Importantly, we found that children's lying behavior was related to their moral evaluations of truthful and untruthful statements. Children who truthfully admitted their transgression were more likely to value truthfulness and give it higher ratings regardless of the situation. In contrast, children who chose to lie tended not to have stringent views about the need to be truthful. Our results suggest that children who hold more relativist views about the moral implications of lying are more inclined to tell lies, whereas those holding more stringent moral views about lying are more likely to confess.

Another noteworthy finding is that, in comparison with the liars and confessors, those children who abided by the experimenter's instruction and did not peek (nonpeekers) gave the most positive ratings for stories in which the protagonist kept a promise and the most negative ratings when the story protagonist failed to keep a promise. It may be that nonpeekers (i.e., children who refrained from cheating) were the most concerned about rules and adherence to them. They might have taken the experimenter's instruction about not peeking at the forbidden toy more seriously than the lie-tellers and confessors, and this concern was strong enough to motivate them to resist the high level of temptation to peek.

Children's perceptions of how the other person will react and feel, especially in politeness situations, can also influence their behavior. In the study mentioned earlier that used the disappointing gift paradigm, we found that Chinese children who told polite lies were more likely to rate such lies positively, and this tendency increased with age (Xu et al., 2010). And in another study described earlier that looked at children's motivations for telling politeness lies, we asked North American children to evaluate the feelings of the lie-teller and the person to whom a politeness lie was told (Popliger et al., 2011). We found that children who themselves told a polite lie about receiving a disappointing gift were more positive in their ratings of the story characters' feelings when the story characters lied than when the characters told the truth. They thought that the person who was told the politeness lie would feel more positive than if they were told the truth. Politeness liars felt that telling a lie to be polite would preserve the recipient's feelings and prevent them from feeling hurt, whereas the children who told the truth were more concerned about feeling they had done the right thing by being honest rather than how the recipient would feel on hearing the truth.

Thus, sometimes our moral standards and behavior match. However, in other situations, they may not. In general, social and moral norms tend to guide our moral value judgments more strongly than social-situational factors, whereas social-situational factors tend to guide our actions more strongly than social and moral norms. When faced with making a decision of whether to tell a lie about a transgression, children's moral values compel them to tell the truth, whereas the social-situational factors of self-protection entice them to tell a lie. This creates a conflict between moral norms and situational factors. Conversely, when children are faced with whether to tell a polite lie, less conflict exists: Both social values and social-situational factors support them in telling such a lie. Consequently, the relation between children's evaluation of lies and their behaviors is stronger when lying appears to serve more prosocial purposes than when lying is self-serving.

CONCLUSION

Psychological research suggests that children's lies first emerge as part of their normal cognitive development. Later development and expression of this behavior is then governed by socialization and moral development. Parents can create a social environment in which children choose to be honest.

As is discussed later in this book, parents can do this through a variety of ways, from the messages they give to their children through talking and through practice, the sanctions they enforce and the praise they use, and the relationship they foster with their child. As you will see in the Chapter 4, parents can also foster honesty by first understanding the child's underlying motivation for lying and then creating conditions that meet the underlying motivation without lying. To help parents understand the underlying motivations that can lead children to lie, the next chapter outlines some of the reasons we lie.

3

Why People Lie

A key way to foster honesty in children is to address their underlying motivations to lie. For example, if a child lies to avoid punishment (e.g., "I didn't spill the drink on the rug"), you could address their underlying fear of punishment by explaining that you understand accidents happen and calmly directing them to help clean it up. I discuss more in Chapter 4 about how to react to lies. However, to understand how to respond, we must first understand why children lie. Without that understanding, we risk responding in a counterproductive way that may increase the motivation to lie. Understanding the underlying motivation helps us to address the motivation and create conditions that promote truthfulness.

Why do children lie? In large part, children are motivated to tell lies for the same reasons as adults. It is just that the content differs. For example, an adult may deny the act of downloading pirated software on a company computer when the server crashes or perhaps lie on their tax return. A child lies because they fear punishment after breaking a vase while playing in the house with a ball when they had been forbidden to do so, or they lie about eating an appetite-spoiling cookie before dinner.

In general, lies can range from being purely self-serving to being purely altruistic. Lies can also be driven by more than one motivation—for example, a lie can serve one's own self-interests while also benefiting another. In this chapter, I review some of the different motivations for lying. Although one can categorize lies in different ways, I have grouped them into these broad categories: lies to escape negative consequences, lies for personal gain, lies for impression management, lies told to be polite, lies told to help another or a group, and altruistic lies. I also discuss false statements that we sometimes label as lies but that are actually told without intention to deceive or only to temporarily deceive in children's jokes, tricks, and play. These categories are not mutually exclusive because we can have multiple motivations for lying. However, having the categories helps to organize and provide insights into the different motivations of lying.

LIES TO ESCAPE NEGATIVE CONSEQUENCES

A primary motivation for telling lies to is to help ourselves. One of the most common lies people tell are *lies to escape negative consequences* or punishment to protect our own interests—to "save our bacon." For instance, we may tell a lie about surfing the internet during company time or to cover up a mistake we made by feigning ignorance on how it happened or who caused it. These are examples of lies told to escape potential negative consequences to self.

> *Understanding the underlying motivation for lying helps us address the motivation and create conditions that promote truthfulness.*

Children often tell lies to escape punishment for misdeeds. For instance, a child who is roughhousing may feign ignorance about how a houseplant was knocked over. A child can lie about brushing their teeth to try to avoid this unpleasant task. A child grabs a toy from their baby brother, causing the baby to cry, but feigns no knowledge of what caused the crying when a parent inquires. A teenager may deny having taken their phone into their room to socialize late into the night against house rules.

In all these examples, the lie is told as a strategy to avoid the censure and approbation that their behavior may have caused.

Researchers in psychological science have reported that these tend to be the earliest lies children tell. In one study, 24 parents kept a diary of the lies their preschoolers told over 3 individual months spaced 2 months apart (i.e., the whole study was 7 months long; Newton et al., 2000). They found that the most frequent lies children told were lies to avoid discomfort and negative consequences to themselves. These lies were often in response to questions, such as: "Did you smash the egg?" ("No!"); or "Who did that?" ("I didn't do it!" or "Someone else, not me"); or "What do you have behind your back?" ("Nothing"). The negative consequences the children are trying to avoid may be punishment but can also simply be the parents' displeasure. Research with adolescents has found that they will tell lies to avoid their parents' censure over issues, such as the friends they hang out with, the activities they do with their friends, or their engagement in illegal activities like underage drinking (Smetana et al., 2009). What young children, adolescents, and later adults lie about may change, but the underlying motivations that compel the person to lie stay the same.

LIES FOR PERSONAL GAIN

Lies to escape negative consequences are not the only type of lies told for self-serving purposes. Other early lies that children tell are *lies for personal gain*, that is, those told to obtain a reward. At first, such lies may be motivated by a desire for material benefits, such as a cookie from the forbidden cookie jar, whereas later, a desire for social rewards (e.g., other's admiration) may motivate children to lie.

Another type of lie that adults and children tell to benefit themselves is told in the hope of instrumental gain. Unlike lies told to escape negative consequences, when people tell lies for personal gain, their primary motivation is to attain some material or psychological benefit. The benefit could be something tangible like money or an object, or it could be a psychological benefit, such as praise. For instance, an adult can tell a lie to get a bonus at work or take credit for a sale made possible by a junior colleague. An adult can lie to the tax collection agency about what their income was to pay less tax or receive a rebate. A parent can lie to a ticket agent about the age of their child to get a discount on the ticket. Children can tell these lies as well. A child can cheat and lie on a test to get a good grade. A child can lie to a parent about getting all their homework done so they can go out and play with friends. A child can claim that they did the tidying up that really was done by the babysitter so the child can receive their parents' approval.

Scientific evidence also suggests that children's lie-telling for personal gain may start to emerge in the preschool years. In one study, children between 3 years and 5 years of age were taught to mislead a puppet about the location of a prize so they could keep the prize for themselves. Four-year-old children were found to be reliably capable of committing this deception (Sodian et al., 1991). In a similar study, 87% of 5-year-olds lied about the location of a prize to the puppet, whereas only 29% of 3-year-olds did so (Peskin, 1992). Another study found that children 4 years and older lie to claim someone else's work as their own to win a prize (Talwar, Crossman, & Wyman, 2017).

In a study in which Canadian parents were asked to keep a diary of their children's lies over 2 weeks, my colleagues and I found that parents reported that lies for personal gain were the most frequent type of lie their children told (Lavoie et al., 2016). For example, a child falsely told her father, "Oh! Mommy said, yes, I can have cake." In a British study of preschooler lies, the researchers also found that parents reported children would tell lies to make false claims of permission (Newton et al., 2000). They similarly gave the example of a young boy having been denied a biscuit (cookie) by his mother, going to ask his father, who did not reply to his question. The boy returned to his mother and claimed, "Daddy says I could have it!" Children also told lies to falsely assert completion of a task, such as: "Have you tidied up your room?" "Yes." There were also instances of young children's giving false excuses like "I'm not tired" to try to avoid going to bed, or "I have a leg ache" to get pushed in the stroller rather than walk.

LIES FOR IMPRESSION MANAGEMENT

Impression management lies, that is, self-presentation lies, are also lies that lead to personal gain. However, they are told for a specific gain: to appear "positive" in the eyes of others or to enhance their self-image with others. Sometime these lies are referred to as "reputational lies." The personal gain desired from such lies is a social benefit in which the person receives social approval or admiration from others. An individual who tells impression management lies wishes to influence how others perceive them in an effort to appear more attractive or accomplished.

For instance, an adult who lies about how large a fish they caught on their fishing trip may wish to impress others and to magnify their fishing abilities. A child may tell others that they are the best in their karate class or can run faster than all the other children can. A child attending violin class may falsely boast to their uncle that they are the best student in the class. In such cases, the child seeks to enhance their prowess and positively influence others' impression of themselves. When these lies are believed, the individual has managed to augment successfully their personal reputation and reap the social benefits. However, once detected, such lies can lead to significantly negative appraisals. This is particularly true when the self-aggrandizing lies stretch the bounds of plausibility, which makes others skeptical. If told repeatedly, such lies may serve to give the person a negative reputation and only enhance the ridicule directed at them.

Another type of lie that is motivated by the desire to manage other people's impression of them is the *face-saving lie*, also called the "bravado lie." In the study of British preschoolers' lies, parents recorded children telling bravado lies in which the children verbally falsified an emotional state (Newton et al., 2000). For instance, a child who was being physically punished claimed, "That didn't hurt!" In another example, a young boy had been asked by a visiting aunt where his father was; he answered that his father was upstairs. However, he was contradicted when his father's voice was heard from an adjacent room. The boy, hearing the evidence that contradicted his previous statement, exclaimed, "My other dad's upstairs!" Notably, this lie led to amusement by the adults present and was not believed.

LIES TO BE POLITE

In addition to lies told for selfish motives, lies can be told to protect or benefit others. One example of a lie told for others is the *politeness lie*: In politeness situations, often the etiquette of culture or the customs governing behavior make telling a blunt truth rude or harmful to the feelings of the other person. For instance, an American adult having a Thanksgiving dinner at a friend's house is asked if they like the friend's homemade pumpkin pie. The pie may have not been to the taste of the guest, but rather than say, "It didn't taste nice. I don't like it," the guest may demure and say, "Thank you. It was very nice." In this case, the guest does not wish to make their friend feel bad by saying anything negative about the homemade pie and conceals their dislike of the pie. Another example is when a friend who has just had a radical new haircut asks if you like their new haircut. You think it is a bad haircut, but to avoid making the person feel bad and self-conscious, you tell them that they look good.

Politeness lies are evaluated less negatively than lies told for self. In certain situations in each culture, telling the blunt truth is unacceptable and rude—like receiving a gift that is undesirable and unwanted. The conventions of courtesy dictate that receipt of a gift is accompanied by expressions of gratitude and pleasure from the recipient. The purpose of these conventions is to prevent offense to the other's feelings. For example, when we receive an undesirable gift, such as a necktie with a fish pattern, for a birthday present, social etiquette requires us not to tell the gift-giver bluntly that we do not like the gift and that fish ties are tacky. Rather, we are expected to express sentiments of appreciation and to conceal any feelings of disappointment or indifference. As a result, when asked, we often use the strategy of telling a lie to maintain amicable social relations and to avoid insult. Research with adults suggests that such politeness lies are one of the most common forms of lies adults tell on a daily basis (DePaulo & Kashy, 1998). They are often considered less negative than other types of lies because they are told without malicious intent and to spare another's feelings.

Children are often socialized by adults to tell politeness lies. As a result, children can be taught either directly or indirectly to conceal any negative feelings and to learn the principles of courtesy to promote social relations and the well-being of another. We often encourage children to tell such lies—not because we want them to be deceptive but in an effort to teach them to be polite. Imagine a child who receives an undesirable gift for their birthday, such as a pair of itchy, wool socks made by their grandma. The child may be expected by the adults around them to express gratitude for the unwanted gift and feign liking it.

Evidence suggests that children start to learn these social conventions of politeness at an early age. For instance, my colleague and I examined young Canadian children's ability to tell lies to be polite. In our study, an adult had a conspicuous mark of lipstick on his nose and asked the child to take a photograph of him, but before the picture was taken, the adult asked, "Do I look okay?" This created a situation in which the children had to decide whether to tell a prosocial lie when explicitly asked about the appearance of the adult or bluntly state that he did not look good. Of the 65 children in the study, 55 chose to lie to reassure the adult that he looked okay for the picture (Talwar & Lee, 2002b). Later, another researcher asked the children if the adult had looked okay before he had his picture taken (to confirm children's true beliefs). All the children mentioned the mark of lipstick on the adult's nose. This is like the situation in which someone has a piece of spinach stuck in their teeth. Do you tell the person and potentially embarrass them momentarily, or do you politely conceal the fact?

Interestingly, when asked why they did not mention it, only 11% of children explained that they had lied because they wanted to avoid causing embarrassment. In this situation, if children told the truth that the adult did not look okay, it is possible they feared facing negative reactions from the adult. Lying would not only avoid unpleasant repercussions but also might please the adult. Children were not lying purely for prosocial reasons for the benefit of another but also to serve their own self-interests. This illustrates the dual nature of some lies. Politeness lies can serve both to promote the interests of others by not harming their feelings and also protect the liar by avoiding the potential negative reactions of telling the unpleasant truth as well as maintaining the social convention of being polite and avoiding embarrassment to the lie-recipient.

On the other hand, children seem willing to lie in some situations, perhaps to protect another's feelings, despite detriment to their own self-interests. In a series of studies, my colleagues and I examined children's prosocial lying using a disappointing gift paradigm (Talwar, Murphy, & Lee, 2007). In these studies, children played a game in which they were promised a gift from a gift basket containing a range of different toys and gifts. On completion of the game, they received an undesirable gift like a bar of soap or a pair of socks instead of a toy. After being left alone for a minute to unwrap the present and look at it, the gift-giver returned and asked the children if they liked the gift. In this situation, children had to reconcile their desire for a better gift with the competing social requirement to be polite.

The disappointing gift paradigm recreates common situations described earlier in which telling a lie is often deemed socially desirable, and truth-telling is deemed inappropriate or rude. Children are often socialized to tell such lies by their parents. Indeed, we found that in this situation, the majority of children lied, claiming to like the disappointing gift, despite later telling their parents that they did not like the gift.

Interestingly, when we did this study, we found that parents often reported being pleased that their child had told the researcher they liked the gift. The parents had not thought of the lie but, rather, the fact that their child had been polite. When parents were in the room with the child as they unwrapped the present, we found that some parents told the child to not express their dislike of the gift to the gift-giver, if they were asked. These parents articulated the convention of not saying unpleasant things about a gift. However, other parents spoke about not saying anything to hurt the gift-giver's feelings and talked about the reason behind the rule; in that case, children were more likely to tell a politeness lie and to make an effort to show positive feelings about the gift. In these cases, children were learning to take the feelings of the gift-giver into consideration and were using lying as a strategy to be polite and preserve the gift-giver's feelings. In contrast, the children whose parents were in the room with them and had not discussed the reason behind the rule were moved to bluntly tell the gift-giver that they did not like the gift.

LIES TO HELP ANOTHER PERSON

Lies told for another person can be prosocial to help another person, but they can still be lies about something negative or transgressive, and they can be antisocial to others in outcome. Lies to help another person, although prosocial in their motivations to help someone, can also help that person escape punishment or negative consequences. Imagine a teen who has gotten into trouble repeatedly at school for aggressive behavior, vandalism, and damage to school property. One more time, and the teen could face suspension. The teen's friend, knowing this, takes the rap to protect their friend from this serious outcome. The friend ends up in detention. Meanwhile, the true offending teenager is spared any serious repercussion because of their friend's concealment and lie. The motives of the friend stem from noble principles of loyalty, sacrifice, and friendship, but the situation surrounding the lie may not be so noble. While such a lie does benefit another, it is not generally perceived as socially acceptable.

Consider another situation that also is not positive. The coach of a team molests one of their young players. The coach is popular, and everyone thinks well of them. The young player also likes the coach, although once the molestation starts, these feelings are complicated by other more ambiguous and negative feelings. The coach tells the child to keep their intimacy a secret and that if anyone finds out, the coach may not be able to continue coaching. The child feels some loyalty to the coach and is manipulated into feeling they need to protect the coach. Hence, when questioned, the child lies to protect the coach and conceal the true nature of their relationship. Here, again, the liar is acting out of concern for another, but the beneficiary of that lie and the actions it conceals are very negative, harmful, and criminal.

Lying to conceal another's wrongdoing can be a selfless act, whereby the lie is told to prevent another from getting into trouble while committing a wrongdoing and thereby incurring the possibility of being in trouble if the lie is found out. Yet children can be more reluctant to tell such lies. For instance, in a couple of studies, researchers examined children's concealment of an unfamiliar adult magician's accidental spillage of ink on a pair of gloves. The children were asked by the adult magician to keep the accident a secret. Overall, most children were unwilling to lie to conceal the magician's transgression. When interviewed about the event, younger children were more likely to keep the secret than older children, who were more likely to tell the truth (Pipe & Wilson, 1994). In these studies, however, the magician was an adult the children had not met before. It is possible that children are less likely to be motivated to lie for a relative stranger compared to someone they know well. If this is the case, children should be more likely to lie for someone with whom they are highly familiar, such as a parent. Under such circumstances, children may feel a greater motivation to conceal a parent's transgression when there is a fear of negative consequences if the truth is revealed.

Two studies examined children's lie-telling to conceal a parent's transgression. In both, the child's mother accidentally broke a forbidden toy and told the child to keep it a secret because she (the mother) might get in trouble. In the first study, researchers found that 5- and 6-year-old children withheld information when asked to keep their mother's secret, whereas younger (3–4 years of age) children did not (Bottoms et al., 2002). It appears that older children, at least, would be willing to conceal a parent's transgression, perhaps out of loyalty.

In the second study, though, my colleagues and I found that children's loyalty to their parents is rather fragile. The majority of children between 3 and 11 years of age told the truth and did not conceal the parent's transgression (Talwar et al., 2004). Many of the children told on the parent immediately, even though the experimenter had not yet "noticed" the broken toy. We varied the conditions under which the child was interviewed to see if children would be more likely to conceal the parent's transgression. Interestingly, children were more likely to lie for the parent after it was clear that they themselves would not be blamed for breaking the toy. Children were motivated to lie or tell the truth about their parent's transgression based on the likelihood that they would be implicated in the transgression themselves. Nevertheless, it should be noted that across all conditions, fewer than 50% of children lied to conceal their parents' transgression. Comparatively, children are less likely to tell lies for others compared to lies told to conceal their own misdeeds.

LIES TO HELP THE GROUP

Lying for the collective is another type of lie that can be told for others. In such cases, a child will lie to conceal a wrongdoing that implicates a group of people who share a common goal or loyalty. For instance, if a group of friends managed to damage a neighbor's property while playing ball on the street, the children may lie to conceal their involvement in the property damage when asked by the neighbor if they saw who was responsible. One study examined these types of lies with children in China. In that study, children in a class had to form a chess team to represent them in a competition. The rules stipulated that they had to pick two experienced players and two novices. The children were left alone to decide who would be on their team. They chose to violate the rules of competition set by the school district and unfairly picked four of the best players to be on their team. Later, they were individually asked if they had followed the rules, and it was found that the number of children who lied increased with age between 7- and 11-year-olds (Fu et al., 2008). However, compared to other types of lies, the number of children who lied was still small. While 11-year-olds were the most likely to lie in this situation, they only did so about 30% of the time. Thus, it appears that children do tell lies for the collective benefit of the group but not at the same rates that they lie for purely self-oriented reasons.

Overall, it seems clear that children will tell lies for others, but, most of the time, they may be motivated to do so only when that lie does not impinge on their own self-interest. The motivation for telling lies to conceal others' transgressions is significantly less salient than the motivation of saving oneself from negative consequences of one's own transgression. Like adults, children most commonly lie for self-interest.

ALTRUISTIC PROSOCIAL LIES

Other lies are told to protect or benefit others that are more noble both in the intent of the liar and in the principles surrounding the lie. These types of lies, *altruistic lies*, are told to achieve another moral principle or action. Consider those that hid Jews during Nazi occupation. Their concealment and deception of the Nazi authorities put them at great risk, yet they did it to protect the vulnerable. In this case, the lie was told in the face of a greater injustice and inhumanity. This lie was a pro-social act, and the outcome was arguably justified. Such lies, told without selfish intent and at potential personal cost to prevent an injustice or other violation can be viewed by some as an exception to the moral prohibition against lying as they aspire to a higher principle of what is just or morally right.

A fictional example of an altruistic lie inspired by real stories comes from the movie *The Good Lie*, which centers on a boy who escapes Sudan to a refugee camp as a result of his brother's lie. In the movie, a group of children is making an arduous trek to seek safety when they hear a marauding troop nearby, and they all dive into the undergrowth to prevent discovery. The boy makes a noise, which alerts some of the soldiers that someone is present. His older brother stands up, indicating it is just he who is hiding, and when asked if he is alone, he answers, "Yes." It is this "good lie" that protects the other children from being discovered, and the older brother is led away by the troops while the rest of the children escape. This is an altruistic lie in which the stakes are high and the cost for the liar is also high. He sacrifices himself to save the others and tells a lie to ensure their safety.

Such lies can also be told in more everyday circumstances in which the stakes are not life threatening. Think of a child at the fair with their younger sibling. They are both at the rifle range. The older child is a good shot, having had several years more practice than their little sibling, and has succeeded in the past in winning a prize. The younger child tries repeatedly but still does not have the skill to win a much desired prize. The older sibling tries again and, once again, is successful. The operator of the range, distracted by others, comes up at the end to get the prize for the successful player. Seeing both children there, the operator asks who won the prize. The older sibling has noticed the little one's disappointment and discouragement. Feeling bad for their younger sibling, the older one tells the operator that it is the younger one who won the prize. The little one's eyes open with wonderment and pleasure when the operator hands them the desired toy prize. The child looks at their older sibling with gratitude for their kindness. Here is a lie told by the older sibling in which they subverted their own interests and gain (i.e., getting a prize) for their younger sibling's gain. This lie is told out of a sense of kindness and empathy for the little sibling. This, too, could be viewed as a prosocial act.

Overall, altruistic lies—those told solely for the benefit of another and with potential costs to oneself—like other types of altruistic behaviors are less common. Unlike other prosocial lies, there is no expectation of reward or benefit to self, such as the avoidance of an embarrassing or unpleasant situation.

FALSE STATEMENTS AS PART OF PLAY

On other occasions, children may make false statements that may be deemed lies. However, the intention is not to deceive or to deceive only for a limited time as part of play, and the truth is revealed soon after the statement.

Tricks

Children tell lies for fun and in jest. In a study by my colleagues and I, we found that the second most common lie that parents reported their children telling were playful trick lies (Lavoie et al., 2016). For example, while watching fireworks with his family, one child exclaimed with a composed face of awe, "Wow! It's so bright, I can see very far. I can see our house! I see Mommy cooking food in the kitchen!" Then, after a pause, he burst out laughing to reveal the truth.

In a British study in which the researcher recorded preschool children's lies, they noted that children told trick lies, such as: "I'm going to write on the floor . . . only joking, Mummy!" (Newton et al., 2000, p. 303). The researchers noted that *trick lies* are characterized by three stages. In the first stage, the child sets up a false expectation or premise. For example, a child might say, "I heard the doorbell!" The second stage is followed by the reaction of the other person. For instance, the parent may run down the stairs to check the door. Then, in the third stage, the child then acknowledges their trick verbally or nonverbally. They may burst out laughing or say, "Tricked ya!" During the first stage, the child appears quite serious and, if questioned, insists on the claim. However, young children often have difficulty maintaining such tricks and cannot hide their "duping delight" for long, often erupting with giggles and giving the trick away.

Fantasy

A discussion about the different types of lies should include children's fantasy stories told in play. Deciphering truth and fantasy can be tricky. Young children are gradually starting to understand the distinction between fantasy and reality at about 3 years of age, and this ability develops between 3 and 8 years of age.

Young children like to make up stories and tell tales. They may blur the distinction in their tales between reality and fantasy. For instance, a 4-year-old may come home to tell you they went on a trip to the zoo today at preschool. They tell a detailed and vibrant story of visiting the zebras and feeding the kangaroos. The child enters into the world of their imagination and play. Indeed, fantasy is normal at this age and is part of a child's imaginary play. Sometimes the parent has to use their knowledge of the world and their child to see the distinction between the fantasy and reality. For instance, a parent may know that their child's preschool did not go to the zoo and is able to recognize the story as the child's imagination. Sometimes it may be that the fantasy could be created as wish fulfillment: The child wishes for something and creates the story around it in their mind. Occasionally, these stories may be mixed up with potential motives for deception, such as an explanation around a transgression. In such cases, a parent can carefully draw the child's attention to the transgression and the rule against it without harshly censoring their fantasy.

As children get older, the fantasy–reality distinction becomes more pronounced. By 6 to 7 years of age and older, a child should be gently but firmly discouraged from telling such stories when confronted about a transgression, and the importance of telling the truth based on what actually happened should be emphasized. However, children's imaginary stories and play in other contexts should be allowed without censure. Children's imaginary play is an important part of their cognitive and social development as well as the fostering of their creativity. It is only in the context of deception that parents should steer children away from their imaginary fantasy stories.

There is another way that children's fantasy stories can come up in relation to their transgressions. Sometimes fantasy stories may be developed in a child's effort to "save face" or to deal with their emotions related to the punishment of their behavior. If you think of the classic story *Where the Wild Things Are*, this is a good example. In the story, the boy, Max, wreaks havoc in his house while wearing his wolf costume. He is sent to his room without supper. Most of the story is about his fantasy of going to a magical island, where the "Wild Things" live. Max intimidates the Wild Things, roaring at them, and is made their king. He romps with them until he stops the rumpus and sends the Wild Things to bed without their supper. Feeling lonely, he gives up his crown despite the protests of the Wild Things, and he sails back to his room to find his hot supper waiting for him. The story is an excellent example of some emotions children may feel when they get into trouble: anger, defiance, loneliness, and sadness at the loss of parental favor. It also illustrates how children can use fantasy and imaginary play to help them process their emotions and play out their desires. Max is able to subdue the Wild Things and command them to his will. He has an unfettered, terrific time, having a big romp with no one to tell him to stop. In the face of his mother's censure, he is able to reassert himself through his imaginary play. Of course, at the end, he returns with desire to be reunited and to reestablish the closeness with his parent, and that unconditional parental love is depicted by the waiting warm dinner for him.

The prevalence of these fantasy lies is not generally reported as high. This may be because usually parents can tell when children are telling stories that are part of their imaginary play and do not take them as intentional acts of deception. Occasionally, however, parents may be unsure of the child's distinction between fantasy and reality, especially with younger children. If no transgression is tied up in the story, usually there is no harm, and parents can let the child enjoy their imaginary play.

CONCLUSION

We lie for a variety of reasons. Our lies can be motivated by more than one reason, and the motivations can overlap. For instance, a teenager who lies about where they were after school may be motivated to lie to prevent negative consequences, such as getting into trouble with their parent, but also to avoid their parents' disappointment or disapproval. The lie could also be motivated by impression management concerns and the desire to appear "good" in their parents' eyes. A child who lies about cheating on a test may fear both punishment and loss of reputation. On receiving an undesirable gift, an adult may lie and say they like the gift to prevent harming the other person's feelings, to not appear rude, and to avoid the person's negative reaction if they told the truth. Lies can be told to accomplish multiple goals and serve multiple motivations.

In general, these motivations are the same for both adults and children. We lie to help protect our self-interests, to get things we want, or to make others like us or think highly of us. Knowing these motivations can help us understand why our children lie. It helps us to reflect on our own behavior and why our "default" to tell the truth can be overruled by stronger motivations. By considering the motivations that prompt dishonesty, we are better able to deal with the behavior, tailor our reactions to our children's dishonesty, and create conditions to foster their honesty.

PART II

Teaching Honesty to Children

4

Stay Calm and Address the Motivation

As discussed in Part I, lying is a serious breach in our social relationships. We are upset when we discover someone is lying to us. Parents often report to me that they are distressed when they catch their child in a lie. It is normal to feel that way when your child lies, and the degree to which we are upset varies by situation. If your 4-year-old tries to tell you that they did not eat the chocolate cookie—yet they have chocolate smears around their lips and on their hands—it's possible you may be secretly amused at this attempt to cover up the obvious misdeed. On the other hand, if your child has just stolen another child's toy and then lies about it, you might be very upset. Or your teenager lies about their social media use, and you discover they have been on sites you do not approve of. We parents need to recognize and deal with these immediate emotional reactions first and then deal with the lie. Once we have dealt with these emotions and can be calm, we are more effective in dealing with the lie.

This chapter discusses why parents need to deal with their emotions first to prevent overreaction and then connect with the child to address the lie effectively. Because lying is considered such a negative behavior, parents (understandably) frequently react emotionally to the lie, which often prevents the child from hearing the message about honesty and may result in an escalation of the situation if the child, in turn, reacts emotionally. Dealing with a lie in the moment of heightened feelings may make a parent act rashly or too harshly. These feelings can often blind us to examine the underlying motivation of the lie so we can address the lie effectively. However, once we recognize we need to stay calm, we can move beyond to the important task of dealing with the lie, correcting the behavior, and healing that bond.

CALM YOURSELF

It is essential for parents to be able to assess their own feelings, recognize what they are feeling, and understand how those emotions may influence how they react. To do this, reflect on how you react in general when something happens that upsets you. Do you feel a surge of anger? Do you feel overly anxious? Or, do you feel crushed? This is important to think about because our actions can be sometimes dictated by our own emotions or concerns without thought.

Reflect on how you feel when you catch your child lying. Do you feel anger? Betrayal (e.g., "How could they lie to me!")? Fear (e.g., "My child is growing up to be a bad person. This lie is a sign of bad things")? Or, perhaps you are concerned about what other people will think (e.g., "The other parents will think I'm a bad mom/dad," "The priest/rabbi/pandit will think I'm not doing a good job raising my child," "My mother will criticize me for not teaching my child right from wrong"). Recognizing these feelings helps you understand what your underlying assumptions are about lying in general and your child in particular. You can then address those assumptions, compare them with what is known about lying and what the actual context is, and deal with them accordingly. Doing so will help you calm yourself in such situations and will also help you frame your reaction in a more positive, constructive way.

In addition to reflecting on how you react when your child misbehaves, reflect on how you react when you have done something wrong or have performed poorly and have received feedback or criticism. Do you look for an excuse? Do you feel incompetent, or do you become defensive? Do you accept the feedback and constructively try to address it? Try to notice and think about how you react to such situations because these reactions are communicating information to the child. How you behave communicates how to deal with negative feedback or censure. Engaging in this reflection also helps you think about how to react and phrase your feedback to the child in a way that will help them learn how to behave. If you always react defensively to suggestions or feel negative feelings, your child may also learn to react in the same way. If you feel bad when you have done something wrong, you can have compassion for how your child may feel, and you can think about ways to com-municate to them—without increasing their sense of shame—how they should behave.

Asking these reflection questions is important not only when the child is a preschooler but also as they grow into adoles-cence. Your reactions and feelings may change over time as your expectations for your child and youth change. You may feel no negative feelings when your preschooler tells you a fib about taking an extra cookie at snack time, but you may feel hurt and upset when your teenager lies to you about who they were with after school. Noticing and acknowledging your own thoughts are the first steps in being able to effectively deal with your child's lies.

It is important for parents to get their emotions in check before they deal with the child's lying behavior and address the underlying motivation. This also allows the parents to think through how they wish to respond to the child and what it is they are trying to achieve and teach the child. For instance, your child truthfully tells you that they do not like the food you made for dinner. Having an outsized emotional reaction can increase the shame the child may feel, leading them to be more likely to keep their feelings hidden and to adopt more secretive strategies to avoid eating your food (e.g., feeding it to a dog). Or, imagine discovering that your child has been lying about going to school and being truant. Responding with an explosion of anger may frighten the child and confirm their decision to lie to cover up. By responding calmly and sticking to the facts of the situation, you can more effectively deal with the lie, the underlying motivations that led to the lie, and the situation surrounding it.

> It is important for parents to get their emotions in check before they deal with the child's lying behavior.

Of course, this is not always easy. There may be times when a parent needs to take a moment to step out of the situation to calm themselves. One time, after a long bathroom renovation, I found my preschool son sitting in the bathroom with a marker in his hands and making artwork on the bathroom walls less than 24 hours after they had been painted. In shock, I gasped loudly, "No! Not the walls!" I immediately realized I was not in a condition to speak to him and turned on my heel to walk into the bedroom for a few moments to calm down. I even shed a tear of frustration at the thought of having to repaint that section of the wall. My reaction was outsized for the misdemeanor my son had committed. He was young and did not know about "walls" and the general rule of not drawing on them. I had never spoken to him about it before. My reaction was fueled by my impatience and frustration over the difficulties of the bathroom renovation, something that was beyond his understanding and was not his fault.

Once I was sufficiently in possession of my emotions and calm enough to react rationally, I then spoke calmly and firmly to my child about not drawing on walls, and I took the marker away from him. My son was alerted to the seriousness by my initial reaction (the gasp had made him sit bolt upright), my withdrawal for a moment, and then my firm but nonaccusatory language that reinforced to him that drawing on the walls was not something we did. He never drew on the walls again. And I learned the important lesson that sometimes taking a moment to control my emotions and stepping out from the situation can help me deal with that situation more effectively.

COMMUNICATE CALMLY TO YOUR CHILD

When reacting to children's lies, the goal is to be dispassionate and calm and to avoid being overly emotional when talking to the child. A parent's frustration and anger about the lie does not help them address the behavior that made the child lie. After a parent has been able to control and address their own emotions and feelings, they can then communicate with the child using a regular tone of voice. Using clear and direct communication about what is expected of the child helps direct the child's attention to the desired behavior and remind them (or inform them if they are young and do not know yet) of the rules. For instance, a parent seeing their child hit their sibling can firmly say, "In our house, the rule is no hitting. No one can hit for any reason. If you break that rule, there will be a consequence." The parent should try to say this in as neutral a tone as possible and may have to repeat it to make sure the child, especially a young child, understands the rules and expectations.

Just because the parent is able to control their emotions does not mean the child will. Children may erupt in protest or sob in repentance. Parents should be prepared for an emotional response from their child. Preparation calls on the parent's own abilities to keep their emotions and feelings in check. In the face of protests that "this is not fair!" parents have to be able to have the fortitude to remain mild but firm in tone while reinforcing the rules.

Parents should not view their child's lying to them as simply a moral infraction and react to that transgression. Parents can see the lie as a sign that an issue needs to be addressed. The child may need help problem solving to prevent the behavior that caused the lie. For instance, a child who lies about not doing their homework may feel compelled to lie about it because they are at a loss on how to organize themselves to do their homework. The lie may be told for impression management reasons because they feel shame or embarrassment at their lack of organizational skills, so they lie to cover up their failure (for more on impression management lies, see Chapter 3).

Realizing that lies can be a sign that there is a problem can help to take the sting out of the lie. Parents can help the child with the underlying problem and to think of the situation as a problem-solving moment.

> *Parents can see the lie as a sign that an issue needs to be addressed.*

If the lie is a serious one about something risky, unsafe, or illegal, the parent needs to address it directly and immediately. For instance, realizing your child has been concealing that they are engaging with others online on sites that have strangers and potentially risky content, a parent must prioritize having a conversation (or multiple conversations over time) about safety online and start teaching the child about how to judge what they see online as trustworthy and appropriate. Children are exposed to a lot of information online, and it is very important that parents provide ongoing help and guidance to help them navigate this online world from early on. However, if a parent only reacts to the concealment, then they are missing this opportunity.

Furthermore, they should consider why the child concealed. Was it because they were worried the parent would stop them from going online? If so, then removing their online privileges could just reinforce their underlying motivation to conceal. Or perhaps they concealed because they were embarrassed? They may have been curious (e.g., to look up something related to sexuality) and then felt shame to let their parents know. If that's the case, then the parent needs to let the child know that they are not judged as being "good" or "bad" for having such curiosity. The parent also needs to create an atmosphere in which the child can speak openly to the parent about their questions and feelings.

Sometimes it may help for the parents to consult with each other first or speak to another trusted adult or family member to problem solve how to address the lie. Giving yourself time to think about how to handle the situation helps you get over the initial upset and fears as well as allows time for rational, careful thought. When the discussion with the child or teenager happens, try to avoid getting into an argument. Instead address the behaviors you saw; for instance:

> I heard you on the stairs last night. And I noticed you were very sleepy this morning at breakfast. But you told us you were home all night. There will be a consequence for that. You are not allowed any sleepovers this weekend. We are concerned about where you went.

Keep your tone matter-of-fact: "We have information, we believe it to be true, and these are the consequences." Keep it simple, listen to what your child says, and remain firm.

Any discipline given to children should be done when the parent is calm and has their own emotions in check. When parents react harshly and punitively, children may not take in messages about the honesty but, rather, become more careful about avoiding harsh punishment. This desire to avoid harsh punishment may lead children to actually learn to become better liars as a strategy to protect themselves from the arbitrary punishment. See Chapter 5 for further details on how to discipline children.

ADDRESS THE UNDERLYING MOTIVATION

As discussed in Chapter 3, most kids do not lie to hurt their parents. They lie because there's something else going on. One way to figure out how to react to a child's dishonesty is to reflect on what motivated the dishonesty in the first place. Look behind the lie to see what is going on. Sometimes, the lie is a mask for a larger problem or reflects a child's lack of knowledge or desire for something. If we deal with the lie only, we miss the reason for the lie and the root cause of the problem. For example, in a serious example of dishonesty, you discover that your child stole a toy from a friend's house and lied about it. If the parent only chastises the child for lying, the message about the importance of not stealing is missed. If a child lies about playing video games at night in their bedroom, only addressing the lie means the parent misses dealing with the issue of video game playing at night. By understanding the reasons that children and people, in general, lie, we can think about ways to reduce that motivation in different situations.

For instance, one parent reported to me that she caught her child sneaking Halloween candy from her stash. After Halloween, the mother had taken the Halloween candy from the child and was allowing her to have only one piece a day. The child lied to conceal her transgression of taking more candy than she was allowed. Seeing her child sneak and lie about the candy, the mother decided to do something about it. After telling her child that it was important that she be truthful, she then asked her daughter what she thought was a fair amount of candy to have each day. In the past, the mother had talked a lot about the importance of eating good, healthy food for your body—"always" foods—and having "some-times" food like candy as occasional treats. The child reflected and said she thought she should have five pieces each day but also eat her vegetables every night at dinner and brush her teeth. After further discussion, it was decided the child could eat three pieces on weekdays and five pieces on the weekend until the candy was gone. After that, there would be no more candy until Christmas.

The result was that her child did not sneak candy and did not lie about it. She did occasionally still ask for more candy, which her mother reported she sometimes allowed. The mother said,

> I figured that by making the conditions for eating candy so restrictive, I was making the temptation to lie very high. After all, I did let her get the Halloween candy to begin with. It wasn't fair to expect her then to not eat it. So I should let her enjoy it within reason, and then when it was gone, we could go back to limits.

Another mother caught her child sneaking potato chips from the cupboard and denying knowledge about what happened to the dwindling bag of chips. Again, this is an example of a frequent motivation for children to lie to conceal doing something they know is against their parents' rules or wishes and to avoid the negative consequences of their parents' knowing. The mother had strict rules about junk food eating and did not allow it. However, she realized that by having the potato chips in the house, she was creating temptation. She had the chips because she liked to have them as a "treat" every now and then. She realized that either she had to make the decision not to have them in the house, or, if she had them, she needed to let the child have them as an occasional treat. In this case, she decided to let him have potato chips as an occasional treat so as not to make the chips tempting "forbidden fruit," She also decreased the amount of potato chips she bought, noting that "if it is junk food for him, it is junk food for me, too."

The previous examples are both related to food. In another example, a mother reported that her son took a clock apart. She found all the pieces later, and when questioned, her son denied it. The child was motivated to take the clock apart out of curiosity, but he had denied it when asked for fear of his parents' anger. In this case, the parents recognized the child's curiosity. They gently talked to the son about not taking things apart and about asking them if he wanted to know about something. They also gently reminded him that he should tell them the truth. The father then went to a thrift shop and bought a few old clocks as well as a radio for their son to take apart. Both parents spent time with the child talking about the mechanics of these different devices, allowing him to see how each worked and how to handle each device. This approach helped to satisfy their son's curiosity and helped him learn about something without creating harm and destruction to something the parents valued. It also took away his need to lie and reinforced that the truth does not always lead to negative results. He learned to ask his parents about how things work and realized he would be aided in his natural desires to learn about the world and how things work. The parents reported that their son grew up to work on electronic devices and later worked with computers.

The preceding examples are all of situations in which the child lied because they feared their parents' negative reactions. Children's earliest lies are often motivated to escape the negative consequences of their transgressions or behavior. This motivation is strong all through childhood, during the teenage years, and into adulthood. A child who spilled their milk on the carpet by accident may lie because they fear a parent's anger or disapproval. A teenager may lie about failing on an exam because they do not wish to disappoint their parents and face their negative reactions. Keeping this in mind, parents can deal with the lie and the motivation behind the lie more effectively. They may reflect on what messages they give their child about achievement and learning as well as how they have reacted in the past to the child's failure on different tasks.

If the child's fear is their parents' disappointment, this is what the parents must address directly. For instance, they can communicate to the child that what is important is that the child make an effort and try their best, and, if the child is struggling, they can ask for help. The parents want the child to succeed and can help the child in their efforts. They may choose to emphasize that is not the grade that is important to them but the child's efforts to learn the material. They may also tell the child that they should never be ashamed to tell the parents if they have failed at something, reassuring the child that no matter what, they love the child and wish to support the child. Letting the child know that the parents do not think less of them or love them less can help address the underlying fears of the child that made them lie.

As outlined in Chapter 3, children tell lies for other reasons, too. For instance, a child may lie about brushing their teeth at night to rush into bed early to get an extended story time. In this case, they may be lying to get more of the "fun time" and avoid doing a chore. Realizing this, a parent can address both the child's teeth brushing habits as well as the lie. The parent may supervise the brushing for a while or give the child a timer to use so they will know how long to brush. The parent can also put a consequence in place, such as no story if the teeth are not brushed.

Even when children lie to protect the feelings of others, parents can address the underlying motivation. For instance, a parent reported to me that she discovered her child had been lying about liking a pineapple cake that the parent had made. She had made the cake repeatedly and had believed it was well liked. Finding out that her child did not like pineapple cake at all and had been lying to her all along led her to feel very upset. However, after she calmed herself down, she reflected on her prior behavior. She realized that when she had made baking "flops," she often acted despondent and engaged in an audible reproach to herself. She realized her son was trying to protect her from feeling bad and wanted her to feel good about her baking. He was trying to protect her feelings and had repeatedly swallowed down cake that he really did not like. When she recognized his underlying motivation, she felt less upset, and she also realized how she should deal with the lie.

When she spoke to him about it, she told him it was okay to tell her if he didn't like something and that not everyone has the same preferences; some people don't like pineapple. She told him that she wanted to bake things he did like, and he had to truthfully tell her if he liked it or not so she could achieve that goal. She also knew—as she told him this—that she had to be prepared to hear the truth and accept it. If it was said in a kind way, she thought she could bear to hear it and not get upset. Later, this parent told me that she had made a big effort to not get emotionally upset when something she baked was not liked, and her son had made an effort to say tactfully if he liked something or not. She also reported that their relationship became even closer after that because they recognized they both cared deeply about the other's feelings. She appreciated her son's concern for her.

WHEN MOTIVATION ISN'T OBVIOUS, LOOK AT THE WIDER PICTURE

Sometimes the motivation behind a lie is not easily seen, and it may require you to look at the broader picture. I was once approached by a parent who was upset because her 12-year-old had lied to his parents about eating his lunch at school. She had discovered he was not eating his lunch and was hungry toward the end of the day. The teacher had reported that his concentration levels were waning in the afternoon. The mother felt upset that her child was lying about his lunch and thought he was taking the money she gave him for the cafeteria and spending it on other things. After the parent talked to the child, the child confessed that he was being bullied by an older teenager who was taking his money from him. The child felt ashamed and embarrassed as well as scared of the bully. He feared that if he told his mother, she would tell the school and the bully would get angry with him. He thought telling would make things worse. So he concealed the bullying and resorted to lying to try to avoid what he thought was a worse fate. Once the truth was discovered, his mother did speak to the school and action was taken. The bully was counseled, and instead of retaliating against the boy, he apologized to him. The child realized that what he feared would happen actually did not happen, and life got better.

This example illustrates the importance of investigating to understand the wider picture and why the child is lying. Because we react so negatively to dishonesty, which we consider a betrayal, it's easy to get caught up in reacting to the act of dishonesty. In the heat of the moment, we can sometimes fail to look at the whole picture and what was motivating the lie.

DON'T SET THEM UP FOR FAILURE

Another way to avoid conditions under which a child will lie is by not inviting them to lie. This is particularly true with preschool children. For instance, if you see your child's juice-stained lips

Ways Parents Can Address the Motivation for Lying

The lie	The motivation	The response
Your child says they ate their lunch when they really were forced to give it to a bully.	The child desires to avoid punishment from the bully and to protect their own image.	Let your child know that they can tell you the truth about their worries because you want to help them, and you can work together to make things better.
Your child lies about how they did on a test.	They did not understand the concepts well and were afraid of getting into trouble for poor performance.	Help your child learn the concepts they are struggling with. Speak to their teacher. Emphasize to your child that they can tell you the truth, and you can help them. By reacting calmly, their expectation of negative reactions is not confirmed.
Your child lies about accidentally spilling milk on the carpet.	The child fears their parent's anger or disapproval.	Calmly ask your child to clean up the mess so that they take some responsibility for their actions. Talk about how accidents happen, and your child can help try to fix it. Let them know that they can tell you the truth and that it is important that they tell the truth.
Your child lies about getting their homework done.	The child wants to go on social media to socialize with friends.	Explain both why it is wrong to lie and your expectations about truth-telling. Give a consequence for not doing homework (e.g., suspension of smartphone use for a reasonable period). Teach your child that it is their responsibility to complete their homework assignment on time.

(continues)

Ways Parents Can Address the Motivation for Lying (Continued)

The lie	The motivation	The response
		You can also help your child succeed by creating space and time to do homework in a public part of the house, such as the kitchen. Provide support and help as needed, monitor homework time initially to be sure that the habit is established, and check your child's work before they are allowed screen time privileges.
Your child lies about their abilities or makes up stories about themselves to their peers.	The child feels a lack of confidence and a need to prove themselves or make themselves appear in a certain way to be accepted by peers.	When alone with your child—not in front of peers—address the motivation of lack of self-esteem or confidence. Calmly tell your child you know what they said is not true. Talk to them about the consequences of "telling stories." Help them to feel better about themselves as they are. Express appreciation for their true accomplishments.

and a juice box on the table, there is no need to ask, "Did you drink the juice?" Or, if you come in on a child scribbling on the wall with a crayon, there is no need to ask, "Did you draw on the wall?" Such questions invite children to try their luck and lie about their behavior in the hope that they will avoid getting into trouble. They wish to appear positively in the eyes of their parents, so they often say what they think will please us. If you ask your child, crayon clutched in hand, who is standing next to the newly scrawled mural in your dining room if they have drawn on the wall, and the child takes the option to deny it, you now have two transgressions to deal with. You have the transgression of the drawing on the wall and the transgression of lying. You also may become doubly upset and react to both transgressions. You may miss dealing with the problem because you are reacting to the lie:

PARENT: Did you scribble on the wall?

CHILD: No.

PARENT: But I saw you! You are lying to me! Why are you lying to me? I can't believe you lied to me.

By not asking obvious questions, you avoid giving them the option to lie, and you can deal with just the initial transgression. Instead of asking them whether they have done something when you already know the answer, focus on the consequence:

PARENT: I see you have drawn on the walls. The wall is not for drawing on. You must clean it up.

Provide the child with a cloth to clean it up. For preschool children, you will have to show them how to do so. They may be unable to clean it up fully on their own, so the expectation should be that they are making an attempt to fix the problem.

Another example comes from a parent who had a very sick son at home. The child asked for grapes to eat, and the father, desirous to get his very sick child something he wanted, went to the grocery store to get grapes. He returned home with the grapes and designated them only for the sick child. However, the father later found that his other son, a younger sibling, had been sneaking the grapes. When he asked that son where the missing grapes had gone, the son denied knowledge. The father reported that he was very upset. He felt that his younger son was stealing from his very sick brother, and he wondered how his young son could be so callous.

After taking a while to reflect on the situation and discuss it with his wife, he realized his younger son just wanted a few grapes, too. In all their worry about their sick child, they had not noticed the younger son's desires. The father spoke to the younger son about the importance of telling the truth. Now recognizing that this younger son was not trying to be "mean" or "callous" about his older brother's health or feelings, he did not punish the younger boy further. Instead, when he next brought grapes home, he made sure to set some aside for the younger son. He also began to create time to spend with his younger son so that the child would feel his father's love and receive his father's attention—and therefore did not need to find less positive ways to get it.

In the preceding example, the literal example of forbidden fruit increased the temptation. Similarly, in the earlier story about the child's sneaking Halloween candy, there was a strong temptation. The child's felt desire for some fruit or candy was not recognized. In these examples, as they realized the reasons behind the behavior and sought to change those conditions, the parents became tolerant of the child's initial secretive and deceptive behavior. As a result of this realization, the child was no longer being deceptive; rather, they were supported in developing desirable behavior.

In some cases, though, a child may not have done anything wrong but now has the option to do something wrong. Consider the example of a child standing next to spilled juice: It may be that spilling the juice was an accident, and no transgression was committed. If the parent sharply asks the child, "Did you spill the juice?" the child may fear getting into trouble. If the child lies about it, the parent now has the transgression of the lie to deal with. Instead, stay focused on the issue at hand: "Looks like you spilled the juice. Let's clean it up together."

At other times, with a number of siblings involved, it may be unclear who did what. For instance, the parent sees a broken toy on the carpet that may have been broken by one or both of the children. Both children tell the parent, "It wasn't me." Instead of focusing on which child is lying about the broken toy, focus on what the children need to do to fix the situation: "All these broken pieces must be cleaned up. I'm asking you both to clean it up." Doing so provides the children with a positive way to fix the problem and shows them that there is no positive consequence for denying responsibility.

While such examples are more common in early childhood, the principle also applies to older children and adolescents. Do not get entangled in issues of honesty by inviting dishonesty. Imagine a situation in which a teenager sneaks into the house 2 hours after curfew. The next day, the parent confronts their child: "What time did you get in last night?" The parent knows the teenager came in 2 hours late because they were listening for the door and the footfall on the stairs. Instead of getting to the issue of where the teen was and the importance of letting the parent know where the teen is and keeping curfew, the parent now has invited their child to lie. The teen may decide to fudge their answer to minimize their lateness and plead that it wasn't really a violation of curfew. Now parent and child are embroiled in a discussion about lying, and the issues of curfew, safety, and communication between parent and child are put off. By the time the parent turns the discussion to these issues, the teen may feel defensive after being caught in a lie or may have shut down and be unwilling to listen to the parent.

By asking the teen the unnecessary question—after all, the parent knows when the teen came in and can just plainly state, "I see you came home 2 hours after curfew last night. It is important for you to keep curfew because . . ."—the parent railroaded their conversation and lost the chance to have a proper discussion with their child about the importance of curfew. It is better to deal with transgressions, rule violations, and other behaviors directly without asking children to needlessly "report" their known behavior.

REFRAME "BAD" BEHAVIOR AS MISTAKES

Children do not always do the right thing. They make choices that are less than ideal. Children learn how to behave, and they will make mistakes. Even adults make mistakes. Adults do lie from time to time and live to regret it. Young children are unable to anticipate long-term negative consequences and may choose to lie as the most expedient way of avoiding immediate negative consequences. For older children and teenagers, they may lie because they are clutching at a poor strategy to mitigate other mistakes they may have made.

Imagine a child who has accidentally broken their grand-mother's ornament. They feel bad, and when questioned, they try to avoid answering the question by lying. In this case, the parent can recognize that the child already feels awful about what has happened, and the parent does not want to increase the shame of it by publicly acknowledging the child's mistake. The parent can respond in a tolerant way that shows consideration for the child's feelings while also upholding the importance of being truthful, even about difficult stuff. If the parent responds in a way that helps the child deal with their feelings and does not belittle or shame them, the child will come to see that, in such situations, they have nothing to fear in telling the truth and that telling the truth doesn't make matters worse.

Keeping in mind that sometimes children's choices are "mistakes" rather than "misbehaviors" allows us parents to reframe the behavior in a way in which we can think about the behavior from the child's perspective and understand why they made that choice. Doing this allows us to respond in a more tailored way to help the child understand the situation and what other choices they can make as well as how those are better choices to make in the future. In this way, it helps us to view their lying not from the perspective of their being "bad children" but from the perspective that they made a mistake, and we can help them learn so they can do better down the road.

TEACH TACT

Being honest does not have to mean being hurtful or rude. We can teach children to balance honesty with the consideration of another's feelings. This may, at times, require a little more effort and thought then just giving a quick, polite lie. It requires some thought about how to avoid bluntness and to temper what you say with sensitivity and delicacy. For instance, if someone gives you a book that you had already received as a gift, instead of, "Oh, I already have this book!" you may say, "Wow, I'm touched! You know what author I like!" Such a tactful statement recognizes their intention in making an effort to get you something you would like and also shows appreciation that they gave some thought to the gift. Sometimes when receiving a gift we do not like, just thanking the person for giving it is enough. We recognize the act of giving: "Thank you for the gift."

If you child tells you, "But I don't want the book. Books are boring!" you can recognize their preference not to have a book but also emphasize we should recognize others' generosity and desire to give, and then show gratitude in turn. We do not have to get anything; people are not obliged to give us gifts, and we are not entitled to get what we want when we want it. Actually—perhaps especially in Western societies—we do get too many things too easily, and that may be our problem. But, I digress. . . .

Teaching tact requires us to help children think about the other person and identify what the underlying intentions and desires are in the social interaction. Was the person trying to do something nice? Were you trying to help the person by giving them feedback that would be useful without crushing them? It also makes us focus on what the virtue is behind the actions.

We can help children by thinking about situations in which giving an honest opinion bluntly may cause harm or negative reactions. You can discuss together what would be possible ways to speak with truthfulness without causing offense or harm. Equally, when your child is bluntly honest, you can help them find a more positive way of saying what they are feeling or thinking. Here's an example: "Arielle, I appreciate your honesty about your opinion. How can you say that in a more respectful, courteous way?"

DON'T SWEAT THE SMALL STUFF

You walk upstairs at bedtime. You see your child dash into bed just before you come in the door. "Did you brush your teeth?" you ask, certain that they did not brush them. "Yes!" You could stop to have a discussion about truth-telling and lies at this time. Perhaps it is a good time if you haven't had that discussion and there is some time left before lights out. It could be a quiet time to have this discussion with your child without interruptions and in a relaxed atmosphere. But it isn't always the time to have the discussion. It may be late, and your child needs to be asleep. They are already showing signs of fatigue. A long discussion now may not be productive because your child's ability to attend and engage in conversation may be depleted. If that is the case, you may just order your child out of bed to get their teeth brushed. You make a note that, going forward, you need to supervise the toothbrushing a little more closely until your child develops the habit.

Or, another time, your child lies about eating their vegetables. You realize you have been trying to force-feed them brussels sprouts and spinach. To develop the healthy habit of eating vegetables, you decide that you must start providing more palatable vegetables like peas and carrots. You supervise your child's eating of those vegetables for the next few weeks to develop that habit.

In both these cases, you are focusing on the target behavior of what the child is lying about. The lie serves to draw your attention to a behavior, habit, or lesson that the child needs to learn, and you redirect your efforts to helping your child learn those behaviors. It does not mean you do not address the importance of honesty. However, by understanding in those moments what the behavior is and what motivates it, you can direct your energies to developing positive behaviors that lessen the motivation to lie.

Similarly, the parent may overlook the child's exaggerations or magnifying of their abilities. Preschool children and children in early grade school often see their abilities in grand terms. They claim they can "run the fastest," or they can "jump so high over buildings," or "I have night owl vision!" These effusions are a normal part of a young child's emerging sense of self as well as their imaginary worlds. As children get older, they are more likely to compare themselves with their peers. Young children often view their abilities in a positive way and magnify those abilities. Such exaggerations may not always require any reaction from the parent, and if they persist, a parent can gently remind the child of a more realistic but still positive assessment of themselves.

DON'T REWARD THE LIE

Another important tip for reducing lying is to be careful not to reward the strategy of lying. Children tell lies for a reason. If they are successful at getting something they want, then that can reinforce the use of lies as a successful strategy to achieve their goals. If you notice your younger child is always making up false stories about getting hurt at school as soon as your older child begins telling you about their day, it may be attention-seeking behavior. So if the parent switches their attention from the older child to the younger child, they are rewarding the younger one by giving them what they want: the attention.

But, by realizing why the child is making up these stories, the parent can respond in ways that do not reward the lie, therefore dealing with the underlying motivation. For instance, recognizing that the child needs their attention, the parent can create time to give the child focused attention. Or, the parent can create a rule that each child is given time to talk about their day on the way home, and that while it is one child's turn, no one else is allowed to speak until it is their turn. The parent then reinforces the rule by repeating it and by giving attention and positive feedback to the child whose turn it is to talk.

CONCLUSION

How we react to transgressions and lies impacts the child. We can react negatively and angrily, which may actually drive them to lie more. Similarly, we can create conditions that encourage them to lie, or we can decrease the motivating circumstances and reasons for lying. By remaining calm and taking a moment to reflect, we are better able to assess the situation as well as the relevant behaviors or details we need to deal with, and we react in way that leads to the child's learning and positive development.

5

Use Positive Discipline

The best approach to honesty is to teach and create an environment in which honesty is valued and it is easy to be honest. I talk about this more in following chapters. However, *we do have to deal with lies when they happen*. Lying is not a positive behavior we wish to encourage. Yet, as discussed in Chapter 3, children often lie in an attempt to escape punishment. This can lead to a vicious cycle of lying and punishment. So how do we effectively deal with lies? The emphasis needs to be on the lie—not the liar.

As a reminder, discipline is not the first step for responding to a lie. First, you must calm yourself and then address the underlying motivation. When parents skip these first two steps and jump straight to the third—disciplining the child—there is little opportunity to gain insight into the motivation behind the lie or the behavior that the lie attempts to conceal. This insight is necessary to address those underlying reasons, thus leading to longer term impact than immediate discipline would.

Three Steps for Responding to a Lie

This chapter focuses on the third step of the process. Discipline strategies that are appropriate and consistent can be used to curtail the negative behavior while teaching the positive behavior. I discuss how to impose consequences and discipline the child within a framework of emphasizing positive virtues in the child.

EXPRESS LOVE

Let's start the discussion on discipline by talking about love. Showing love to your child, engaging with them, and having a loving response are foundational aspects of parenting that lead to more effective and positive discipline. When the parent regularly gives the child positive, focused attention without distractions and responds promptly and lovingly to the child's cries or emotional upsets, the child feels valued and strongly connected to their parent. This forms a strong emotional bond between the parent and the child. Within the context of that loving and caring relationship, the child develops a sense of themselves and a desire to maintain that relationship. Thus, when the child is firmly corrected by their parent with whom they have a loving relationship, they are motivated to fix their behavior. In this context, the parent often does not have to resort to overly harsh words or punishment because their censure and somber attitude are enough to alert the child and focus the child's attention on correcting the desired behavior.

You will be more successful in disciplining your child if you have a warm and close relationship with them. When parent and child have a positive relationship, there is a "bank" of good feelings. The parent can draw on that bank when they have to correct the child for misbehavior. A child who knows they are loved is more likely to behave appropriately and listen to their parents. Children are more likely to comply with, pay close attention to, and do onerous tasks when they have a positive relationship with their parent—when they feel accepted and loved as well as trust their parents. This is important for children and adolescents. Doing small things to make sure we spend time to nurture and strengthen that bond with our child is important and makes a difference when we must talk to them seriously about misbehavior. For children, this could include talking to them about their day in the car as you drive home or spending time reading at bedtime together. For adolescents, this can include eating a family meal together, going shopping, working together on projects around the house, or doing some shared activity.

UNDERSTAND THE DIFFERENCE BETWEEN DISCIPLINE AND PUNISHMENT

When we think of "discipline" as parents, we may automatically think of "punishment" because both concepts involve giving an unpleasant consequence in response to bad behavior. Indeed, the two terms are often used interchangeably in popular discourse. But many psychologists differentiate the two terms.

Discipline Versus Punishment

✔ Discipline	✗ Punishment
✓ Takes a proactive approach	✗ Is a reactive approach
✓ Teaches the child to behave according to the rules by focusing on a future behavior	✗ Inflicts suffering or penalty for past behavior to change future behavior
✓ Has logical or natural consequences for wrongdoing	✗ Is "paying for their mistake"
✓ Puts kids in control of their behavior	✗ Puts the adult in control of the child's behavior
✓ Gives the message: "Here is what you can do/should do instead"	✗ Gives the message: "You must stop doing that; it's wrong"
✓ Relates the consequence to the offense	✗ Does not directly tie the consequence to what happened

Discipline, which comes from the same root as "disciple," means responding to bad behavior in a way that trains or teaches the person. Children are still held responsible for their behavior, but the consequences are meaningful and related to the behavior. In contrast, *punishment* emphasizes suffering over teaching; it is when there is a negative consequence as retribution for bad behavior that does not necessarily to teach them how to behave in the future.

For example, when a child has lied about cleaning up their toys, a parent may discipline with a verbal reprimand and reminder of the rule of telling the truth: "Don't tell lies. We tell the truth in our house. And we clean up after ourselves. Now, I am going to watch you as you clean up this mess." And the parent enforces the cleanup, so the child engages in the desired behavior with supervision. With consistent reinforcement and patience, the child learns the expectations and how to behave accordingly. If the child continues to not comply, the parent might add a consequence for noncompliance, such as no screen time or that the child can't go play at the park until their toys are cleaned up. However, the important element is consistency and teaching your child to learn that when they make choices to behave certain ways, there are consequences, and they can learn to be responsible for those consequences. This fosters their autonomy and helps them to develop the ability to make positive decisions about how to behave and be responsible for their actions.

Punishment, in contrast, focuses only on the negative consequences. In the example of the child lying about cleaning up their toys, a parent could shout at or spank the child. This response delivers negative consequences for the behavior, but the person who punishes the child becomes responsible for the child's behavior. Thus, the parent takes the responsibility rather than put it on the child. The child does not gain any information about how to make the right choices in the future and how their behavior can have consequences to themselves and others. They only learn that if they get caught lying, they will get in trouble. So, they just learn "don't get caught."

Examples of Discipline and Punishment in Different Scenarios

Scenario	Discipline	Punishment
Child lies about driving the car when they did not have permission.	Parent points out that because the child made the choice not to follow the rules, the child is not allowed to use the car for a week.	Parent makes the child do additional household chores for a week.
Child lies about doing their home-work because they were chatting with friends.	Child is not allowed screen or phone time until they finish their homework.	Parent grounds the child and gives them extra math work to do.
Child lies about drawing on the wall.	Parent communicates the rule about not drawing on walls. Parent removes the crayons and asks the child to help wash the crayon off the wall.	Parent yells at the child and spanks them for being naughty.

Punishment can promote compliance out of fear of punish-ment from you. Your child only learns to avoid lying to you because they are afraid of the punishment you will give. How-ever, this learning is not necessarily generalized to situations when you are not present. When your child is with others or they think that you will not know, they have no reason to comply. This is because if the main reason a child chooses to not lie is out of fear of being punished, then when the child believes the likelihood of punishment is negated, there is no other compunction to prevent lying.

> Children need to learn to fix their mistakes, not just learn to pay for them. Children need to assume responsibility for their actions.

Punishment, such as spanking, may not have the long-term desirable effect of teaching children to be honest. Physical punishment like spanking is a form of power assertion. A considerable amount of research has shown that spanking can be a harmful type of punishment. Such techniques take children's focus away from seeing the consequences of their behavior. It can teach the lesson that physical force and domination over others is a way to get people to behave the way you want them to. Compelling evidence from psychological science shows that power-assertive methods of discipline are related to immediate obedience but may undermine children's internalization of moral standards and increases the risk of behavioral and mental health problems in the long term (Gershoff, 2002, 2019). Children are more likely to behave when their parents are around to avoid being hit, but they have not necessarily been taught why they should behave that way, leading them to misbehave when parents are not there. In contrast, parents who are proactive in providing clear instruction, support, and limit-setting in a supportive and firm manner are more likely to have children with fewer problem behaviors over time.

Psychological scientists found that mothers of toddlers who showed committed compliance (i.e., a measure of internalization defined by enthusiastic adherence to a parental agenda without need for intervention) in a cleanup situation were more likely to use gentle guidance, such as reasoning, suggestions, and polite requests (Kochanska & Aksan, 1995). They were also less likely to use threats, physical punishment, and commands. When mothers used these forceful, negative control strategies, researchers found it was negatively related to child internalization. In other words, children whose mothers used threats and physical punishment had less self-control and were unable resist playing with a forbidden toy when alone. Parents who are warm, responsive, and consistent in their expectations have a more positive influence on children's internalizing moral conduct.

One study demonstrated how punishment may backfire when it comes to children's honesty (Talwar & Lee, 2011).

In this study, my colleague and I had two groups of children who went to private schools in a West African city. One group was from a school that used harsh punishments, such as pinching the children, slapping their heads, and beating them with a stick. These harsh punishments were used to respond to a range of offenses, from getting a math question wrong to being disruptive in class. The idea behind administering these punishments was that children need reinforcement to learn, and physical punishment effectively teaches children not to misbehave. The other was a group of children from the same city. In this group, children attended school where discipline included time-outs (i.e., standing outside the classroom) and verbal reprimands, and for more serious offenses, children were taken to the principal's office.

Children from both schools participated in a temptation resistance paradigm in which they were told not to peek at a forbidden toy (for more on this paradigm, see Chapter 2). As was found in previous studies with children in North America, the majority of children peeked. However, when children were asked if they peeked, a different pattern of results emerged. Just more than half of the children whose school did not use a corporal punishment lied about peeking, whereas almost all the children in the corporal punishment school lied. Furthermore, when children's ability to maintain the lie was examined, children from the corporal punishment school were significantly better at maintaining their lie during follow-up questioning. These findings suggest that children from the corporal punishment school were not only more dishonest about their peeking behavior than those from the noncorporal punishment school were but also more advanced in their ability to tell convincing lies.

These findings also suggest not only that there are limits to the effectiveness of physical punishment in teaching honesty but that physical punishment may actually backfire as a way to deal with lying. When punishment that is mainly directed at compliance and is potentially harsh—even for minor offenses— is used, children may learn that if they have done something wrong, they have nothing to lose by lying. They will be punished for the transgression if discovered, but if they lie and lie convincingly, they may be able to conceal the transgression and completely avoid punishment. When children perceive the consequences balanced in this way, lying becomes an attractive strategy to lessen the negative impact on themselves and to potentially protect themselves from perceived harm.

In situations in which there are inequalities and injustices in an oppressive and hierarchical system, individuals may use strategies like deception to resist and to protect themselves. While adults and adolescents view deception, in general, as undesirable, they also see deception as an acceptable strategy to deal with unfair restrictions imposed by those in greater power and control (Perkins & Turiel, 2007; Turiel, 2002). On a smaller and more personal scale, children, when exposed to harsh punishment as a means to achieve their compliance and exert control over them, may turn to dishonesty as a means to protect their own physical and psychological selves.

DON'T SHAME THE CHILD

We have to be careful about how we respond to the child's misbehavior, in general. It is often easy to respond to misbehavior or bad behavior with anger, aggression, shaming, and punishment, such as spanking. Such negative effects may not be confined to just physical punishments like beatings. Giving children "tongue lashings" can also be very bad. We must be careful to not use abusive words that "beat" the child psychologically or belittle them in front of others. This includes harsh verbal chastisements that center on the "badness" of the child and diminish the child to make them feel shame or belittled. We have to deal with the lie-telling behavior but not make the child feel that they are a liar. If we call them a liar and make it about the child's being bad, they may incorporate this into their self-identity. "I am a liar. If I am a liar, what do I have to lose by lying?" We need to avoid saying things like, "Why can't you be more honest?!" Such statements that make it about the child's personality can be shaming.

Shame is different from guilt. While *guilt* is the feeling that "I did a bad thing," *shame* is the feeling that "I am a bad person." When we feel guilt, we feel remorse and regret. We feel empathy for the person we have harmed, and we are motivated to repair the damage through good behavior. Guilt

Guilt Statements Versus Shame Statements

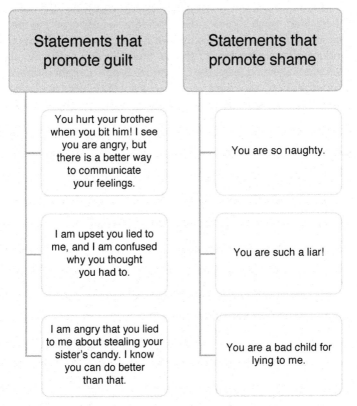

Statements that promote guilt	Statements that promote shame
You hurt your brother when you bit him! I see you are angry, but there is a better way to communicate your feelings.	You are so naughty.
I am upset you lied to me, and I am confused why you thought you had to.	You are such a liar!
I am angry that you lied to me about stealing your sister's candy. I know you can do better than that.	You are a bad child for lying to me.

can motivate us to take constructive steps to not repeat the mistake or offense in the future. In contrast, when we feel shame, we feel worthless, and we are motivated to either shut down or lash out at those shaming us; we are *not* motivated to improve our behavior.

For instance, in one study, toddlers played with a doll whose leg fell off while they were playing with it (Barrett et al., 1993). The guilt-prone children tried to fix the doll and approached the researcher to explain what happen. The children who were shame prone avoided the researcher who had given them the doll and did not voluntarily disclose that they had broken it. This is an important point when it comes to lying. Because there is so much stigma around being a liar, especially in the minds of children and youths, we have to be careful about inducing strong feelings of shame. Shame is a negative moral emotion. Shaming leads the child to feel bad about themselves and does not foster their honest behavior. If children are belittled regularly or made to feel deep shame about themselves, they may lie more to avoid such negative feelings.

Children are more likely to experience shame when parents express anger, withdraw their love, or assert their power with punitive punishment. Children may conceal their misdemeanors or their choices because they fear their parents' reaction. However, this may be amplified if the reactions by parents are particularly harsh or punitive, or if they "morally damn" the child. When this is the case, the child may decide that concealing and lying are better choices than telling the truth to avoid the threats to their self-identity. Lying is a concealing behavior that can help them avoid such feelings, and they will be motivated to become better at it.

It means that sometimes a parent may wish to deal with the deception privately when it is just them and the child present—away from an audience of others. This way, the child does not feel embarrassed or ashamed in front of others. If a young child or teenager feels shame in front of their peers or others, they may shut down emotionally and just want to get out of the situation without really listening to the parent.

When talking about the incident, it is better to refocus behavior on what is needed. If a child is acting in an unacceptable way, tactfully remind them of the desired behavior. If you have been talking about virtues, in general, as part of a moral education program, you can ask them questions, such as: "What virtue were you forgetting?" or "Which virtues would've helped you do the right thing?" or, in a more direct way, you can remind them, "How could you have been truthful in that situation?" You can also talk about what prompted the situation and the child's lie—for instance, why the child felt angry at their sibling, which led to the child's hitting their sibling and then lying to say they did not. In this way, parents can help and support the child to express their feelings of frustration and find more positive ways to deal with those feelings in the future without having to then lie about their behavior. The parent can help the child without the child's feeling humiliated about who they are and not internalizing feelings that promote negative ideas about the self (e.g., "Mommy thinks I'm a bad person").

> *When talking about the incident, it is better to refocus behavior on what is needed. If a child is acting in an unacceptable way, tactfully remind them of the desired behavior.*

AVOID PERSONAL CRITICISM

When we correct children, we should be careful with the language we use. As discussed earlier in this chapter, we want to be careful not to induce strong feelings of shame in the child, which can be counterproductive to the child's learning and developing sense of self. We must try to avoid criticism that attributes dishonesty as a character trait (e.g., "You are such a liar!"). Research has shown that criticism that attributes failure on performing to a desirable standard can be especially problematic for the child's learning. For instance, researchers found that when children received person-centered criticism (e.g., "I'm very disappointed in you") about their lack of ability on academic tasks, the children developed negative ideas of their intelligence and their ability to do the tasks (Gunderson et al., 2018). Children were also less likely to persist at tasks. When parents used *process criticism*, which attributed failure to lack of effort, it led children to develop a healthier idea of their abilities to develop and improve.

USE POSITIVE DISCIPLINE

The goal of discipline is to teach the child right from wrong. For my purposes, I am referring to discipline that involves training the child to correct and mold their behavior. The emphasis is less on controlling the child and more focused on providing the scaffolding and structure to develop, over time, the child's internal self-control, behavior, and understanding to make positive choices.

You may have heard the term "positive discipline." What does that mean? In reality, the principles of such discipline require communicating expectations to children, praising good behavior, and correcting the child rather than "punishing the child" and giving the child attention not just when they are behaving badly. Importantly, it does not mean letting the child do whatever they want when they want.

Discipline is essential part of training a child and being a parent. Parents cannot simply adopt an attitude of nonresistance toward children and let them do as they wish when they wish. Parents must endeavor to inculcate gently and patiently the principles and behaviors that they wish their children to exhibit. The parent is the first educator of children, and it is through the parent that children often learn the moral principles and conduct that they go on to develop as adults. Without proper guidance and discipline, children will not learn how to behave.

The Do's and Don'ts of Positive Discipline

Do's	Don'ts
• Do focus on teaching the child. • Do respond to misbehavior calmly and dispassionately. • Do label the bad behavior. • Do emphasize what to do ("Please tell the truth"). • Do, when possible, give children a chance to "fix" their behavior or to experience the natural negative consequences of it. • Do make the consequence proportional to the "crime." • Do clearly communicate rules and intended consequences before rules are broken. • Do follow through with the intended consequence after a rule is broken.	• Don't focus on making the child suffer. • Don't respond to misbehavior with anger, aggression, shaming, and punishment. • Don't label the child as a "liar," "cheater," and so on. • Don't emphasize what not to do ("Don't lie"). • Don't always determine how the child will "fix" it. • Don't withdraw love or affection. • Don't give negative consequences for a rule you have not communicated beforehand. • Don't "let things slide" after you've communicated a rule and the intended consequence for breaking it.

Children need parents to set boundaries, give them guidance on how to behave, and explain the expectations about how to behave carefully and simply. Parents can then follow through with punishment, if necessary, in ways that are appropriate to the child's age level of maturity.

With very young children who are 2 or 3 years of age, we must be extremely gentle and patient. We can gently guide them to tell the truth with simple messages about its importance, and we can praise for honest behavior. If a child lies to cover a transgression, we can help the child to learn how to behave and gently remind them to be honest about their behaviors.

Consider this example: Three-year-old Oonagh scribbles on the wall and lies when asked if she did the scribbling. Her mother can take away her crayons from her, telling her firmly that drawing on the wall is forbidden. She can also say, "Please tell me the truth." At such a young age, firmness is necessary, but too much force will not incline Oonagh to be more likely to tell the truth in the future. If Oonagh repeatedly scribbles on the wall, her mother may choose to take Oonagh's crayons away for a time or impose some other suitable consequence. But when it is clear Oonagh has carried out the misdemeanor, her mother may avoid regularly asking Oonagh to report on her behavior because this may invite her to be dishonest. Instead, Oonagh's mother concentrates on correcting the behavior that is causing Oonagh to conceal and lie. She may not only discipline Oonagh about the scribbling on the wall but, realizing her daughter's desire to draw on a large scale, put up a blackboard to draw on or put up large scrolls of paper for the child to make a mural on. In such a way, the child learns that drawing on the walls is not allowed but is given another outlet for her desire to draw that is acceptable and does not cause harm to the walls.

Parents should not be afraid to firmly direct the child to correct their behavior. Children who are left to themselves with no guidance are in limbo, trying to figure things out for themselves. Or they grow up to think they can do whatever they please, putting their own needs before the needs of others. Failure to exercise discipline at all can hinder the development of moral standards. Therefore, it is important that children receive good discipline because it helps them to acquire their own self-discipline that is necessary for a successful life.

USE THE COMPONENTS OF POSITIVE DISCIPLINE

No one discipline technique will work every time for every child. Different techniques work better for different children. One must consider the temperament of the child, their behavior, and the situation. Also, as the child becomes older, the parent must adapt the techniques they use.

Avoid disciplining reactively. Wait until your emotions abate and then address the lie. When you are not in the heat of the moment and have calmed down, you are better able to discuss honesty with your child and impress on them its importance. You also are able to think more calmly of what the appropriate consequences for their behavior are.

Instruct on What Should Be Done

First, frame instructions as "do's" rather than "don'ts." When disciplining children, we often tell them what *not* to do. We need to tell them what to *do*. Rather than saying, "Don't lie," you can say, "Please tell the truth." This helps children to learn what the right behavior is. Whenever possible, disciplining the child within a framework of emphasizing the positive virtues and behaviors that you wish the child to exhibit can help that child learn what is expected of them. When communicating to your child, try to be direct and specific. If it is a lecture, the child may stop listening. Keep your communication focused and to the point.

Impose Consequences

When imposing consequences for the child's behavior, be careful to make them proportional to the actual crime. Taking away privileges or possessions or making restitution may be reasonable consequences for telling a lie. As discussed earlier in this chapter, when punishments are given harshly and arbitrarily, children may actually become more inclined to lie. In an atmosphere involving a severe and strict approach to discipline, children may develop the ability to lie as a protective measure. Make sure the consequence is fair and appropriate.

Give Children a Chance to "Fix" It

When we mandate a punishment for the child, we are taking control of the situation and externally dictating the consequences of this behavior. This is necessary for parents to do at times to correct the child's behavior, and within the framework of clearly communicated expectations and guidance on how to behave, this approach can help the child develop positive behaviors. However, in some cases, as children become older and are able to appreciate the consequences to others of their dishonesty and the impact on their relationships, we can put the responsibility back on them and give them opportunity to "fix" the situation. Children need to learn the consequences of their behavior and to fix their mistakes, not just learn to pay for them. Children need to assume responsibility for their actions.

When you take away a privilege or spank a child, you have taken the responsibility of the child's actions on yourself. You have made it your job to make the child pay the consequence. The child may feel that now that they have paid for their misdemeanors, they are free to continue without thought of how they will avoid or solve the problem that caused them to lie in the first place. By holding the child responsible and accountable for their actions, they learn how to behave responsibly and honestly.

The story of Alysha is an example of this approach. Alysha threw her ham sandwich into the garbage can at school. The teacher found it and asked who did it. Alysha shook her head when her teacher looked at her. The teacher finally settled on another student as the culprit (a student who got into a lot of trouble for being naughty), and that student was punished and had to stay indoors for recess. Alysha's mother heard the story because the student's mother had complained to her that her child had been unfairly punished. Alysha's mother asked her daughter if she knew about what had happened. Alysha confessed to her mother that she had thrown the sandwich out because she had not liked it, but she had not confessed to the teacher.

What motivated Alysha to throw out her sandwich? What motivated her to lie to her teacher? Alysha did not like ham sandwiches anymore but felt that her mother would be upset if she said she did not like the lunch her mother had made for her. So, rather than take the uneaten sandwich home, she threw it in the garbage, expecting that to solve the problem. However, on finding the sandwich, her teacher reacted with clear annoyance and anger. Children were often punished in the class, so Alysha feared getting into trouble. She denied throwing out the sandwich to avoid her teacher's negative reaction and punishment. As a result, the teacher unjustly decided another child had done it, and that child received punishment. Alysha felt guilty. When she told her mother what had really happened, she felt relief mixed with trepidation. Her mother was careful not to react with anger or hurt feelings about the unwanted sandwich. She patiently and firmly talked to Alysha about what had happened and the importance of telling the truth.

In this case, Alysha could have been truthful on two occasions. First, she could have truthfully brought the uneaten sandwich home and told her mother she did not like it. Such honesty may not always be comfortable. Later, when she did hear about the sandwich, Alysha's mother reassured Alysha that she could always tell her mother if she did not like a particular food and that they could find a solution (e.g., packing a different kind of sandwich, Alysha's agreeing to eat half of the sandwich, Alysha's getting to pick one item for her lunch each day). In this case, Alysha's mom did not discipline Alysha further for this part of the dishonesty because she saw that Alysha had already become cognizant of the unpleasant consequences of throwing out her sandwich.

The second occasion when Alysha could have told the truth was when the teacher asked who had thrown away the sandwich. Instead, Alysha denied throwing the sandwich away and let the other child take the blame, Alysha's mother asked her what she was going to do to "fix it." At first, Alysha did not have an answer, but with her mother's help, she made a card to apologize to the other child and offered to do his classroom chores (i.e., wiping the blackboards) for the day as reparation. She also confessed to the teacher and offered to stay in for recess. In this way, Alysha took responsibility for her actions and faced the consequences of her dishonesty. It also served to teach her a valuable lesson on the cost of dishonesty and how much easier it would have been to have just told the truth in the first place.

Letting children come up with a way to fix the problem or make reparation can be a powerful way to let them learn how their actions affect others; it also provides them with a constructive way to experience the consequences of their behavior. Children learn to problem solve and seek a solution to right their wrongs and repair relationships. However, for younger children like toddlers and preschoolers, they will usually not be able to come up with a way to fix a misdemeanor. Children in elementary school can be encouraged to think of "fixes." Children in middle childhood from about 8 years and older can usually come up with solutions.

If a child cannot generate any suggestions or carry out the solutions, then parents may need to intervene. Parents can ask the child, "How are you going to fix this?" Give the child a little time to think about it; if they are stuck, parents can help a little with suggestions. Children should be encouraged to start thinking for themselves and generating ideas with parents guiding them. In Alysha's case, she did not think of anything at first other than to answer, "Tell them." However, with her mother's gentle encouragement, eventually she came up with the suggestion of making an apology card. When her mother probed further if there was anything Alysha could do to make up for the lost recess, they eventually generated the idea of Alysha's doing some of the other child's classroom chores. One of the best ways to develop children's capabilities to be honest is to point out the impact of the child's behavior on the other person and, when possible, give children opportunities to repair the relationship.

Let Children Experience the Negative Consequences of Their Behavior

There are times when we do not need anyone to intervene and impose penalties on us because the consequences of our actions are severe enough to correct our behavior and teach us what not to do. For instance, in the example of Alysha, the act of throwing out her sandwich and denying it led to such unintended consequences to others that it induced strong feelings of guilt and regret for her actions. Alysha did not need further discipline from her mother. The results of her behavior and the efforts required to fix the situation afterward were so much greater than if she had told the truth about the sandwich at the beginning that Alysha needed no further lesson on value and the preference for being honest—even about something you feel uncomfortable admitting.

However, not all actions lead to immediate or easily discernible negative consequences to the child. In those cases, parents ought to intervene and may need to impose consequences. Children do need to learn that the choices they make have consequences in life.

Make the Consequence Proportional to the Crime

Applying negative consequences are sometimes necessary. In *Raise Your Kids Without Raising Your Voice*, author Sarah Chana Radcliffe (2009) gives the example of speeding in a car. Sometimes people will not check their speed without threat of a penalty. For many, the threat of penalty is enough for them to keep their speed in check. However, some have to experience that penalty to learn and adjust their behavior. The point is, at times, we may need to feel the pinch of a negative consequence to be truly motivated to correct and change our behavior. Negative consequences can help when the consequences are reasonable and are not unnecessarily punitive.

We need to make sure that the consequences align with the severity and frequency of the behavior. As discussed in Chapter 4, in toddlerhood and early childhood, we need to allow for "mistakes" when we first catch children lying. This is also true with older children who have not exhibited dishonesty frequently before. By considering the motivations behind the lie, we may sometimes choose to address the underlying motivator to eliminate their need to lie. Or it may be that the underlying motive was a positive one (trying to prevent someone from feeling bad or to help a friend), even if the final choice of action was not the best choice. We may choose to not apply a negative consequence for the lie under such circumstances and to remind the child of the importance of honesty.

Certainly, the first time a child is caught telling a lie, you may decide no consequence is necessary. If you have a young child who you have not talked to about honesty before, this may be your cue to start having those conversations. If you have talked about honesty before, you can remind the child about its importance and make a request: "We don't lie in this house, because we value honesty in each other. We tell the truth instead." You can communicate what the incorrect behavior is and why it is incorrect, and request the child do that behavior: "I ask you to tell the truth." If the child then repeats the undesired behavior, such as lying again, you can say, "Yesterday, I said we do not lie because we value honesty in each other. We tell the truth. From now on, I want you to tell the truth. If not, X will happen."

Whatever the sanction or consequence you say will happen; you must fulfill that promise of a negative consequence and carry it out. It should be applied calmly, not with anger or emotional upset. If you do not fulfill it, you will lose credibility for the future, and the child will feel it is never necessary to do what you ask. However, ensure that the penalty suits the misdemeanor. The most a child should lose is a privilege or a possession, not parental love. Using the example of the speeding ticket penalty: First offenses should receive a warning. Later offenses may require a ticket-level penalty (e.g., loss of privilege or possession). And only in extreme and rare cases would a "go to jail" consequence be handed out for defying authority. Such severe penalties should be used only very occasionally and may never be necessary at all for some children.

Discipline for Both the Misdeed and the Lie When Children Lie to Cover a Misdeed

When children are lying about a transgression, there is the transgression and there is the lie. It is important to teach children that honesty is always valued, even about misdeeds, but *lying about a transgression leads to double trouble.* (See Chapter 6 for how to talk to children and use stories to illustrate how to be honest about a misdeed.) This means clearly outlining to children when they are receiving consequences what the consequence is for. For instance, if an 8-year-old breaks a vase and confesses it to you, you may say,

> I am unhappy you broke the vase with your ball. I have told you clearly that you are not allowed to play with the ball in the house. However, I am glad that you have come and told me truthfully about breaking the vase. We can clean it up together, and you can use your pocket money to help me buy a replacement.

You have highlighted the consequences of their breaking the rule as well as appreciation for their choosing to be honest about the transgression.

However, if the child lies about breaking the vase, you may say,

> I am unhappy you broke the vase and lied to me about it. I have told you clearly that you are not allowed to play with the ball in the house. And I do not like to be lied to about it. It is important that you always tell the truth.
>
> Since you broke the vase, you must clean it up and use your pocket money to replace it. And since you lied about it, it shows me that you are not behaving like a responsible person right now, so I will take your ball away for 1 week, and we will discuss again what it means to be responsible and trustworthy. If you had told me the truth about breaking the vase, I would have been upset about the vase, and you still would have to help replace it, but I would have been pleased that you took responsibility for what you did and told the truth.

For a child in early childhood, the explanation could be shorter. The main point is to give your child an extra consequence for lying. If your teenager defies curfew and lies about it, a parent can take away their electronics for a day or ground them for the curfew offense and give them an extra penalty as a result of their lie.

Listen to Your Child

Give your child, especially a teenager, a chance to speak. It is not an invitation for excuses but an opportunity to identify the problem your child was having that they used lying to solve. You want to hear, as a parent, what made the child feel they needed to lie. By allowing the child to explain, it can help you understand the context around the lie, and you can make informed decisions about how to deal with the lie. Importantly, it also allows the child or teenager to engage in a conversation to problem-solve and fix the situation.

Praise Good Behavior

An important part of discipline is the flip side: praising good behavior. If parents only give attention to the child when they misbehave, the child may be implicitly encouraged to misbehave just to receive attention. Even if children receive attention from their parents, if they never receive praise for being honest, then they learn only part of the message parents wish their children to learn: The child learns that being caught lying is bad. The lesson there is that lying is not a desired behavior, but it doesn't teach that honesty is a valued behavior. Children are left to logically conclude that it is important not be caught lying, and if you are, you will be punished; therefore, the goal is to lie when you think you can reasonably not be caught. The value of being honest, even if no one will know that you are lying, is not inculcated in children unless they actually witness those around them appreciating and praising honesty.

Discipline is more effective when children are also taught the correct behavior and receive acknowledgment for that correct behavior. If children are raised with both discipline and meaningful praise, they will, over time, require less discipline as they develop and internalize moral standards of behavior that guide their own choices and decisions on how to behave. (See Chapter 7 for more on how to praise children effectively.)

Tell Children What Behavior You Expect Ahead of Time

Also key to effective discipline is setting expectations of what you expect from children. Talking in advance to them about situations can help them know what is expected of them. This can mean general conversations about how to behave, how it is important to tell the truth, and why not to lie. If we do not have these conversations with children, we leave it to them to figure out how to behave, and they may misjudge the situation or make the wrong choice. (See Chapter 6 for more about how to talk to children about honesty.)

General conversations give them an overall framework of what is good and bad. However, this may not help them deal with specific situations. You are not going to be able to think of all future situations that the child may face when they have to decide to tell the truth or lie, but you will know some of the most likely ones. You can talk about such situations to the child in advance (not in the heat of the moment, reacting to the child's lie), and you can discuss with them how they can react; how they can speak with kind, truthful words; or how they can be brave and tell the truth about a misdeed. Talking ahead of time about such situations can prepare the child and provide the groundwork to help them resolve moral dilemmas when faced with them. It also gives you the framework to refer to when you correct the child.

CONCLUSION

Discipline through love means using positive reinforcement when children act appropriately. However, there are times when acknowledgment and praise are not enough to eliminate inappropriate behavior as well as times when a child needs to be counseled or chastised using means based on reason and to a degree that is necessary. Parents must use their wisdom to decide how to correct a child as needed so as not to overly punish a child for a minor infraction. They should use gentleness and patience as children are learning how to behave.

Parents also must recognize that young children need to be taught about honesty and may not realize the negative consequences of their behavior. Children in middle childhood and adolescents need to be encouraged to find ways to take responsibility for their own actions and to find solutions to fix and repair relationships. The child who is dealt with in a hostile and punitive manner either through harsh beating or vilification is more likely to learn to fear their parent, be motivated to avoid such punishments by concealing more, and learn to not listen to their parents' lectures. Discipline should be always be tempered with gentleness and patience as well as with loving care rather than from a place of anger and violence.

6

Talk to Children About Honesty

We must teach honesty. Children will not learn about the values and behaviors we wish them to show if we do not actively encourage and teach them. If honesty is important to us, then it should be something we talk about to our children, and we can do so in many ways—for example, by sitting them down and discussing the value of honesty. But there are also so many informal ways that we can talk about honesty throughout the course of the day and our lives. No matter how it is done, it's essential to speak to children about honesty for them to understand its importance and how to effectively use it in interactions with others.

Talking to children about honesty and allowing them to ask questions, reflect, and think about honesty provides them with the ability to understand and internalize the importance of this behavior. It also helps them to figure out what "honesty" means and what it looks like in different circumstances. Taking the time to have these conversations is a significant way parents can connect and communicate with their children. Holding these conversations in a supportive way in which the child is able to interact with the parent can be a positive and reinforcing approach to teaching children honesty and developing their capacities to be honest. Importantly, this means *having a conversation*—not lecturing your child but allowing your child to ask questions, give opinions, or provide examples.

In this chapter, I describe different ways to talk about honesty with your child. First, I discuss how we must consider what it is we wish to teach our children and what honesty means to us in our lives and practice. By taking the time to reflect, we can then approach conversations with children with more authenticity and greater purpose. Next, I discuss when to have such conversations and to consider the context and attention of your child. I then discuss how to use stories to start conversations about honesty and what elements in the stories to discuss. These are often longer, more sustained discussions between adult and child. I also address how we as parents can emphasize honesty and the teachings we have previously given our children as relevant events occur in our daily life. I discuss how moral reminders like promises and messages about consequences of honesty can serve to help guide children in their day-to-day decisions about how to act. These conversations and practices are not a one-time fix that ensures your child will always be honest. They do not always have an immediate effect and do not mean your child will be honest all of the time. However, over time, such conversations along with other practices, such as seeing others practice honesty, will teach your child about honesty and *how* to be honest, leading them to be more honest adults that many of us grow up to be.

QUESTIONS TO ASK YOURSELF

When teaching children about truthfulness it can be useful for us to spend some time reflecting on how we feel about honesty and how we practice it. Here are questions to consider:

- Why do I value honesty?

- Am I always truthful? What are the circumstances when I am not? What do I think about that?

- Are there times when it may be okay to deceive? Am I okay with my child's deceiving under those circumstances? Why or why not?

- How does my child currently exhibit truthfulness?

- What aspects of showing truthfulness can I help my child work on?

Asking these questions can help us reflect on our own values and what we wish to communicate (and also practice; see Chapter 8). Our private answers to these questions can help us in thinking about what it is we wish to say to children and what it is we want to emphasize to them in our conversations and help them with.

Have compassion for yourself and know that you and your child are not perfect. This exercise should not be one of personal recrimination or of conscious self-delusion. Essentially, it requires one to be truthful about oneself to oneself. This can lead to uncomfortable insights or questions. It may lead you to change your behavior to be more aligned with your answers to these questions and your expectations. I ask these questions to myself repeatedly as I encounter new situations as a parent and as an adult. I hope that reading this book will help you to address these questions and resolve your conundrums. By engaging in this reflection and investigation, we can figure out how we wish our children to be, how we wish to embody those values and behaviors we want in them, and how to align our words and deeds more closely with our chosen principles.

WHEN TO HAVE CONVERSATIONS ABOUT HONESTY

All too often, we find ourselves talking about honesty when the child has been dishonest. And there are good reasons to talk about the importance of honesty and to remind children about the value of honesty at these times. However, such communications are usually not conversations with the child and need to be brief to avoid lecturing.

Conversations about honesty should be held at times when the child is not personally involved in lying. Discussions about

Talking About Honesty

Right after your child lies:	At other times:
• Keep it brief. • Just give a reminder about honesty. • Know that the child may be defensive.	• Take more time. • Have a discussion and ask questions. • Know that the child will be more open to discussion and questions.

lying and honesty when the child has just lied may lead to defensiveness and fear of negative consequences, which prevent the child from truly thinking about the concepts, the reasons for it, and the behaviors attached to such principles. By having these discussions at different times than when the child is implicated in lying, parents are more likely to encourage open discussion. Also, by having such conversations at other times, we are able then to briefly refer back to these discussions and the values we've talked about when we do catch a child not always living up to those principles.

You can choose to have these conversations about honesty on different occasions and at different times. Sometimes they will be about your child's own behavior. At other times the focus will be on another person's behavior, such as a child that they play with. Children may also hear about items in the news or through advertising that bring up conversations about honesty. Or, you may see someone being honest about something and comment on it.

We can also have formal conversations about honesty. If your family regularly discusses virtues, or if you engage in a formal moral education in your home or through religious or community settings, you can set aside time as part of those regular discussions to discuss honesty and the importance of honesty. Or, if children receive character or moral education in a community or school setting, parents can make sure that they reinforce such conversations by bringing it up at home and asking the child to reflect on what they have learned and discussed

in those settings. Even if children do receive character education or religious instruction outside of the home, a vital part of
children's learning and reinforcement of that learning are conversations with parents. For such educational programs to be
effective, they must be presented in conjunction with parents'
teaching and children's learning at home.

Honesty also can and should be talked about in informal
moments. These are not planned times but arise out of the
day-to-day activities of your life. The key is to notice these
opportunities. All too often, we are so busy that we do not
notice moments when a person has been honest (when they
might have chosen to act otherwise). These conversations can
arise when your child honestly confesses something to you,
when you observe another being truthful, when you are reading
a story, or when you are watching a television show or see
something on the news.

We encounter numerous instances of honesty daily, and
we cannot not stop to talk about them all. However, now and
then, a case stands out that has the child's attention (like in a
story), and these are good times to pause to reflect on how
honesty was used and why honesty is important. Particularly
important to notice and occasionally discuss are moments
when we witness someone being honest about something
that may be difficult to admit (and which others might lie about).
Examples include making a mistake; doing something wrong;
or feeling something that may be contrary to another's feelings
or desires, such as saying honestly that you do not really like
fishing to your parent who has been keenly taking their children
with them on long fishing trips.

When encountering these day-to-day interactions, we can
do two things to emphasize the value of honesty. First, we
can observe what the person did and voice appreciation or
approval. For instance, maybe you saw someone honestly tell
a shop cashier that they gave back too much change, and the
person handed it back. You might comment on what the person did by drawing your child's attention to the behavior and
reflecting positively on it: "That man noticed he had received

too much money back, and he honestly gave it back to the cashier. That was good." Just simple reflections like that from time to time show that you do notice honesty and that it is something you value and appreciate.

The second and more elaborate way is to discuss after the incident why the person acted the way they did: "Why do you think he gave the money back?" "Would anything bad have happened if he didn't?" And if child reflects and then answers, "Not really" because the clerk hadn't noticed, you could follow up with: "Then why do you think the man said that?" You can focus on the person's behaviors and intentions. Preschool children may have difficulty answering these questions and need your help: your providing guidance and explanation about the act. However, let the child express their thoughts and build on that:

CHILD: The man didn't want to be bad. He wanted to be good.

PARENT: Yes, he wanted to be good—to tell the truth.

When talking to children about honesty, one conversation is not enough. Returning to the topic over and over at different times and stages is necessary not just to reinforce the message but also to discuss different aspects and situations. It is easy to have a conversation about the importance of honesty and how "honesty is the best policy," but the nuances of what that looks like and means in different situations as children get older need to be discussed. In addition, as children grow, they will come across different lies others tell or accusations of deception by others that will lead to new conversations.

Discussions about honesty can also arise from what is happening around the child in the wider society. For instance, parents or children may bring in topics of honesty when discussing advertising and the methods advertisers use to present their products. Or, if a child hears a news report about a politician's being called a liar, they may have questions, especially if the politician has been seen in a favorable light by others around them or has the weight of authority and respect. A child whose friend innocently gives incorrect information may label the other as a liar. In this case, the parent may have a conversation with the child about the differences between mistakes and lies. The parent could draw the child's attention to what the other's knowledge and beliefs about the matter were as well as the intentions of the person who gave the false information.

> *When talking to children about honesty, one conversation is not enough. Returning to the topic over and over at different times and stages is necessary not just to reinforce the message but also to discuss different aspects and situations.*

Sometimes these conversations are short and, at other times, longer in duration. However, the key is to not prolong them such that they become onerous or incur resentment. This is particularly true as children become older and grow into adolescence. Older children in middle childhood and adolescents are more likely to actively engage in longer conversations, especially if they are allowed to take the lead in the conversations to ask questions and give opinions. For younger children, the conversations may be shorter in duration but more frequent, depending on the child. For instance, a young preschooler who does not yet distinguish a mistake from a lie may label and accuse others of lying, which may prompt more frequent conversations for a time. A child who is competing with a younger sibling may start using lying as a strategy to advance their own interests, prompting more necessary conversations about how to share, what is appropriate behavior, and the importance of truth-telling. Children in middle childhood who understand the importance of honesty and its value in their home may arrive home from school perplexed and disturbed by witnessing a friend's lies to others.

While children in toddlerhood and early childhood, simple moral messages, including "lying is wrong," are sufficient. As children grow and experience lying by others, they will need longer discussions. School-age children should be encouraged to think more deeply about the implications of different children's of lies. As they grow throughout childhood and into the adolescent years, for children to develop their own internalized principles and conscience, they must be able to think about the reasons for such declarations. Children benefit from these extended discussions.

STORIES

You can enter into such conversations in a number of ways. As discussed earlier in this chapter, these conversations can be prompted by the actions of others or questions your child raises. One way that is particularly effective as an entry point to discussing honesty with children is using stories. Stories provide examples of what the behavior looks likes in different situations and helps with emphasizing the importance of honesty.

In general, stories teach children about the world around them. They are powerful tools that teach us social messages because they engage our attention and provide vivid illustrations of, as well as encourage a deeper understanding of, people's actions, motivations, feelings, and beliefs. Stories have been used for centuries to pass down and teach values and warnings. They also are entertainment. Young children hear about the value of honesty in many storybooks. For older children in middle childhood and adolescents, they come across such themes in various books they read.

A parent can choose to read to their child stories in which a character faces a decision about honesty and lying. The parent can encourage the child to reflect on these concepts by asking what the character should do and why. Younger children may give brief answers, whereas older children may be encouraged to generate different responses that the character could make and discuss the implications of different strategies for all the characters involved. Having discussions about honesty and lying are likely to be more effective than just simple declarations that lying is wrong. The parent should encourage their child to reflect on the feelings of characters involved, and for them to develop greater understanding, it is important to let them generate responses and their own explanations. Parents can then discuss with the child those responses and encourage further reflection.

Often in our conversations with our child, we dwell on lying's being bad. However, to help children understand how to embody honesty, we need to help them see what that looks like. Thus, stories in which they see that the character is honest are helpful in providing them with illustrations of an alternative behavior to lying. Children need examples showing how to behave in situations in which lying might be tempting to do as an easier way out. Stories are a powerful device for providing examples of how to behave, especially for younger children. Many stories address honesty and lying; see, for example, the lists in Rodriguez (2017) and Bookroo (n.d.).

Tell Positive Stories

Children are often taught about honesty through morality stories and moral discussions. From an early age, children are exposed to an abundance of stories and fables. These stories serve as a means of socialization and as a tool for conveying cultural values.

Honesty is one of those moral lessons that has been depicted in story and fable. In one of the studies done by my colleagues and me, we examined the effects of hearing these stories on children's behavior. The study involved North American children between 3 and 7 years of age, and we read one of four classic stories to the children (Lee et al., 2014). We used the well-known stories of "Pinocchio," "The Boy Who Cried Wolf," and "George Washington and the Cherry Tree" as examples of stories told to teach children about the consequences of lying and the virtue of honesty. The first two emphasize the virtue of honesty and the negative consequences of lying. In the third story, "George Washington and the Cherry

Tree," George cuts down his father's cherry tree with his axe, and later, when he tells his father the truth about cutting down the tree, his father praises him for his honesty rather than punishing his misdeed. We told children these stories to see if it would influence whether they would lie about their own transgression. The fourth story was the "The Tortoise and the Hare," which is not about the moral virtue of honesty but of persistence; we included it as a control condition.

Before being read the story, the children had participated in the temptation resistance paradigm in which they had been told not to peek at a toy while the researcher went to fetch the storybook. A video camera caught if the children peeked or not. When the researcher came back, the toy was put away, and the child was read one of the four stories. After the children listened to the story, they were asked if they had peeked at the toy while the researcher was away.

As we have typically found, the majority of children will peek at the toy, and older children are more likely to resist temptation compared with younger children (see Chapter 2 for more details on the findings). However, when the children who had listened to the story were asked if they had peeked, the result was interesting. Those children who had been told the control story "The Tortoise in the Hare" mostly lied, which we had previously found is typical at this age. We found the same for those who heard the "Pinocchio" story and those who heard the "The Boy Who Cried Wolf." The children who heard either story were not more likely to tell the truth about their peeking behavior. However, children who had heard the "George Washington" story were more likely to tell the truth. Approximately half of these children confessed to the transgression of peeking at the toy. These results suggest that there was something about this story that had influenced the children's decision to truthfully report their own transgression.

Why was this the case? One possibility is that, unlike "Pinocchio" and "The Boy Who Cried Wolf," "George Washington and the Cherry Tree" emphasizes the virtue of honesty and depicts the character telling the truth with resulting positive consequences. To test this possibility, we ran a second experiment in which we changed the story of "George Washington and the Cherry Tree." In our modified version, rather than extol the virtue of honesty and positive consequences, the story highlighted the negative consequence of lying. In the modified story, George Washington lies to his father by telling him that he did not cut down the cherry tree. His father later discovers the truth and punishes George for lying. His father takes away George's axe and tells him he is very disappointed in George because he told a lie. We wanted to see if this story would influence children's truth-telling about their peeking behavior in the temptation resistance task. We found that when children heard this modified story, they were not more likely to tell the truth compared with when they had heard the control story. In other words, when the "George Washington and Cherry Tree" story was modified to no longer focus on the honesty and positive consequences, it no longer had a truth-promoting effect on children's behavior.

As children grow, for them to develop their own internalized principles and conscience, they must be able to think about the reasons for such declarations. The stories may help children to engage with these internalized moral principles and connect them with their choice of behaviors. It may be that the positive moral story is effective because it both provides a model of how to be honest about a transgression and demonstrates how adults might be pleased to hear the truth in such a situation (see Chapter 8 for more on how modeling behavior can impact children). Unlike the other two stories, which emphasize the consequences of lying, "George Washington and the Cherry Tree" emphasizes the positive consequences of honesty. It was the emphasis of the positive consequences of honesty and highlight of its virtue that had the greatest impact on children's actual honesty. When children heard a story that emphasized positive outcomes for being honest, they were more likely to be honest about their own transgression.

> *Stories like "George Washington and the Cherry Tree"*
> *show how we can be honest, even in the face of potential*
> *punishment and disapproval. Such stories show what*
> *it looks like to be truthful and the potential positive*
> *outcomes of being truthful.*

What to look for in stories are elements that demonstrate honesty and positive consequences for choosing to be honest. Stories that emphasize negative consequences of dishonesty can help serve as cautionary tales for lying. However, stories in which the liar is punished or has some unfavorable outcome, although salutary tales, do not critically demonstrate honesty. If we think about truth default theory (as described in Chapter 1), we can understand why this is the case. Although these stories help us understand why lying is bad (like "The Boy Who Cried Wolf") and understand the value placed on honesty in our society, they do not give information on the "how" of being honest. When confronted with a situation in which one's self-interests are threatened and telling the truth is harder than fibbing, we may cross that threshold and override our truth default. As discussed in Chapter 1, although adults and children know it is wrong to lie and rate lying negatively, they may still lie in a situation in which they fear negative consequences to themselves. These motivations can be strong enough for them to abandon the principle of honesty for the more immediate benefits of dishonesty.

Stories like "George Washington and the Cherry Tree" show how we can be honest, even in the face of potential punishment and disapproval. Such stories show what it looks like to be truthful and the potential positive outcomes of being truthful. Those are key elements in teaching children to be honest: showing them *how* it is done and how it can lead to positive effects. These elements address the motivational conflict that children may experience in situations in which they have done something wrong and are torn between confessing and lying.

Have Discussions

Talking about the honesty of characters in books can provoke inspiring and instructive discussion. We can ask children to reflect on the stories—for example, "When have you had a similar experience?" or "When have you experienced someone being dishonest with you in your own life?" and "How did that make you feel?" These stories are useful as a way to illustrate honesty and dishonesty as well as the consequences of such behavior. For preschool children, conversations that emphasizes the main message help underscore the point: "What did X say?" "Is what X said true or was it a lie?" "What happened to X?" "Was it good that X lied/told the truth?" "Yes, it's important to be honest. . . ."

Ask questions to ensure the child has followed the story and understood the key plot elements. Ask them reflection questions about what the characters did and said, as well as what happened as a result. Preschool children may need help to come up with answers. Encourage any attempts they make and add on any information they missed:

PARENT: What did Cassie say?

CHILD: She said, "No."

PARENT: That's right. Cassie said no when she was asked if she took the cookies. And was that the truth?

CHILD: No.

PARENT: No, it was not the truth. She said she did not take the cookies, and she did. She told a lie.

For children in middle childhood, encourage them to generate the answers as much as possible and to be patient as they try to think or express their thoughts. Sometimes when children are asked, "What do you think?" or "What do you think Cassie should have said?" it takes further probing and gentle patience for the child to be able to form their thoughts on a subject and express them. Sometimes they may be unable to give you an answer out of shyness or uncertainty. Be patient; don't rush in to provide the answer immediately. Silent pauses are okay; don't force them to answer if they just can't think what to say. With time, they will gain greater confidence in voicing their ideas.

MORAL REMINDERS

When we are talking to children, we can nudge them to be honest. Research shows that moral reminders can be effective at thinking again about what our moral principles are. Often when we are interacting and engaging with others around us, we are reacting to different situations and conflicting motivations. We do not always take the time to think about what our values and principles are. We sometimes just react—and sometimes in a way that is contradictory to our values and principles. We may live to regret these actions.

One way to ensure that we act according to what we value is to be reminded of those values. In that way, moral reminders can serve to help us remember how we wish to act. Some research suggests that moral reminders work. In a study in which my colleagues and I asked children between 3 and 7 years of age if they had peeked at a forbidden toy, we found that when we first asked the children to promise to tell the truth, more children told the truth and confessed to peeking compared with when they were not asked to promise first (Talwar et al., 2002). We repeated this study when children were asked about someone else's transgression. Once again, we found that when we asked children to promise to tell the truth, they were more likely to truthfully report the transgression (Talwar et al., 2004).

Promising to tell the truth serves as a moral reminder about the value of honesty and the importance of being honest.

It also asks for a commitment to being honest. However, it does not work all the time. Some children still told a lie. It may be that such moral reminders help us to remember our values when there are not stronger motivations that lead us to protect our own self-interest.

If you need a straight answer about something you are concerned about, asking the child to promise to tell the truth before asking them a question increases the chance that they will. However, it is not a guarantee that you will hear the truth. It is not a magic antidote that ensures honesty! You only have to think of people who give false testimony in legal trials or at public inquires to know that if motivations to conceal the truth are strong enough, they can trump other commitments like being honest. Moral reminders are not always effective. We may choose to lie because we evaluate the benefits of the lie to be greater than those of the truth. However, children, especially young ones, do tend to take promises seriously. This is likely even more the case when parents have consistently kept their promises, and the children feel trusted. Nevertheless, you should not use such a tactic indiscriminately and frequently but, rather, sparingly for crucial moments. You do not wish to overuse the tactic because it may lose its efficacy.

Moral understanding may only affect our behavior under some circumstances, such as when the conflict between our self-interests and moral principles is reduced or when the moral rule is made salient. When the moral consequences of lying are less evident and the benefits of lying to self are glaringly obvious, a child or adult may lie without thinking about the moral standards to which they adhere. An adult who arrives at work late and is confronted by their boss immediately uses the strategy of lying by saying they were stuck in traffic (instead of admitting to oversleeping) to reduce the boss's disapprobation. This lie is quickly told without thinking about the importance of honesty or the adult's moral views on the topic. However, in another situation in which the moral rule is more uppermost in the mind or there is more time to think about the appropriate behavior, the adult is honest. Children are the same. Merely asking them to promise to tell the truth can serve as a reminder of the importance of honesty.

MESSAGES ABOUT THE POSITIVE CONSEQUENCES OF HONESTY

People are heavily influenced by what they believe will happen as a result of their behavior. External and internal factors shape people's expectations of what the outcome will be as a result of their actions, which, in turn, influences their decisions on how to act.

Young children are strongly influenced by the guidance and encouragement from others, and parents in particular. Thus, external factors can heavily influence their behavior. This can include expectations about punishment or the pleasure and approval from an authority figure. We can also be influenced by internal factors, including our own internalized sense of what is right and wrong. Thus, we can be motivated to act to please ourselves by doing the right thing. How these expectations influence behavior may vary in different contexts and may change over time. As children internalize the moral standards taught by their parents, these internal standards can play a greater role in determining their behavior.

In an Australian study, psychological scientists asked children 5 to 10 years of age to predict the likelihood that a story character would lie or tell the truth in different situations (Wagland & Bussey, 2005). The researchers discovered that when punishment was expected for the transgression, the children predicted that both external encouragement (referring to the experimenter's satisfaction) and internal encouragement (referring to the child's own self-satisfaction) would increase truth-telling compared with no encouragement. However, children did not expect any change in truth-telling when hearing either appeal when no punishment was expected.

In one study, my colleagues and I looked at the impact of reminding children between 4 and 8 years of age about honesty in contrast to expectations of getting into trouble for their transgression (Talwar et al., 2015). In this study, like before, children were told not to peek at a forbidden toy. Later, the adult researcher reminded the children about the importance of telling the truth, saying, "If you tell the truth, I will be really pleased with you. I will feel happy if you tell the truth" or "It is really important to tell the truth because telling the truth is the right thing to do when someone has done something wrong. It is really important to tell the truth."

In the first condition, the reminder "If you tell the truth, I will be really pleased with you. I will feel happy if you tell the truth" emphasized the approval of the adult, an external motivator. In the second condition, the reminder "It is really important to tell the truth because telling the truth is the right thing to do when someone has done something wrong. It is really important to tell the truth" emphasized the feelings of personal satisfaction of achieving one's principles, an internal motivator. In a third condition, there was no message about honesty. We found that both the messages about honesty led more children to be honest compared with when no message was given.

However, when we had the same conditions but also increased children's expectation that they would be in trouble for peeking, moral messages had less of an impact: Just a few children were honest. Of the two moral messages, only the external motivation of the adult's approval continued to have some impact, but its effects were attenuated by children's concerns about getting into trouble. Taken together, the findings of these studies indicate that messages that emphasize the positive consequences of honesty rather than the negative consequences of dishonesty can promote honest behavior in young children.

So here you see how the messages we give that emphasize the positive consequences of honesty—whether internal or external—can influence children's decision to confess their transgression. However, the findings also demonstrate that when the concerns about protecting one's own self-interest—in this case, not getting into trouble—are salient in the child's mind, such moral reminders may lose their potency to influence.

> *Messages that emphasize the positive consequences of honesty rather than the negative consequences of dishonesty can promote honest behavior in young children.*

The messages may also impact children differently according to their age and prior experience. Young children, especially those under the age of 8 years (although it may vary from child to child), are very motivated to please authority figures. Our research showed that telling children that you will be pleased with them if they tell the truth increases the likelihood that they'll be honest. However, older children and adolescents tend to care a little less about pleasing authority figures and can be motivated more by their own internal sense of what is right. With age, if these moral principles have been emphasized and youths have internalized them, messages that remind the children and draw their attention to their own principles of what is right and wrong may be powerful.

Here are the basic steps for having a conversation about honesty:

- **Explain what honesty is.** For young children, a simple definition is fine. For older children and teenagers, you can have more elaborate discussions about what it means to be truthful to yourself and to others, and why.

- **Explain why honesty is important.** For very young children, a simple explanation is fine that emphasizes the goodness of honesty. For older children and teenagers, you can discuss different contexts, the feelings of those involved, and the consequences.

- **Explain how to practice honesty.** Children need help to understand how to practice honesty. For young children, you can provide examples of how you can practice honesty in your life. For older children and teenagers, they can generate examples and discuss how they think honesty can be practiced in those situations.

Example Statements for a Conversation About Honesty

Step 1: Explain what honesty is	"Being honest is being truthful and trustworthy."
	"When people are honest, they will not lie, cheat, or steal."
	"Honesty means admitting mistakes even if you know someone may be angry or disappointed with you."
	"Truthfulness is speaking and acting with truth. You do not lie about anything big or small even if it may be hard to tell the truth at times. When you are truly yourself, you show people your true self and share what is true to your heart."
	"Honesty means telling the truth and doing what we believe is right. It's okay to keep your promise or tell the truth. Honest people always make an effort to be fair and just. If you have nothing nice to say, it's better not to say anything at all."
Step 2: Explain why honesty is important	"Honesty is important because it builds trust."
	"When people lie or cover mistakes, others can't trust them."
	"When people aren't honest with themselves, they pretend that something doesn't matter when it does, or they exaggerate to impress others."
	"When you're honest, you do not try to fool others. You only make promises you can keep. You make your mistakes, you admit your mistakes, and you try to fix it."
Step 3: Explain how to practice honesty ("You are practicing honesty when . . .")	"You say what you mean and mean what you say."
	"You make promises you can keep."
	"You admit your mistakes."
	"You refuse to lie, cheat, or steal."
	"You tell the truth tactfully."
	"You do not try to impress others by making up stories or exaggerating."
	"You accept yourself as you are."

(continues)

Example Statements for a Conversation About Honesty (Continued)

Step 4: Give examples	"You accidentally break one of grandma's figurines when playing. You might feel upset and worried that she may be mad. What does honesty look like?"
	"You are talking with friends about the sports you play, and you find yourself exaggerating about how well you can play a sport. What would honesty look like?"
	"Your friend asks you if a new dress looks good on her, and you think it doesn't. What does honesty look like?"
	"You forgot to do your homework, and the teacher asked where it is. What does honesty look like?"
Step 5: Role-play ("Think about a time when you were honest or saw someone else being honest or dishonest. . . .")	"When is it most difficult to be honest?"
	"Why might you try to impress others by exaggerating?"
	"How do you feel when someone else exaggerates?"
	"How does honesty help friendship grow stronger?"
	"What does it feel like to always tell the truth and keep your word?"
	"What does it feel like when someone lies to us?"
	"Why is it important to be honest?"
	"How can you show truthfulness at home?"
	"What ways do you show truthfulness to your friends?"

- **Give examples.** You can also give examples to your child and talk about how to be honest in those examples.

- **Role-play.** You can practice and teach honesty through role plays. You can do this with one child or a group of children.

Check out the chart with example statements you can use in your conversations.

CONCLUSION

Having conversations with children about honesty serves to teach them about what it means to be truthful and how they can practice honesty in different situations. You can start these conversations in a number of ways. Stories that show charac-ters being honest in different situations can help demonstrate to children the how, why, and what happens next when being honest. There are many stories in folklore and literature about lying and honesty. However, stories that model honesty (in which the character tells the truth—at least eventually) and show the positive consequences of honesty as well as the importance of truth-telling may be particularly helpful to illustrating the desired behavior to children.

Parents can also ask questions that may make the child think about acts of honesty or dishonesty themselves and why it was good or bad. You can discuss the intentions behind different lies and truthful statements. You can discuss how some lies may be told with good intentions or to be kind. Conversely, sometimes blunt truths can hurt others and are told with the intention to be cruel. You can discuss if such statements are good or bad and what are the ways to be kind or help with words.

These discussions promote children's moral reasoning and considerations of other's feelings and perspectives. They also help them reflect on positive ways to deal with moral dilemmas when they wish to be both honest and kind.

7

Acknowledge and Recognize Honesty

Another important and powerful way of fostering honesty is to acknowledge it when you see it. We recognize lying, and it has consequences. Do we remember to recognize honesty? All too often we notice children being dishonest, and we draw their attention to it. However, we are less frequent in drawing their attention to their honesty. If we don't recognize it, then all the conversations, stories, and messages about why honesty is important become less effective.

Children often get bad credit for lying and little good credit for telling the truth. We should focus on the what "to do" instead of just giving attention to the "don'ts." We often tell children what we don't want them to do, which actually focuses their attention on the very behavior we wish them to avoid. "Don't lie" and similar statements focus on dishonesty. Using positive attention for the behaviors we want them to do places the focus on honesty. In this chapter, I discuss the importance of catching children being honest and giving positive reinforcement for such behaviors. I discuss different ways to comment on children's honest behavior through acknowledgment, appreciation, and praise, and I offer tips on how to use praise effectively to teach them the value of their honest behavior.

CATCH THEM BEING HONEST

We notice what our kids do, and we can catch them doing things we do not want them to do. We can catch children telling lies, but if we want to teach them to value honesty, don't forget to catch them telling the truth. An important way of communicating to children about honesty is to look for opportunities to acknowledge when they tell the truth, especially in situations in which it might have been easier for them to lie. When your child tells you the truth about something they have done, take a moment to show that you appreciate their honesty by saying, "I'm really glad you told me the truth." Acknowledgment sends a powerful message that you value honesty.

Catching honesty is hard to do. The problem with honesty is that it is often a behavior we don't notice. As discussed in Chapter 1, we have a default to be truthful and expect that others are being truthful in their communication most of the time. As a result, we tend not focus on it. It is natural for us to not notice it. We frequently are focused on other things when someone's being honest, such as what they are being honest about. Too often, we just react negatively to what they have done (i.e., if it was a transgression). In general, people tend to focus on exceptions to rules, and lying is an exception to our truth default. Thus, we have a natural tendency to notice such behavior and to overlook truthfulness. However, we have to consciously acknowledge the truth so the child can recognize what constitutes honesty. Indeed, given the ubiquity of honesty in our communication, in many instances of honesty throughout the day, it may not be necessary to acknowledge it. However, we should look out for two types of situations to catch honesty.

The first is when it is may be more expedient and protective of one's self-interest to lie, whereas telling the truth is the more difficult choice. When children are honest in these situations, we want to catch and acknowledge that behavior. When we catch them in that behavior and show that we see it and honor it, we're communicating to the child the value of that behavior as well as allowing them to see themselves as someone who practices that behavior. That helps to increase their self-esteem and encourages them. It can reinforce the behavior.

The second situation we want to "catch" is when they truthfully share their feelings with you about something that you may feel differently about or may not like. They may share with you that they do not like what you packed for their lunch, or perhaps they do not really enjoy going on planned trips to art galleries and would prefer doing outdoor activities, or they don't want to go to church early on Sundays anymore. When they tell you their true feelings, especially when it is said respectfully, it is important to notice it. Perhaps you do not want your teenager to stop going to church, and you may have a discussion with them about it before deciding on an appropriate response or action. It may be annoying for you to discover that you child is not enjoying your carefully crafted sandwiches and would prefer something else. Before you launch into a full discussion about what to pack for lunch that satisfies your nutritional desires and the child's taste buds, "catch" and notice that your child was honest with you and was comfortable enough to share how they felt. The key to catching honesty is to notice it before your attention is swept away to deal with whatever the issues are at hand.

ENCOURAGE AND COMMENT ON CHILDREN'S ACTS OF HONESTY

When we do catch children being honest, we can comment on it. Judith Suissa, a moral philosopher, pointed out that when we praise children, we are engaging in an interaction with our child and introducing them into the moral community that we all live in. When we praise our child for clearing the dinner plates or passing the ball in soccer practice, we are teaching our child about "what matters and what matters less; what is worthwhile and what is less worthwhile; what is morally significant and what is not" (Suissa, 2013, p. 11). By commenting on and showing appreciation for different behaviors, we convey to children our moral sense of the world—of what is good and what is bad. As Suissa pointed out, emphasizing to your child the importance of being top in their class "implies that other people are there to be competed with and beaten" (Suissa, 2013, p. 15). What we comment on, what we give our positive attention to, and what we show appreciation for shapes the way children start to see the world and how they should interact with others in it. For me, this point is an important one as a parent. It means that I need to reflect on the moral messages I give the child and how I acknowledge and appreciate the child's behavior to be in conformity with the moral principles that I wish to teach. If honesty is important, then it is a behavior that I should recognize. If I do not, its absence makes it unimportant.

There are three ways to comment positively: acknowledgment, appreciation, and praise. When we notice children's honesty, our comments and encouragement communicate to the child that they have acted in a positive way. We positively reinforce their behavior. In the next few sections, I talk about ways we can recognize honesty and encourage them in their acts of honesty. Acknowledgment, appreciation, and praise are all related terms and are all ways to reinforce behavior. Although they overlap—with praise encompassing acknowledgment and appreciation—I initially discuss them separately to illustrate that there are different ways and degrees to which we can comment on children's honesty.

Three Ways to Comment on Honesty

1. Acknowledge

"You told the truth."

2. Appreciate

"Thank you for telling the truth."

3. Praise

"Good job telling the truth, even when it was hard."

Acknowledge

In some cases, just acknowledging the behavior creates a teachable moment that makes the child aware of their behavior and their ability to be honest. Acknowledgment is when we make a simple observation about the behavior. We often use acknowledgment for children's inappropriate and wrong behaviors, such as: "I see you were messy again" or "I notice you're telling lies." However, we can be less likely to acknowledge appropriate behaviors.

Simply acknowledging appropriate behavior is often a powerful step toward maintaining those behaviors. You can acknowledge the desirable behavior—for example, "I see you told the neighbor that it was you who broke his windshield. That was honest of you"; or "That showed honesty when you confessed to your teacher that it was you who broke the pencil sharpener"; or "You told the truth to your teacher about not doing your homework"; or, simply, "You are being truthful."

When you comment on the behavior, it can be helpful to label it. In particular, it can highlight to the child their actions if you acknowledge their behavior at the time they do it. For instance, you can say, "I see you are being honest about the mistakes you made." Labeling the behavior and acknowledging it demonstrate to the child what the desirable behavior is that they have performed, and they learn to recognize it as a desired behavior.

Appreciate

Expressing appreciation involves thanking a child for doing something that pleases you, such as: "Thank you for helping"; or "Thank you for waiting patiently while I was speaking to the neighbor"; or "Thank you for being honest about how you feel"; or "Thank you for being honest about where you were this afternoon." Appreciation not only communicates what the desired behavior was that the child did but also conveys a model of showing gratitude or pleasure at the behavior.

> *If children only receive attention from adults when they do things wrong, they will behave that way just to get some attention—any attention—from their parents and the adults around them.*

Appreciation can be communicated not only through words but also through gestures. Parents can show appreciation with hugs, smiles, or other gestures of approval. You can hug, pat, smile, or wink at a child because they have performed a desirable behavior. My grandfather used to wink to show his approval. A wink from him made you grow 2 inches taller and square your shoulders in pride and determination to continue doing more of the same behavior that warranted the wink. Gestures of appreciation, whether verbal or nonverbal, give children important positive feedback about their choices and behavior. If children only receive attention from adults when they do things wrong, they will behave that way just to get some attention—any attention—from their parents and the adults around them. However, by giving them positive attention and praise when they behave in ways we want them to act, they are more likely to persist and repeat those behaviors.

Praise

Praise is when a parent comments on a child's behavior with a positive evaluation of that behavior. It is a direct and positive statement of approval, and it is one way in which parents convey moral messages to children about what we value. The goal of effective praise is to help children learn right from wrong and to discover how to improve behavior. We want them to develop their own guidance system. By commenting positively, we can help them develop that system. However, how we praise children can affect them positively and sometimes negatively.

Decide Which Works Best: Praising Character or Praising Behavior

There has been some uncertainty over what type of praise works best to reinforce honesty: praising a child's honest behavior (e.g., "I'm glad you told the truth about making the mess") versus praising a child's honest character (e.g., "I'm glad you are so honest"). As children develop between preschool years up to 8 years of age, praising their character may give them important feedback about themselves as they develop their identity and sense of self (Rudy & Grusec, 2020). However, by the time children reach 10 years of age, the differences between praising their character and their actions may no longer be important. For parents, what is clear is that praise helps children integrate prosocial behavior into their sense of self and fosters a sense of competence in these skills.

One study that examined praising children's generosity can give us insight into how praise may influence children's pro-social behaviors (Grusec & Redler, 1980). In this study, 7- and 8-year-olds won marbles in a game. They then had the opportunity to donate some of their marbles to poor children. After they had donated some of their marbles, the experimenter commented, "Gee, you shared quite a bit." Children then received process-oriented reinforcement praise: "It was good that you gave some of your marbles to those poor children. Yes, that was a nice and helpful thing to do" or they received praise for the disposition-oriented praise: "I guess you're the kind of person who likes to help others whenever you can. Yes, you are a very nice and helpful person." In a control condition, children received no praise. Children were then given the opportunity to share more. Children who had received either praise, both the process and dispositional, shared more. A few weeks later, the experimenters gave the children a chance to give more. Children whose character had been praised were more generous than children whose actions had been praised. Praising their character may have helped internalize generosity as part of their identity.

> Praise helps children integrate prosocial behavior into their sense of self.

Another study suggested to children 3 to 6 years of age that they could "be a helper" or invited them "to help." It was found that children who were told they could be helpers were more helpful with an experimenter than those who were told they could help (Bryan et al., 2014). The researchers also examined cheating behavior in adults. They found that when adults were told, "Please don't be a cheater," they were less likely to cheat than when they were told, "Please don't cheat." In these studies, the authors noted that by using a noun wording in the praise, it framed the behavior as something that was a positive part of their identity. They suggested that children (and adults) desire to feel positive about their identity, and such praise makes them motivated to act in ways that are part of that positive identity.

In another study, 5-year-olds who were told that they had a good reputation for being a "good kid" were less likely to cheat than children who were in a control condition and had received no information about their reputation (Fu et al., 2016). Using a temptation resistance paradigm (see the description in Chapter 2), the researchers found that while younger children peeked to find out the answer in a guessing game at the same rate in both conditions, 4-year-olds waited longer to peek when they had been told that they had a reputation for being good.

Although these preceding two studies did not examine praise specifically, the findings suggest that dispositional labeling may lead to a change in self-perception. It may be that such praise helps to highlight to children that their actions are a reflection of their character, and, subsequently, they incorporate that into their moral choices of how they act.

However, considerations on how to use praise should be taken depending on the age of the child. For instance, researchers found that for 5-year-olds, there was no effect of praise on their behavior (Grusec & Redler, 1980). Children shared similar amounts across all conditions, including when they received no praise. The researchers found that for school-age children—8 years of age—increased prosocial behavior was observed only after the children received praise where they were labeled a prosocial person. However, they reported that 10-year-olds increased prosocial behavior regardless of whether the experimenter praised their prosocial action or labeled them a prosocial person. Similarly, a subsequent study found that 8- and 9-year-old children engaged in more prosocial behavior after praise for being a prosocial person compared with praise for prosocial action or no praise (Mills & Grusec, 1989).

It may be that praise is particularly influential in a critical period when children are developing a stronger sense of identity. Giving children 8 years old and younger praise, especially praise about having an honest character, helps them incorporate that into their self-identity and can encourage them to sustain that behavior. Giving them praise can provide a framework for children to gradually to internalize the moral principles and become established in their daily actions. As children get older and have a stronger sense of identity, it may matter less whether the praise focuses on honest behavior versus honest character. More research is needed to better understand how praise impacts prosocial behaviors at different ages.

Praise for Effort Rather Than Intelligence

Notably, parents should avoid praising one character trait to promote honesty: intelligence. Research shows that praising a child's intelligence (e.g., "You must be smart at this") rather than effort (e.g., "You must have worked really hard") leads them to view intelligence as a fixed, unchangeable ability. As a result, when they face difficult tasks in the future, they are less likely to work hard and more likely to cheat out of fear of failure and the idea that it will mean they are "not intelligent." In contrast, when children are praised for their effort (e.g., "You're a hard worker") rather than intelligence, they are more likely to persist at a task and work harder—and less likely to cheat—because they see challenging tasks as opportunities to learn.

CONSIDER THESE TIPS FOR USING PRAISE

When using praise, parents need to keep several general principles in mind. These principles include being specific; avoiding false, insincere, and excessive praise; avoiding comparative

The Do's and Don'ts of Praise

Do's	Don'ts
✓ Do be specific. ✓ Do give attention. ✓ Do focus on psychological rewards more than on material ones. ✓ Do give unconditional love.	X Don't give false and insincere praise. X Don't give comparative praise. X Don't praise in absolute terms.

praise; staying clear of absolute terms; giving attention; focusing on psychological rewards rather than material ones; and giving unconditional love.

Be Specific

Praise should specify what the behavior is. Use descriptive terms to direct the child's attention to what they have done that is being positively appraised. An example is: "That was good that you were honest and told our neighbor it was you who broke his windshield. I'm proud of you." Other examples include: "You did a good job washing up the dishes"; or "I'm really pleased to see you try so hard working on your project"; or "Ali, you made an effort to tell the truth about what you did, even though you knew you may get into trouble. That was showing integrity. You did a good thing telling the truth."

Using general praise does not convey to children the information about what was good, and they do not learn what the desired behavior is or how to act. Consider these examples: "It was helpful how you picked up your toys after your friend left and tidied up" versus "Good job" and "I like the way you are using different colors in your drawing" versus "This is so amazing!" The first phrase in each example specifically tells a child what they did that was worthy of praise and labels it in terms of the positive behavior. Praise should be used to communicate to the child what it is that they are doing that you appreciate.

Giving general praise like "You're a good girl" or "That's a great job" can be too broad to make it easy for the child to decipher what made them good or what made the job great. General praise conveys positive attention but does not teach the child what specifically makes them receive that positive attention and what the desirable behavior is. Overreliance on this general praise may emphasize the importance of "pleasing" the parent without the child's internalizing any specific information about what they did that was good. Children will desire to receive more of that attention and thus do things to receive that praise without learning the principles behind them. It is important for the child to learn that it is honest behavior that is praiseworthy as well as why it is desired. If an older child or teen tells you where they were hanging out with others after school—a place that they know you would prefer they did not go to—you can praise the child by saying, "It was honest of you to tell me about where you were. It makes me feel better to know where you are and that you are safe."

Avoid False, Insincere, and Excessive Praise

Avoid empty praise. Praise should be sincere and reflect the child's actual efforts. Parents should refrain from using false, exaggerated, or insincere praise (e.g., "You are a genius for answering that question!" or "You are the greatest boy in the world!") Even young children can detect insincere praise. Research has found that if praise is perceived as false by a child, it can have paradoxical effects on the child's perceptions of their ability and negatively affect their self-esteem (Brummelman et al., 2017). Praise that is inflated or exaggerated, such as, "You made the most incredibly amazing drawing," compared with noninflated praise, such as, "I found your choice of colors in the painting beautiful," had a negative effect on older children and predicted lower self-esteem over time.

Parents may feel tempted to exaggerate or make their praise overblown so that the child will feel better (e.g., "Your drawing is amazing!"; or "You did incredibly well at this!"; or "You are a genius for getting that question right!"), but such praise can backfire. If what the child has done is something relatively simple or easy, the child may actually infer that you think they are not that capable (e.g., "If I am praised for this easy thing, then they must think I can't do much better"). Take, for example, a child's telling the truth about something that they have no reason to lie about. If you were to suddenly and exuberantly praise them for what to them was an unremarkable behavior (e.g., "Wow, you told the truth! It is just so amazing how honest you are being"), they may feel that you did not have high expectations for their honesty.

Furthermore, researchers found that children who have initial lower self-esteem to begin with are particularly vulnerable to the deleterious effects of inflated praise, whereas children with initial high self-esteem are more likely to have higher rates of narcissism after hearing inflated praise (Brummelman et al., 2017). Inflated praise may make at least some children feel pressured to continue displaying the "excellent" behavior, which may lead some to feeling unable to live up to the standards set for them. Parents should keep in mind not just how they deliver the praise but also how the child who hears it interprets it. Some children may be more adversely affected by certain types of praise than other children.

We need to be careful not to overuse praise so that it becomes meaningless or that it leads children into complacency and pride. We can reflect on our own use of praise and our individual children's view of themselves to wisely determine when to encourage, admire, and praise the child. We must not confuse the use of encouragement and praise with giving unwarranted admiration, which can have a negative impact on the child. Children's good acts like being honest about something they did do merit comment. However, exaggerated praise and excessive admiration can be harmful to the child.

Praise should be deserved and genuine. Children know when it isn't. It cheapens the praise in the child's mind. And the person giving the praise seems less truthful.

Avoid Comparative Praise

Parents should also be careful not to use comparative praise. For instance, imagine you had a new haircut and someone said to you, "Oh, your hair looks good *now*." Comparative praise can be a backhanded compliment that makes a person feel bad and negatively affects their self-esteem about how they used to be. For instance, telling someone that they look so much better now makes them feel bad that they looked terrible before. Telling a child, "You're much more honest" communicates to the child that they were a dishonest person before, which may make them feel bad. Instead of their hearing your praise, what they hear is a criticism of the past behavior. It is better to use straightforward words of praise that clearly identify what they did right in that specific moment. Those words convey the teaching that the behavior is good and that it is what they did to earn such praise.

Avoid Using Absolute Terms

Avoid making absolute statements, such as "You are always honest"; "You are the most honest child in the class"; or "I'm glad you told the truth. I wish you would be more honest all the time." These statements put a lot of pressure on the child that they may not be able live up to or make them feel more insecure about your positive attention.

Give Attention

If you are giving a child praise, give the moment the attention it deserves. Make sure that when you deliver the praise, the child is attending to you and you are attending to the child. Giving praise while you are distractedly dashing about the kitchen can let the praise be lost as a passing, unimportant comment. Take a moment to pause to deliver praise. This is something you wish the child to know you think is important. Look at your child or teenager. Making eye contact allows you to create that connection and helps them to see the importance of your message. You may wish to gently touch the child and smile. Then praise your child.

The best time to comment on child's behavior is when the child is already engaging in the desirable behavior. By noticing the behavior, it lets the child know that this behavior is important to you. For instance, you can say, "It's good you are being honest about the mistakes you made."

Focus on Psychological Rewards Rather Than Material Ones

A word about rewards: Rewards can be either psychological ones (e.g., positive attention, hugs, kisses) or material ones (e.g., a food treat, money, a toy). Psychological rewards can be used to reinforce any positive behavior. However, I do not recommend using material rewards to reinforce honesty and other moral virtues. Regularly giving children material rewards for honesty runs the risk of leading them to be honest only when they expect to "get something." Researchers have found that giving material rewards for prosocial actions, such as sharing, reduces children's overall tendencies to be altruistic and results in less prosocial behavior in the future. We do not want children being honest only for reward. However, acknowledgment, appreciation, and praise communicate that being honest is intrinsically worthwhile for its own sake, and they have no dampening effect on children's prosocial behavior.

As a side note, although material rewards might be used judiciously for other types of behaviors (e.g., cleaning one's room), nonmaterial rewards are still better. One excellent type of nonmaterial reward is to give extra privileges. For example, parents might let the child stay up 30 minutes later to play a game or watch a show if the child completes chores. Or parents might use a point system or a bean jar system in which the child gets a point added to a chart or a bean in a jar every time they listen without a reminder. After the child meets a certain criterion (e.g., earns a certain number of points, a full jar of beans), they get to do something fun that you can do together. In my house, we use nonmaterial rewards like taking trips to the zoo, museum, or waterpark; watching a movie together; or engaging in other activities we decide on in advance. A judicious use of a material reward was when I used a new scooter as a reward for my son if he learned all his times tables and was able to answer 200 questions correctly in one try. Once he met that goal, he would be able to get a new scooter to replace his broken, old one.

The key is to use these rewards thoughtfully and deliberately—with planning and discussion with the child ahead of time. Do not offer a reward on the spur of the moment, in times of crisis, or out of desperation (e.g., do not say, "I'll give you $5 if you clean up your mess now" just before company arrives for dinner).

> *Regularly giving children material rewards for honesty runs the risk of leading them to be honest only when they expect to "get something."*

Give Unconditional Love

An important point about the efficacy of using any type of praise, acknowledgment, or appreciation is that it is given within the context of the parent–child relationship and is effective when the child feels unconditionally loved by their parent. Unconditional love is when we say things like "I love you" or "I am so glad you are my son," or we do something nice for the child for no particular reason. Examples include making their favorite meal, giving them a little treat when you play together, joking with them, laughing together and sharing moments of humor, hugging them or affectionately touching them when we listen, showing interest or sympathy and support, or sharing an activity together like watching a movie or shopping or baking. These behaviors convey our acceptance and love of the child. They are important for giving the child a sense of security and a bond of love.

Such behaviors are often easy with younger children because they are small and cuddly. However, with older children and teenagers, we may not be able to scoop them up and cuddle them the same way as when they were toddlers, but we can still do things that convey our unconditional love and approval of them. This is important for their own sense of well-being, self-identity, and self-esteem. Also, creating a bond between the parent and the child creates the framework on which all other teaching guidance and discipline rest. Actions of unconditional love are *not tied* to children's doing specific behaviors or acting in a certain way. Children do not have to do something to receive our unconditional love. When we show unconditional love to children and give them positive attention, they feel that love and acceptance.

Parents have to be careful about using conditional forms of positive attention to reinforce behavior (i.e., giving their child attention, approval, and love only when they comply with your wishes or behave in a desirable manner). Occasional use of such techniques may help to guide the child's behavior and reinforce their desired behavior. However, it becomes a detractor to the child's development if it is the only type of positive reinforcement the child ever receives, and they never receive positive attention that is unconditional. In this case, the child learns to behave only for your positive attention because it is the only way they will receive it. Furthermore, one should not pair them together—for example, by saying, "Mommy really loves you for listening to me and doing what I say!" It implies that you only love the child when they listen to you at certain times; that is, your love is conditional on their behavior. If you separate them, it is healthier: "Mommy really loves you" and "I really like it when you listen to me." If the child receives signs of unconditional love and positive attention regularly, then the use of acknowledgment and praise can be effective in motivating children to engage in specific behaviors until their behaviors become self-reinforcing.

CONCLUSION

Catching children being honest can be an effective tool for reinforcing and teaching children how to be honest. You can catch them being honest by acknowledging the behavior, expressing appreciation, and praising them for being honest. By doing so, you communicate to the child important information about themselves and about what is important to you. It can positively (as well as negatively) impact their self-worth.

There are ways to do praise badly. Giving children conditional attention, giving them inflated or false praise, or giving them general praise does not help them internalize the principles of honesty or increase their honest behavior in the end. However, when used in a judicious way, praise can have positive effects. What matters is the way you give the praise. When you "catch them being honest," the recognition emphasizes to children what you value and what behaviors are valued.

8

Walk the Talk

Don't just talk; walk the walk! Make sure you are modeling the behaviors you want your children to show. It's no good lecturing them about the virtues of honesty and then taking them to the movies and lying about their age to get cheaper tickets. When you give back extra change, when you keep your promises, when you admit making mistakes and tell the truth—these are all powerful messages about how to be honest. What you do underscores the message of how you value honesty and how you practice honesty. A powerful teaching tool is your own behavior.

In this chapter, I discuss how what we do sends messages to children. First, I talk about what is communicated to children when our words and actions do not match and how we as parents can reflect on the messages we wish to give children through our actions. I describe some of the common lies parents tell and how these lies impact children as well as the importance of keeping promises to build and maintain trust. Parents are not perfect, just like children are not perfect. Taking time to think about our own behavior and to develop patterns of behavior that embody the messages we wish to communicate to children helps us to walk the walk and feel better about ourselves.

WHEN WORDS AND ACTIONS DON'T MATCH

If we tell children that being honest is important and that we value honesty, it contradicts that message when we then lie. By not behaving in accordance with what our stated values are, we tell children that it's okay to say one thing and do another. We essentially give the message of "it's okay to fudge it sometimes, especially if nobody notices." So when we do not practice honesty, we undercut our message about the importance of honesty. It also says that what we do is different from what we say. When our words and actions are in alignment, it gives greater potency and credibility to our words than when they are out of alignment. When they are not in alignment, children learn to nod and spout out homilies about the importance of honesty just like adults, but they learn to be no better when it comes to putting it into practice.

In contrast, acting in the way that we wish our children to behave demonstrates to them how to be honest and also reinforces the message that we value honesty. Children learn a lot by watching and observing what the parents do and say in different situations. If our behavior is congruent with what we are saying, then our messages become stronger, and the likelihood of learning a lesson becomes greater.

> *Children learn from watching others around them.*

To illustrate how observing the impact of other's lies affects children's own behavior, I describe two studies that demonstrated this influence on children's decisions to lie or tell the truth. In one study my colleagues and I conducted with Canadian children, we looked at how seeing someone lie or tell the truth would influence their own behavior (Engarhos et al., 2020). In this study, children witnessed another person break the researcher's eyeglasses. Later, when the researcher looked for her glasses, the person either confessed to the breakage or they lied and said they did not know how the glasses got broken.

Similar to real-life experiences, these truths or lies were subsequently met with positive or negative verbal reactions. In some cases in which the transgressor told the truth about breaking the glasses, the researcher responded positively, thanking them for telling them. At other times, there was a negative outcome: The researcher was upset with them for breaking her glasses. Similarly, when the transgressor lied, this resulted in positive and negative consequences. In one condition, when the transgressor lied about breaking the glasses, they were believed, and they avoided making the researcher upset. In another condition, the transgressor lied but was not believed, and it resulted in negative reaction from the researcher.

Later, after observing the lie or truth of the transgressor, children participated in a temptation resistance paradigm in which they were told not to peek at the answer of a trivia test question and had the opportunity to tell the truth or lie about their own behavior. We found that while most children between the ages of 5 and 8 years lied (as is typically found at this age), fewer children lied when they had previously observed the transgressor lie with a resulting negative outcome or when they saw the transgressor confess with a positive outcome. Children's observations of another's behavior and the consequences that resulted when they lied or told the truth influenced their own decisions to lie or tell the truth.

In another study with Chinese children, researchers found that 5-year-olds who observed a classmate receive praise for confessing to cheating were more likely to confess to cheating themselves. However, those who saw a classmate confess to cheating but receive no praise were not more likely to confess about their own cheating behavior (Ma et al., 2018).

As these two studies illustrate, children learn from watching others around them. When they observe the associated consequences of telling the truth or lying, this observation helps inform them about the benefits or risks of being honest, which, in turn, can influence their decision making about whether to lie or tell the truth. Children observe others and learn from these social interactions which types of behavior are considered praiseworthy, and then they use that information to guide their own behavior.

REFLECTION

Often the job of parenting requires us to confront our own behavior, our own values, and how we act and wish to act. It's no different when we think about honesty. Do we behave honestly? Sometimes little lies can creep in because it's easier to just lie than to tell the truth. Think about when a friend invites you over to their house, and you don't want to go because they always end up talking about topics that you find really boring or aggravating. However, you don't want to say that to your friend, and it makes life easier if you just tell them that you're busy already that Friday night. That's an easy lie. They don't come back with any questions, and you're off the hook without having to think of a way to decline and not hurt your friend's feelings.

We can tell the easy lie sometimes without thinking. I know one father who, every time a telemarketer called, would tell the telemarketer that he was just a guest visiting the house, and the call would immediately end. It was a really quick and easy way to shut down the telemarketer spiel. These lies may not cause a lot of harm, and they may even preserve the feelings of others. However, we do need to reflect on the lies we tell and how they jive with the messages we give about when to tell the truth or when not to. Our behavior tells the "real" story to kids. Is that the "story" we want to tell? Does what we do sit well with how we wish to behave?

We need to be careful about our own behavior. When we tell lies, children may observe them and derive messages on how to behave. In particular, a parent wants to avoid having a child perceive the parent as being false and hypocritical. For example, take a parent who talks about how horrible their neighbor is, how the neighbor is such a bore and is obnoxious, and how the parent dislikes how the neighbor looks after their garden and lawn. Then imagine that parent speaking to that neighbor, and the child observes their parent praising the neighbor's lawn care and how wonderful that person is in general. This type of hypocrisy teaches the child false pretense and fakery. It also models backbiting, showing a smiling face to the person, but when the person is gone, ridiculing them and criticizing them. Such behavior models a form of dishonesty and hypocrisy; it suggests to the child that such behavior is acceptable.

Furthermore, parents should be careful about asking their children to keep secrets or lies. For example, a parent goes shopping, buys a new gadget, and later instructs their child not to tell the other parent about the purchase because they'll become angry. The parent is making the child a partner in their concealment. Or, imagine a parent who, although admonishing their child for being deceitful, later enrolls the child in the parent's own deception when someone comes to the door, and the parent tells the child to announce that the parent is "not at home." The child has been told to do one thing and watched their parent do another thing. Verbal prescriptions on how to behave lose their potency when they are unaccompanied by actions that mirror those words.

On the other hand, when children observe parents being truthful and behaving in a trustworthy manner that leads to positive outcomes, this can be a powerful teaching tool. In this way, parents' can influence their children's honesty positively or negatively through their own behavior. If children see their parent telling lies to get something they want (e.g., "Oh no! This is not a cola! It is really just black water, and you wouldn't like it"), then they see that such lies can lead to desirable out-comes with no negative effects.

COMMON LIES PARENTS TELL

Parents tell lies to children sometimes, too. If one looks at Twitter or other social media feeds of parents, it is not uncommon to see parents share the lies they tell their children. Often these are lies told by parents as a way to behaviorally control children (e.g., "If you cross your eyes, they will stay that way"; "The store is all out of cookies"; "The internet company shuts the internet off at 6 p.m.") and get them to comply with parents' directions (e.g., "If you don't come now, I will leave you here"; "Stop crying! The police will come to make sure that you behave if you don't stop crying now"). Parents can also tell lies to their children to prevent negative feelings (e.g., "No, the hamster didn't die; he just went to a hamster retirement home") or to promote positive feelings (e.g., "Look! See the rainbow! The rainbow came out just for you!"). In general, these lies may be told by parents who, most of the time, are honest but use this strategy occasionally to help them in the moment to manage their children.

In a study conducted with American undergraduate students, most reported that their parents strongly promoted honesty and discouraged dishonesty. However, their responses also suggested that parents tell lies to children. Of the undergraduates, 88% indicated that their parents had told at least one lie to them, and they provided examples. Some undergraduates reported that their parents sometimes told lies to promote positive feelings and preserve their child's feelings—like complimenting a child's cooking even though the outcome was "terrible." However, some undergraduates reported their parents also told lies to control the child's behavior—for example: "If you go outside alone, a witch will fly off with you" or "If you don't pay attention, the bogeyman will steal you" (Heyman et al., 2009, p. 357).

In a second study, the researchers asked U.S. parents to evaluate their own parenting practices in relation to different examples of lies. Overall, the parents reported strongly encouraging honesty in their children. However, parents also gave positive evaluations to lying in some contexts. Many of the parents rated positively at least one of the lie scenarios they read. They also gave examples of lies they told their children. For instance, one parent reported that

> I was attempting to get my four year-old daughter out of the bathtub. . . . I told her that sitting back down was going to make the germs she'd just washed off think she really liked them and would cause them to jump back on. (Heyman et al., 2009, p. 360)

Another example given by a parent was this:

> My son never lets me leave him. One night my husband and I had dinner plans. When my friend Linda called, my son asked me "Who is it, Mommy?" An idea came to my mind. I said, "Oh it was my friend Linda. The witch got her. You will have to stay with your brother so daddy and mommy can go help her." I did it because I didn't want him to cry when I left and ruin my dinner. (Heyman et al., 2009, pp. 360–361)

In another study involving a sample of parents from the United States and China, the researchers asked parents about their use of lies to encourage behavioral compliance in their children. They found that most parents (84% in the United States and 98% in China) reported having lied to their children to influence the child's behavior (Heyman et al., 2013). Parents in both countries reported telling lies to their children to encourage them to eat—for example: "You need to finish all your food or you will get pimples all over your face" (p. 1179)—to make them leave a place or stay at a specific location. They also lied about spending money—for example: "I did not bring my money with me today. We can come back another day" (p. 1179). The most common lie told in both countries was the practice of falsely threatening to leave a child alone in public if the child refused to follow the parent. This likely reflects the universal challenge parents face in trying to leave a place against their child's wishes.

In another study conducted by my colleagues and I, we asked Canadian parents if they thought it was ever acceptable to lie and what they taught their children about lying. About half of parents indicated that lies to protect others were sometimes acceptable, whereas a very small percentage of parents (8% of our sample) reported that it was never acceptable to lie (Lavoie et al., 2016). Some examples of lies parents encouraged their children to tell were: "I told her to lie about her age so she can get into an amusement park for free" or "Don't tell Daddy the dog peed on the floor" (p. 6). A small number of parents reported that it was acceptable to tell lies to protect another or for altruistic purposes. Generally, how parents reacted to their children's lies and how they encouraged or discouraged their children's lying were consistent with their verbal messages about lying.

IMPACT ON CHILDREN

Do parents' lies really affect children? As illustrated in the study described earlier (Engarhos et al., 2020), a child's observation of another person lying or telling the truth can have an immediate impact on the child's behavior and influence their decision to tell the truth or lie. Other research also indicates that there may be long-term impact for some children who repeatedly observe parental dishonesty. In another U.S. study, researchers found that the majority of undergraduate students reported that their parents only told occasional lies to them and that their parents mostly told them prosocial lies, which they perceived as not being serious or destructive, or not affecting them negatively (Cargill & Curtis, 2017). The undergraduates also said they would be more likely to use this kind of deception with their children. Notably, the researchers also found that 5% of undergraduates reported that their parents frequently lied to them. Importantly, they found that as undergraduates' perception of parental deception increased, satisfaction with their relationship with their parents decreased.

These findings suggest that a small amount of lying may not affect the child–parent relationship, but it does give the message that occasional lying is okay. However, when children perceived their parents as lying frequently, it impacted their relationship with their parent and eroded the trust in that relationship.

> Parental lies, if used regularly to influence children's behavior and emotions, may have long-term negative effects.

Furthermore, a study with adults found that greater exposure to their parents' lying to them in childhood was associated with increased dishonesty toward their parents in adulthood as well as increased severity externalizing problems, such as aggression, rule breaking, and disruptive behavior (Setoh et al., 2020). Thus, it seems likely that parental lies, if used regularly to influence children's behavior and emotions—especially in a manipulative way to exert power and gain compliance—may have long-term negative effects on children's psychosocial functioning into adulthood.

COMPASSION FOR PARENTS

Parents need to be compassionate with themselves if they occasionally tell their toddler a lie to gain compliance. In the heat of the moment of dealing with a toddler in a busy place, sometimes we grasp at quick strategies. The parent who told their child that the chip aisle was closed to stop the child from grabbing chips probably did not scar their child for life. The parent was just desperate to get out of the store because it is quite hard to grocery shop with toddlers in tow. However, if that parent frequently tells such lies and often gains compliance through lying, this could have a long-lasting effect.

Many parents lie as a last resort when they feel at their wit's end and beleaguered. Rather than spending time beating yourself up, think more proactively for the future. What are some longer term strategies you can put into place to ensure your child's compliance?

CAVEAT

Events or details happen in life, and a parent may wish to protect their child from them. For instance, the parent may refrain from discussing in front of their young child something distressing in the news to avoid the child's becoming anxious or overwhelmed. There may be arguments among family members. Or perhaps something happened to you before you arrived home, such as being mugged or losing your job.

If you child asks about such events, be honest with your child. However, you do not need to give them every detail if it is not age appropriate, but you do not need to lie either. We do not need to overburden the child with adult concerns or worries, or with details that will make them worry for your or their own safety.

PROMISES

Keeping promises and abiding by one's word is an important part of being trustworthy. We want children to be trustworthy and honest. We teach them to keep their promises. Young children understand the obligatory nature of promises at a young age. In a study with children between 3 and 5 years of age, researchers found that when a partner failed to uphold a promise of sharing stickers with them, the children protested against the broken promise (Kanngiesser et al., 2017). In another study, the researchers found that when children promised to continue a cleaning task, they persisted longer cleaning on their own and mentioned their obligation compared with those who had not made a promise (Kanngiesser et al., 2017). Thus, children as young as 3 years of age understand the importance of making and keeping promises, and they are upset by the breaking of promises. Promises are important to children and are important to the bond between adult and child.

One of the most effective ways to teach children about trustworthiness is through observing the parents' actions. Parents who regularly evade or break promises become untrustworthy in the child's eyes. The failure to keep promises has a detrimental effect on children's training. Parents should attempt to avoid the injustice of broken promises to their children. They should make promises with the true intention of keeping them and with the consideration that they are obtainable.

If you are not sure you can fulfill a promise, then it is better not to make the promise. But, if you make a promise, you should make every effort to keep it. This means thinking before you promise something because sometimes promises are impossible to keep or are for things that a highly likely to be unobtainable. Before promising anything to a child, the parent should first judge whether that promise can be fulfilled.

> Parents who regularly evade or break promises become untrustworthy in the child's eyes.

It is understood that on occasion, something beyond your control prevents the promise from being fulfilled. For instance, you promise to take the child to the public outdoor pool tomorrow afternoon. When the time arrives, a thunderstorm prevents you from being able to fulfill your promise because the outdoor pool is closed. Under the circumstances, it is alright to explain to your child that the situation was beyond your control. Children can learn that sometimes events are beyond even their parents' control. If you happen to know the weather forecast and that there is a likelihood of a thunderstorm tomorrow afternoon, you can say to the child, "I promise to take you to the pool tomorrow afternoon provided there is no thunderstorm."

Promises made with negligence or without the intention of really carrying them out should be avoided. Promises should not be made to the child to get them to do what you want them to do with no intention of keeping your side of the bargain. In this way, such promises are a tool to deceive the child. Broken promises model that what you say and do don't have to be the same. Broken promises also sow in the heart of the child the seed that one does not have to be trustworthy at all times.

For example, think of the child who is upset watching their parent get ready to go out. The child doesn't want to be left at home and wants to go with the parent. To quiet the child down so the parent can finish getting ready to leave, the parent promises the child a treat of candies that they'll bring home when they return later. They make this promise knowing that they probably will forget about the candies or may even have the intention initially to get the candies, but this intention will fall away quickly once the parent leaves. Their main purpose for making that promise is to quiet the child and stop their crying. The child believes the parent, wiping away tears and trying to be happy so that the parent will not be upset with them and potentially take the promise of candies back. They keep their side of the bargain by being quiet and waiting patiently for the parent's return.

When the parent returns, the child excitedly greets them at the door, looking to see what the parent is carrying. "Did you bring the candies?" The parent responds that they were too busy to get the candies; or something happened that made them forget about it; or the shop was closed, and they couldn't go to another one. The parent has some excuse. "But don't worry," the parent says. "Next time I go out, I'll buy you some for sure." The child is left feeling disappointed and hurt. Repeated bouts of broken promises teach the child there's nothing wrong in failing to keep a promise. It also breaks the bond of trust between the child and the parent.

CONCLUSION

There are two methods to teach children: the *direct method* in which we instruct, explain, and talk to them; and the *indirect method* in which we show them. How we behave—how we demonstrate to children what it means to be truthful—is a powerful way to teach children. If we are truthful and practice honesty in our daily lives, children will see it. Furthermore, our words and teachings about the importance of honesty will be more potent.

These two methods go together and mutually reinforce the message about how to act. We often give a lot of thought about what we say. We equally need to give a lot of thought about what we do. However, remember: We are not perfect. If we slip up, then repair and restore—and start again tomorrow.

9

Encourage Open Communication

Open communication is a vital part of encouraging honesty in children and is important at all stages. For instance, teenagers who feel they can talk with their parents about what is happening in their lives or what is bothering them are more likely to tell their parents details about their lives. One of the main reasons children conceal and tell lies is because they feel like they cannot trust their parents to listen to them without being negative.

In this chapter, I discuss the importance of creating a parenting relationship in which children feel confident about talking to their parents. This chapter briefly reviews and discusses how different parenting styles can influence children's tendency to be honest or dishonest in different social situations and how specific parenting methods can help foster honesty. I discuss the behaviors that parents need to exhibit to promote open communication with children, including using reflective listening, acknowledging feelings, using consistency and firmness in rules, and being detached rather than reacting. I also discuss how parents can foster a climate of open communication through developing the practice of family consultation that involves all the members of the family. By having a warm, responsive relationship with children while still having well-defined standards and expectations, parents can create a family environment that fosters honesty. Promoting such an atmosphere is something the whole family can engage in and provides opportunities for everyone to be heard and consulted.

UNDERSTAND PARENTING STYLES

Different parenting styles and parenting practices can affect children in general and, more specifically, create conditions in which they may be more or less likely to be honest. Scientific research has focused on two dimensions of parenting practices: responsiveness and demandingness. Both are important, and here's why.

Responsiveness is the degree to which parents accept and respond to their child's emotional and developmental needs. This includes being warm, loving, and supportive. Everyone has the basic need to feel loved, valued, and respected. Parents communicate all three in many ways throughout the child's life. This is a central part of parenting and is the foundation on which the parent–child relationship should be built.

Demandingness is the degree to which parents provide clear rules and expectations, and then correct their child's behavior through patient, careful training. Demandingness is important for providing the child with a framework for growing and developing. I use the analogy of a young vine. As a vine like a Virginia creeper develops from the seed, pushing green shoots out of the earth, it is pliable and can easily be trained on a lattice or other scaffold to grow into the desired location. However, if the plant is left on its own for some years, it will likely grow along the ground in an unruly manner and find whatever it can to climb up. If the gardener comes later and tries to train it up a scaffold or trellis at this stage, the "wood" of the plant's stems is less pliable and more likely to snap or break.

Based on the dimensions of responsiveness and demandingness, there are four general styles of parenting:

- *Authoritative parenting* is the most effective style. It is high on both demandingness and responsiveness. Authoritative parents have firm expectations and standards that they expect the child to meet, but they are also warm and encourage their child to think for themselves to develop a sense of autonomy.

Parenting Styles

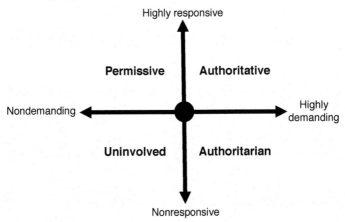

- *Authoritarian parenting* is high on demandingness but low on responsiveness. This parenting style emphasizes the blind obedience of the child, the use of strict rules and discipline, and the use of punishments to control the child that may, at times, include power-assertive techniques (e.g., using harsh punishment or coercion to enforce child discipline) and withdrawal of parental affection.

- *Permissive parenting* is low on demandingness and high on responsiveness. Permissive parents are emotionally warm and sensitive to their children's needs but are reluctant to enforce rules and discipline.

- *Uninvolved parenting* is low on both demandingness and responsiveness. Uninvolved parents show little interest in their children either in terms of setting rules and discipline or in emotional warmth and responsiveness. This type of parenting has a detrimental effect on children's development and is strongly associated with negative outcomes for the child's future.

The actual scope and expression of these dimensions may vary across parents, families, and cultures. Generally speaking, authoritative parenting creates the most positive and supportive environment for children to develop in. Authoritative parents support children with both love and warmth as well as provide firm rules and standards. This parenting style helps children grow into well-adjusted, socially responsible, and independent people who have positive social relationships, as is illustrated in the research on children's honesty and the development of their moral behaviors. One study found that parental control led to less lying in preschool-age children (Ma et al., 2015). In another study, my colleagues and I found that authoritative parenting led to less antisocial lying in preschool-age and early school-age children (Talwar, Lavoie, et al., 2017).

As children get older, though, the relationship between parenting behaviors and children's honest reports may become more nuanced. For instance, research with adolescents has found that those who were honest and told their parents about engaging in prohibited behaviors, such as smoking and drinking, perceived their mothers as high on maternal warmth and knowledge (Cumsille et al., 2010). These youths also had the fewest problem behaviors compared with other adolescents who lied and concealed. When adolescents expect disapproval from their parents about their activities, that expectation can lead to their intensifying the strategic use of lying about behaviors in an attempt to reduce negative consequences to the self. This, in turn, can lead to a cyclical pattern in which poor relations with parents leads to more lying, which worsens the parent–child relationship.

For example, researchers found that while secret-keeping in adolescents led to a poorer relationship with their parents, this was a bidirectional relationship because having a poorer relationship with parents can also lead to an increase in secret-keeping in adolescents (Dykstra et al., 2020). Adolescents who do not trust or feel supported and understood by their parents may be more likely to conceal their activities from their parents. Similarly, researchers found that frequent lying by adolescents was strongly related to less communication with parents and higher alienation (Engels et al., 2006). The more the adolescent children lied, the less the parents knew or asked about children's behavior. On the other hand, when there was a warm, intimate, and satisfying relationship between the child and parents, the youths were less likely to lie to their parents.

MAINTAIN OPEN COMMUNICATION

Communication is important to creating a climate in which people feel comfortable being honest. In climates in which communications are frequently warm, supportive, and positive, individuals tend to feel more comfortable, which can help lessen their fears about disclosing the truth or speaking about their feelings or actions honestly. When it comes to communication, though, there are general rules, including modeling good communication within the family, spending one-on-one time with your child, asking your child for input, encouraging children to talk about both negative and positive emotions, acknowledging your child's feelings, and listening to your child without interruption.

Model Good Family Communication

If communication in the family is considerate and kind, it models a respectful style of communication. This means paying attention to what others in the family express. It means not just talking but also taking the time to listen to what other members of the family have to say. Open and honest communication facilitates family members' being able to express their varying opinions, differences of ideas, or wants as well as their love and admiration for each other.

When the adults in the family interact with each other and with their children in such a way that respect is given to each person, it creates a climate in which individuals in the family feel they can express themselves honestly while still speaking in kind and respectful terms as well as feeling accepted and loved. In such a climate, families are better able to resolve inevitable problems and challenges that arise in every family. For all members of the family, it important to speak in respectful tones without harsh criticism or in demeaning terms.

Spend Quality Time With Your Child

Spending quality time with your child gives them opportunities to engage in conversation. Show that you want to learn more about your child's interests: Ask questions about what they like to do and be genuinely curious about the things they are interested in. If your 6-year-old enjoys making crafts, get crafty. If your 10-year-old likes playing a specific video game, then take an interest in it and learn about it. If your 14-year-old likes a certain band, listen to the music and get to know who the musicians are. If your 15-year-old is hanging out on a certain social media site, get to know that social media site (you don' t need to stalk them; just be familiar with the things that are important in their lives).

Take an interest in their interests and find ways to do shared activities. You may establish certain activities that you do together and can carry throughout their childhood into the teenage years, such as baking, going fishing or camping, or playing video games together. Be equally open and alert to new opportunities to share time with your child as they get older and as their interests and activities change.

Ask Your Child for Input

Let the child be part of the solution: Ask your child to give input to solve problems. Doing so allows the child to have some say in the rules as well as the outcomes when rules are not respected. While toddlers may be unable to give you input and preschoolers may have difficulty coming up with suggestions, you can scaffold these abilities for them by helping with suggestions and encouraging them to be active participants rather than passive recipients.

Older children and teenagers have more to say. Giving teenagers more autonomy in making decisions can help them in their attempts to develop their own sense of self-identity and put into practice the moral principles they have developed.

Encourage Talk About Positive and Negative Emotions

We often do not like to hear about negative feelings and may sweep children's expressions of these feelings away. However, it is important to allow children to talk about their feelings. Equally, sometimes we quell children's jubilant expressions of joy and positive emotions. Listen to them, and let them know they can express what they feel and think. Avoid criticism when your child is sharing their feelings and thoughts.

A child who knows they will be heard and listened to is more likely to communicate rather than shut down. Within a family climate of mutual respect and kindness, family members can communicate with each other and listen to each other.

Acknowledge Their Feelings

When children do express negative feelings, acknowledge those feelings. You may not like what they are feeling, or you may wish they would not feel that way. However, you address those feelings by first acknowledging them. A child who says, for example, "I hate my brother" is expressing their upset and anger at their sibling. A parent may wish to rush in and negate that feeling with, "No, you don't!" You may not want your child to say such things, but you can acknowledge that, in that moment, your child feels upset: "I know you are angry with your brother."

In another example, a child may come home from school and tell their parent, "No one likes me!" Many a parent will want to immediately make it better for the child: "That's not true! Many people like you. I like you. You father likes you. Your sister likes you. Jennie likes you . . . [et cetera]." What the child is expressing is a feeling they are having at that moment. It may be different from how you perceive the reality, but it is what they are feeling. To help our child address those feelings and what they are about, we have to accept what they are feeling. We need to be prepared to hear what they feel without trying to discount it. If the child feels heard and accepted, they are more likely to listen to your counsel afterward and find positive ways to deal with their feelings.

Don't Interrupt Your Child

Allow your child to finish what they are saying before you thoughtfully respond. Sometimes parents jump to the conclusion of what their child is saying and interrupt with their follow-up thought before a child has finished saying it. Pause and allow the child the time to finish their thought. With preschool children and even children in early grade school, you may need to pause often as the child tries to assemble their thoughts and the words to express them. A teenager, too, may take their time to work themselves up to saying something that they feel trepidation about expressing. Do not rush in to finish the child's thoughts for them; instead, patiently allow them to find the words to express them. If they need help with a word, you can interject it if it helps them continue to the end of their idea.

As children get older, they may use more complicated and longer sentences. You may infer what it is they are trying to communicate or wish to respond or refute something that has been said before they have finished expressing their entire thoughts. Here again, it is wise to let the child or teenager fully express their ideas before responding. They are more likely to feel heard and more likely to listen in return. Let them speak and hear their perspective. Be curious to learn what your children thinks about things. Adults should listen to what children and teenagers say and not be judgmental if they wish to really know the child's thoughts and feelings. By taking the time to actively listen, adults are more likely to be able to respond thoughtfully and to understand the child's perspective, which, in turn, can lead to more positive, supportive communication as well as better problem solving.

KEEP UP COMMUNICATION IN THE ADOLESCENT YEARS

Parents can have greater difficulty keeping open communication in the adolescent years. When children were younger, you had more control over their lives and knew what their activities were. Adolescence is a time when children seek more autonomy and are more often engaged in activities away from home. In adolescence, the main source of parental knowledge is their adolescents' sharing of information and disclosure of their activities. By keeping communication open, adolescents feel like they can disclose and confide in you.

While in childhood, you were the governor as the parent; in adolescence, you become more the advisor or counselor as teenagers seek autonomy and try to make some of their own choices. At times, you will need to counsel the adolescent to help them understand that certain behaviors and conduct are inappropriate. Parents of adolescents, though, should not treat their offspring as though they are still only children. Rather, they need to see them as the emerging adults they are developing into.

When serving as a consultant (discussed in more detail in the Engage in Consultation section), avoid the use of harsh words and ensure that your actions are characterized by courtesy. You should never belittle your adolescent or their ideas. By speaking to them in respectful tones and not with harsh and angry words as well as treating them considerately, you are modeling to them the respect that you wish, in turn, to receive from them. Expect them to talk to you in the same way. This should be well established in your family as the only acceptable way to communicate.

Parents should be able to accept the legitimate and logical demands of their adolescent children. They should answer their adolescent's questions as capably as they can and allow the child to engage in conversation and express their own opinions. Although adolescents increasingly seek autonomy and the ability to make their own decisions, they are unable to make all their own decisions yet. You can explain the reasoning behind your decisions, and you can increasingly engage them in the decision-making process.

Parents should allow the time and opportunity to engage in open conversations on different topics that are of interest to the adolescent. Doing so allows a positive exchange that is not always centered on rules or decision making and helps maintain, a warm and positive relationship between the parent and child. These consultations are more conversations than lectures: The adolescent is an equal partner in the discussion and exchange of ideas. If all conversations between the parent and teen are always about the enforcement of rules, or they become debates about what are acceptable activities or behavior for the teenager, there is no time to create connection. Teens are increasingly involved in their own lives and the lives of their friends, so parents may have to work harder to create spaces and times to have conversations and engage with their teens. This is vital to maintaining strong relationships. This is vital for everyone in the family.

> While in childhood, you were the governor as the parent;
> in adolescence, you become more the advisor.

When clashes do happen, take time to pause and wait for the situation to abate. Then you can approach your teen calmly. By being calm, a parent is more likely to be able to engage in constructive conversation with the teenager, and there is more likely to be a positive outcome.

SET RULES AND COMMUNICATE EXPECTATIONS

Setting clear rules is an important part of creating conditions for honesty. Using rules and clearly communicating expectations of how family members should behave can help reduce a lot of the stress in parent–child relationships and help with maintaining open communication. However, a key condition to ensuring rules are effective is pairing them with an emotionally warm, open, and accepting relationship. When a parent and child have a strong, emotionally warm relationship, rules can help reduce arguments and daily discussions about how to behave. The child or teen feels that they are respected and appreciated, and that they will not be harshly and unjustly punished.

Rules need to be reasonable, but they should not be used excessively. When rules are reasonable and communicated clearly and firmly, children and teens—within the context of a warm relationship—are more likely to ask your permission or disclose if they have broken a rule. The child or teen will see you as warm and nonpunitive but firm with rules; thus, they will have a greater respect for those rules.

Research with adolescents who are often testing the boundaries of parents' authority has found that when adolescents respect parents and feel that their parents are warm and nonpunitive, they are more likely to feel that parents have the right to set the rules; are more likely to respect the parent's authority; and, consequently, are more likely to be truthful. Of course, that may not stop the teen from arguing and debating the rule. And even youths who have a great relationship with their parents may do something they don't want to tell their parents about and lie.

For instance, a common push–pull between parents and adolescents these days are the use of smartphones and other digital devices. Youths can often hide their activities online if they think their parents would disapprove. When parents are more open and discuss the different issues related to digital use in a way that allows for youths to feel like they are part of the conversation (rather than just being talked to), they are more likely to listen to their parents' concerns and take them more seriously. Equally, the parents need to understand the motivations and attractions that different online sites may have for youths so they may address those motivations (see Chapter 4 for more details on how to skillfully deal with motivations). Some online risky behavior actually results from the youth's feelings of inadequacy or isolation, or from peer pressure. This is another reason to keep the lines of communication open: so that you know what is happening in your teenager's life, and your teenager feels they can share even their negative feelings with you.

While parents may make the rules when children are little, when the children are teenagers, parents can include them as part of the discussion. Older children are able to problem solve and can be invited to make suggestions. Doing so can also help them learn to create self-imposed limits and regulate their own behaviors. So, for instance, they can suggest reasonable limits for screen time use, and these rules can be set with their input. When parents engage in more negative parenting practices, such as harsh and authoritarian parenting, adolescents are less open with their parent.

Rules create a framework for children to operate within, thus helping to reduce behavior that is inappropriate, transgressive, or problematic. When children do break those rules, they are more willing to understand and expect the consequences. Within a warm and loving relationship, children are more likely to internalize moral standards of behavior, more likely to accept parental authority to enforce the rules, and more likely to accept the repercussions of their behavior. Rules will be violated, and children may be motivated to lie about those violations. However, when parents have established a strong, trusting relationship with their child that emphasizes principles of responsibility, fairness, and concern for others, rules can decrease the motivation for children to lie.

A study conducted by U.S. researchers illustrates how teenagers' perception of their relationship with their parents and their ability to communicate openly influenced their views of the acceptability of lying to their parents (Gingo et al., 2017). The researchers presented adolescents with vignettes about adolescents lying to their parents. In some vignettes, the parents were described as usually listening to their adolescents' perspective during disagreements and including the adolescent in joint family decision making. In other vignettes, parents made decisions unilaterally and were uninterested in listening to the adolescent. In these vignettes, the parents had directed the adolescent not to engage in a particular act, but the adolescent does engage in the act and lies about it. For example, an adolescent called Patrick wishes to date a girl called Liz. His parents do not like Liz and tell him not to see her even after Patrick tries to convince them that he should be able to date her. Patrick does date Liz without his parents' knowledge, but he tells his parents he is dating someone else. In another example, an adolescent lies about riding a motorcycle that his parents explicitly forbade him to ride. In such a case, the concern for the parents was for the safety of their child.

Overall, while adolescent participants evaluated lying in the motorcycle story as unacceptable, they were more accepting of Patrick's lie about dating. Adolescents saw actions that were in the personal domain (e.g., who to date) as less under the legitimate control of parental authority. However, in other types of acts, such as those that involved safety or social conventions, adolescents accepted parental control over such activities and judged deception as unacceptable. They also viewed the directives of parents who had a mutual relationship with their child and listened to the adolescent's perspective—compared with those who unilaterally made decisions without interest in hearing the adolescent perspective—as being aimed at protecting and looking after the adolescent's well-being.

Adolescents were more likely to endorse deception as acceptable in responding to parents when a unilateral relationship existed rather than when a mutual relationship existed. When the relationship was mutual, adolescents rejected deception because it would damage trust and harm the relationship. However, when there was a unilateral relationship, adolescents noted that lying was not risking a relationship because of the lack of trust or closeness. As one participant reportedly said, "Why shouldn't she lie? It's not like she'll have a worse relationship if she does, they're not close, and it's already terrible" (Gingo et al., 2017, p. 874). Thus, the findings of this study suggest that when parents engage in mutual discussion and decision making with their teenager—that is, the teenager is able to give their perspective and be heard, and the parents and teen have open communication and mutual respect, adolescents are more likely to see their parents as legitimate authorities.

In another study, researchers asked Chilean adolescents between 11 and 19 years of age whether they would fully disclose, partially disclose, avoid the issue, or lie for six scenarios (Cumsille et al., 2006). The scenarios included situations that could be seen as both personal (i.e., an individual can make their own choice) and about safety (i.e., legitimate concern about the safety and well-being of the individual). For instance, the researchers included scenarios about hanging out with friends that the adolescent's parents think are problematic, being with friends when adults are not around, where the adolescent goes with their friends, what time the adolescent should get home at nights, smoking, and drinking. Adolescents were asked what their typical behavior was for each scenario when they disagreed with their parents: tell all, avoid the subject, tell part of truth, or lie.

> *Within a warm and loving relationship, children are more likely to internalize moral standards of behavior and accept parental authority.*

Teenagers who responded that they would tell all reported higher levels of obeying parental rules, believing in parental legitimacy to set rules, agreeing with parents, and perceiving their mothers as high in warmth or support and knowledge about their children. They also engaged in the fewest problem behaviors. In contrast, those who frequently chose the option to lie had the opposite trend: low levels of positive attributes and high levels of problem behavior.

GIVE THEM SPACE

Treating a child of any age with respect and giving them opportunities to have some autonomy is important. For toddlers, this may mean letting them choose between two types of cereal for breakfast, walk a little way instead of riding in the stroller, or wear their swimsuit all day under their clothes. As children grow into early childhood and middle childhood, they develop their own interests and engage in imaginary play that they share with their peers. You may catch them whispering to each other about their games or laughing over their shared jokes. They will not always want to share these with you. Allowing them space to grow and develop their own self-identity is important. You can monitor their interactions with others without always interfering or being in the middle of their play. However, as children become preadolescent and transition into adolescence, they may increasingly seek greater privacy. This is a natural part of development. As they reach puberty, their desire for privacy becomes more acute, and as they grow older, adolescents increasingly operate outside of their parents' abilities to directly supervise them, changing how and when parents can guide their behavior.

Respecting teenagers' desire for privacy can encourage them to be more honest and open with you. Teenagers who feel trusted and that you are not getting into their business all the time will feel more comfortable telling you about their lives rather than feeling the need to keep things hidden. This is not to say that parents should never ask for any information from their teens. Parents still need to know the whereabouts of their teens and information pertaining to the teen's well-being and safety. Parents should be concerned to know that their child arrived safely at their friend's house or where their teen is on a Friday evening. However, parents do not need to demand to know what their teen talks about with their friends. When asked, adolescents often feel that parents have a greater right to ask about information about their activities with their peers rather than personal information, such as what their peers are like or what they talk about.

Teens who feel that their parent is prying too much may be more likely to start keeping things about their life hidden. They may become more likely to shut down communication and to avoid giving you details about their lives. By asking only for information you need to know, you are more likely to keep the lines of communication open.

Research shows that parents tend to have greater knowledge about their teens when the family climate is positive and warm, and the parents do monitor but stick to more routine types of questions about activities. This sort of family climate is associated with increased positive well-being in adolescents. However, when parents engage in more intrusive and negative parenting, adolescents tend to clam up, restricting the amount of information they share, thus leading to parents' having less knowledge about their teens' lives.

Children and adolescents tell lies and use deception as a way to circumvent what they see as intrusive or illegitimate parental control. When American adolescents believe that the issue at hand is personal and not harmful (e.g., choice of who their friends are), they are more likely to reject the legitimacy of their parents to intervene or set restrictions (Smetana et al., 2009). In such cases, teens are more likely to see deception as a legitimate means of resisting parental control. Adolescents commonly report telling both lies and keeping secrets as a way to obtain autonomy while avoiding parent–child conflict. They tell lies and conceal to prevent parents from knowing and monitoring their behaviors.

For instance, another study in which researchers presented American adolescents ranging from 12 to 16 years of age with hypothetical vignettes in which parents and adolescents in each story disagreed over different activities further illustrates motivations of adolescents to disclose or conceal information (Perkins & Turiel, 2007). In all of the stories, the adolescent wanted to do something, and the parent objected to the activity, so the adolescent lied about what they were doing. Some stories involved issues of fairness, such as parents' objecting to an adolescent's wanting to be friends with someone of another race, or issues of harm, such as a parent wanting the adolescent to fight with another student who is teasing the adolescent. Other stories involved personal choices, such as the parents' objecting to the adolescent's dating someone the parent does not like, or the adolescent's wanting to join a club that the parents think is a waste of time. Some stories involved potential harm to the adolescent either academically—for example, in a case in which a parent objects to the adolescent's choice not to finish homework—or in physical welfare, such as a parent's objecting to the adolescent's choice to ride a motorcycle. In another story, the adolescent committed a misdeed like breaking a cell phone in anger.

Adolescents were asked if it was alright (or not) for the adolescent in the story to do the activity in secret and not tell their parents. They were also asked if it was alright that the parents expect the adolescent to do the activity. For the most part, the rejection of parents' directives to engage in racial discrimination or to harm another was based on the ideas that the acts are wrong or unjust and that they caused harm to others. In such cases, to follow the directives of the parents was seen as morally wrong, and deception was acceptable to avoid such a violation. It is not only moral concerns that lead adolescents to accept deception; most also thought that it was acceptable to deceive parents about directives in the personal realm. The adolescents considered parents, in these situations, to be engaged in unwarranted control and justified deception on the need to maintain boundaries of personal jurisdiction. However, in scenarios involving potential harm to the adolescent, adolescents thought that parents are right in asserting their responsibilities and evaluated parental directives positively. So adolescents are not always dismissive of the legitimacy of parental directives, and they do not have a general or global orientation that it is alright to deceive parents.

PREPARE FOR HOW TO REACT TO UNCOMFORTABLE TRUTHS

Another important quality that parents and adults must develop is to be detached when listening to children's confessions or when they raise objections to certain rules. Rather than be reactive, it is best to be able to listen and communicate in a calm, dispassionate manner (see Chapter 4 for a discussion on how to remain calm). Here, the point I wish to raise is that part of maintaining open communication with your children is being able to listen to what they have to say and not shutting down the conversation by reacting too negatively or too soon, or because you feel unable to handle hearing what they have to say. If you want to encourage and foster your child's honesty, you must be prepared to hear things that are not always nice or comfortable. As outlined in Chapter 4, to do this, you want to keep your tone of voice neutral and not emotional when you respond to your child, and you want to be clear and direct in your communication.

We have to be prepared to hear things about our children's behavior we may wish are not true. A child who tells you that last night they hung out with their friends at the park and were drinking alcohol has told you the truth about something they could have lied about. You may not be pleased that your child is engaging in underage drinking, or hanging out with friends you think are unsuitable, or loitering in a place you do not feel is safe after dark. You may react to these facts. However, it is important to remember that your child told you, and you know the truth rather than a cover-up story. If you want your child to be honest, it means that you need to be prepared to hear that your child is not always behaving perfectly. It is okay to feel upset about your child's behavior. That is natural and normal. But in the moment when your child is telling you the truth, you need to be ready to hear it—for better or for worse. Would you prefer to hear the truth and know what is happening with your teenager, or would you prefer they lie and be hanging out in an unsafe area in the dark? A parent has to ask themselves these questions. If you want honesty, you have to be prepared to hear the truth and appreciate that the truth was told. Then deal with it.

Trying to create an environment in which there is open communication between all members of the family requires parents to cultivate the ability to, at times, detach from their own immediate feelings and reactions so they can actively listen to what their child is saying and understand the child's feelings, perspective, and potential fears. Let the child finish what they have to say before responding to help prevent the child from shutting down. Also keep in mind that they may have trepidation about telling you the information, and if they see you react in a way that confirms their fears, they may stop before they have told you everything.

In my research lab, my colleagues and I have often heard from adolescents that they are afraid to tell parents about cyberbullying because they fear their parents' reaction and the potential consequence that in reaction to the news, their parent will take away their smartphones. Adults need to be mindful of potential fears that the child has and create an atmosphere in which the child can fully disclose. That means creating an open-door policy such that the child feels like they can tell the parent anything. You also need to have conversations with your child throughout their development on the issues of honesty and lying. You want to communicate that "we want you to feel free to be honest with us, regardless of what you have to say." Another part of having these conversations, especially as the child gets older into the preadolescent and teenager years, is then being prepared for honesty.

ENGAGE IN CONSULTATION

A good practice to develop in the home is *consultation*. This is a practice that adults in the family can learn to do between themselves, and they can train their children to engage in it as well. For young children in early childhood and early grade-school years, most of the consultation is between parents or between those caregivers in families who play a significant role. However, with age, children can be included in discussions and decisions that affect the family or the child in particular. For instance, children older than 8 years may be part of a family discussion about where to go for a holiday or how they can help their community's charity drive. They can be consulted about what after-school activities they want to do or what clothes they will wear for a family wedding. As children get older and approach adolescence, they become increasingly capable of playing an active and even energetic part in these consultations. Letting teenagers take an active role in these consultations and giving opportunities to lead different family activities can empower youths who have the energy, enthusiasm, and desire to be actively involved in their lives and world.

Family consultations can be formal "family meetings" or informal discussions that arise from the needs of the moment. However, the principles of a family consultation are that it is a time for candid, dispassionate, and cordial discussion. Through consulting together, the family can make collective decisions; consulting promotes the unity of the family. In such a way, it can strengthen the bonds of trust and love between members of the family. It also allows a variety of opinions and new insights to be brought forward and examined dispassionately so the family can take decisive action or clarify certain matters. Importantly, if the discussion descends into argument or stagnation, then it should be deferred to another time. Consultation should be used as a means to create harmony and allow for diverse perspectives of the family to be integrated into the family's understanding of the issues at hand.

During the practice of consultation, parents can let their adolescent express their opinions or talk about things they wish to do in the future; the parents should avoid interrupting and silencing the youth. They should also be careful not to make all decisions without the youth's input. An adolescent who doesn't feel that their opinion has been adequately considered or their feelings consulted may be more likely to resort to deceptive means to get around such decisions, which they do not see as legitimate. With respectful and considerate parents, the adolescent may be able to see different aspects of the subject under discussion and come up with suggestions and solutions that consider these perspectives.

By acquiring the habit of consultation in the family and the deliberation of important matters from an early age, adolescents develop into social citizens capable of deep thinking.

Parents can learn to consider the feelings, emotions, and needs of their children to learn their intentions. Through the exchange of thoughts and views, the truth, to some extent, can be discovered. Also, through this process of consultation, adolescents are less inclined to feel that their parents make unjust orders and are authoritarian adults who issue decisions without considering adolescents' own wishes and points of view. This practice increases the rapidly maturing adolescent's ability to grasp with the complexities of problems under discussion, and youths are more likely to submit to any decision arrived at as a result of the consultation.

CONCLUSION

Creating an environment in which members of the family can talk, discuss, and communicate with each other in an atmosphere of love and trust is vital to fostering truthful and candid expression. Children who grow up in such an atmosphere are more likely to feel their voice is heard and that their feelings, choices, and perspectives are respected. They are more comfortable sharing their feelings, thoughts, and details of their lives.

As children get older and enter adolescence, and assert greater autonomy and engage in more activities outside the home, this sort of environment becomes increasingly important. Warm, loving parents who set clear expectations for their children, allow them opportunities to think for themselves and participate in decision making create an environment in which honesty is the default and any motivation to deceive is often negated.

10

Build a Foundation for Character Development

In this chapter, I talk about abilities and skills that we should develop in our children to help support our lessons about truthfulness and the importance of honesty. While lying develops as a normal part of child development, children are also developing abilities that counter dishonesty, and parents can help foster these abilities.

Specifically, I discuss the importance of developing children's empathy, perspective-taking, self-control, and conscience—all essentially are the building blocks of character development. For each, I explain the ability and give examples of what it looks like in children. I also suggest techniques parents can use to foster these abilities in their children. By strengthening these abilities in children, the children will develop internal tools that will foster their honesty.

I end the chapter by talking about how teaching honesty within an overall framework or orientation on morals and virtues can support children's truthfulness as well as their development to become morally strong adults. The behaviors and virtues I speak of not only help children to be honest but are also important for their own development of character and their ability to engage with others in positive ways.

Building Blocks of Character Development

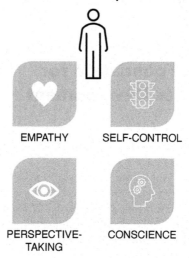

EMPATHY   SELF-CONTROL

PERSPECTIVE-   CONSCIENCE
TAKING

EMPATHY

Empathy is the ability to feel another's pain or sadness. When children understand what another is feeling, this can generate feelings of sympathy and acts of kindness and helping. Empathy is a central moral emotion that allows us to understand how other people feel. It is considered a central skill of emotional intelligence and has a profound impact on our social relations with our family, peers, teachers, and everyone we meet. We need empathy in our daily lives, and we need to foster that capacity in our children.

Through empathy, a child learns to become sensitive to others' needs and feelings. Children who are empathetic are more likely to help those who are hurt or are in difficulty. They are more likely to treat others with compassion and kindness. They are more likely to recognize the impact of emotional pain on others. And they are less likely to be mean to others or act aggressively toward others. In a nutshell, they act more *prosocially* toward others.

Let's look at an example of empathy. Aaron watched his little brother cry and fuss as his mother got his brother ready to go to the doctor. Aaron bit his lip and looked worried: "He is scared of the doctor. He doesn't want to get his shots," he told his mother. Then he ran upstairs and returned with the favorite stuffed bear that his brother took to bed with him every night. Handing the bear to his little brother, Aaron said, "Here, have Mr. Snug 'ems. You can squeeze him. I didn't like getting my shots either. I took Bunnybud with me when I got my shots, and it made me feel better to squeeze him." He then gave his brother a squeeze.

In this moment, we see Aaron's ability to recognize his little brother's distress and empathize with his fears. Aaron can reflect on how his brother feels and use this understanding to try to help his brother and address his needs. Aaron's empathy for his brother acts as a catalyst for his gesture of kindness and caring when he brings his brother his teddy bear for solace.

> *Empathy can lead us to tell the truth in ways that are kind and considerate of another person's feelings.*

We clearly want to develop this skill in our children. Feeling empathy is a powerful emotion that can connect your child to their conscience and to their sense of what is right and wrong. A child with empathy is more understanding of, tolerant of, and compassionate toward others around them.

Exploring Empathy and Honesty

Empathy is an important skill to have to develop prosocial behaviors and to be a caring individual. Research has consistently shown that children who are higher in empathy are more likely to act prosocially. It is important to be honest and compassionate: The truth can be told in ways that help others or in ways that can intentionally hurt others.

Consider this example: Your teenager gives you their essay to read. You can see they did it quickly; it is sloppy in its style and organization, and it is not well written. You can tell them that the essay "needs work" and offer supportive advice or specific suggestions that can help them revise it. In this situation, the truth can be supportive and helpful as well as lead to positive change. Your child hears the truth without it causing significant harm to their sense of self or leading to feelings of helplessness. Framed within a broader framework of positive communication and messages about the importance of learning—trying and trying again without fearing failures—the youth's overall abilities will grow and be better for this honest communication.

However, the same sentiment can be expressed in negative terms. You can tell your teenager that they are a "slacker" and speak in derisive and derogatory tones about them and their work. In such a case, the teenager feels only negative feelings and may see no avenues for improvement. They may choose to stop listening to you, to not make the effort to revise the essay, and to avoid your scrutiny in the future as much as possible. The honest communication that their essay was not to the standards you expected has been communicated in a way that only leads potential harm to the youth's self-esteem and does not support their learning or development.

Empathy alone, though, does not always promote moral behavior. For instance, if a child has difficulties controlling their emotions, and their feelings become too intense, they may experience personal distress, leading them to focus on their own needs rather than those of others (see the later section titled Provide Emotion Coaching on how to help children deal with negative emotions). However, when empathy is focused outward on the feelings and needs of others, it can lead the child to develop feelings of sympathy and concern for others, which can lead to helpful actions.

People sometimes tell a prosocial lie because they wish to spare another's feelings. For example, a person may lie about liking the pumpkin pie their friend proudly baked for them. People tell lies because they empathize with the negative feelings that the truth may cause. However, empathy also leads us to be honest, too. We tell the truth because we know what it would feel like if we were lied to. Empathy allows us to understand how it can feel to discover someone has violated our trust and deceived us. In addition, it can lead us to tell the truth in ways that are kind and considerate of another person's feelings.

In a study my colleagues and I conducted in my research lab, children between 7 and 11 years of age played a computer game against another player who was a research confederate (someone who was part of the study). The winner of each round of the game received a prize. The confederate lost every single round and became increasingly sad in one condition or just remained indifferent in another condition. For the last round of the game, the confederate asked if the child would say that the confederate won so the confederate could get one prize. It was left to the child to decide how to act. We also had parents fill out a measure of children's empathy.

We found that most children would share their previously won prizes with another player who was feeling distress for losing, and those who shared had higher levels of empathy (Nagar et al., 2020). They acted prosocially to help alleviate the person's sadness. We also found that some children would tell a prosocial lie, saying they had not won the last game so that the distressed player would receive a prize. Those who told these prosocial lies also had greater empathy. So having empathy for others can lead children to act in ways to help others and help ease others' distress, and this can include some-times telling a lie to help another person.

In another study done in the United States, researchers found that 7- to 11-year-olds were more likely to spontaneously tell a polite lie to someone who was feeling sad than to someone who was feeling neutral, with this differentiation being most prominent among 10- to 11-year-olds (Warneken & Orlins, 2015). As children become older, their abilities to understand and empathize with others increases. Thus, children are able to interpret another person's emotional experience as different from their own are able to use this understanding to behave morally and in ways to help someone feel better.

Lies told to protect others' feelings or to help others are a common feature of our interpersonal interactions. This type of dishonesty is not evaluated as negatively as other acts of dishonesty, but we still value honesty overall. Having empathy can lead us to use lies in a more prosocial way; however, understanding how others feel can help us learn to be honest in a more tactful and kinder way. The blunt truth, though, can hurt sometimes, too. If you wish your child to avoid telling prosocial lies—those told to protect another's feelings and to be polite—you need to help them to find ways to be tactful (see Chapter 4 for a discussion on teaching children tact).

Developing Empathy

Children naturally start showing empathy in the preschool years. That's when they start being able to recognize their emotions and understand other people's emotions. However, empathy is a capacity that must be nurtured in our children. Nurturing empathy in a child simply means to help them learn to become sensitive to the needs and feelings of others. Like a good gardener, we must tend to the empathy of our children for them to bring forth beautiful flowers and delicious fruits. The good news is that empathy is a skill that can be developed with a little encouragement. Here are some ways to foster empathy in your child.

Provide Emotion Coaching

Emotion coaching helps children develop the ability to cope with their own negative emotions. Feeling negative emotions can sometimes prevent us from thinking about others. This, in turn, can lead to the decreased likelihood of helping others because the person is too distressed with their own negative emotions. We can help children by acknowledging rather than dismissing their negative feelings. A discussion about how they are feeling, what caused those feelings, and what effects those feelings are having on them and others can help them to constructively cope with those negative feelings.

Demonstrate Empathy Toward Your Child

It is important to notice the child's feelings and listen with empathy. Acknowledge what is causing the emotion and label how the child is feeling. Then, find a resolution for the child's needs. In this way, we are modeling empathy to our children. Seeing us showing empathy toward both them and others demonstrates and teaches children how to show concern and empathy for others. Here's an example:

CHILD: I do not want to go to the doctor's. I hate it there.

PARENT: I understand that you don't like it there [noticing and acknowledging the emotion]. Whenever you have a doctor's appointment, you are afraid they are going to give you a shot [labeling the emotion]. This time you won't have to have a shot [finding a resolution].

Teach Children to Recognize and Label Emotions

Children who are more empathetic are usually more emotionally literate. They can recognize and express their emotional states and those of others. You can label your feelings and the feelings of others easily as part of your day-to-day conversations. For instance, you might say, "I am feeling sad because I am missing my friend" or "The child at the playground was very frustrated when he couldn't go on the swings. He did not want to wait his turn. That made him yell. How do you think the other children felt/how did you feel?" By encouraging children to reflect how another person feels, you are helping them to build capacity to develop empathy and "feel" what others are feeling. Just watching another's actions is not enough; the child needs to be encouraged to imagine how the other feels.

Teach Children the Vocabulary to Name Feelings

You can foster children's emotional vocabulary by using "feeling questions" about their emotions. Here are some examples:

"You seem worried/nervous about something. What is the matter?" "You seem really angry/upset? What is bothering you?" "What did you do today that made you happy/proud?"

Read to Children and Discuss Feelings

Reading to children is another great opportunity to talk about feelings and emotions. Even older children who can read enjoy time together reading chapter books like *Harry Potter*. You can ask the child how the characters feel at different points and why they may be feeling that particular emotion—for example, "How do you think Cinderella felt when she was told she could not go to the ball?" or "What do you think Harry [Potter] felt when his aunt locked him under the stairs?" Encourage the child to reflect on different emotions and the causes of different feelings.

Play Games That Make Children Think About Feelings

For little children, you can draw faces of different basic emotions for the child—a happy face, a sad face, an angry face, and so on—and label them. Older children can be asked to draw someone who is happy or sad or expressing some other emotion. The child then can be asked why that person is happy or sad. If the picture is of a sad person, the child can be asked what someone could do to make that person happy. Older children can play games in which they have to think of related synonyms or antonyms of a particular emotion. For instance, you might ask, "What are other emotions similar to anger (e.g., furious, irate, livid)?" or "What is the opposite of anger (e.g., calm, peaceful)?" You can ask older children to identify times when they felt angry, name body signs that suggest a person is angry (e.g., flushed cheeks, pulled-in brows, clenched fists), or describe a time when they saw someone angry and why they felt angry.

Recognize the Child's Kind Sensitive Actions to Others

When you see your child showing empathy and caring toward another, make sure to recognize it and praise the behavior—for example, "It was so caring the way you held your baby brother's hand while he had his shots. I think it really made him feel better." This simple reinforcement can be a powerful and effective way to enhance your child's behavior and demonstrates the effect on others. Pointing out to your child the impact of their behaviors is important so the child develops a sense of how they can make a meaningful difference in other's lives.

You can also recognize empathy in a child when

- they show sensitivity toward the needs and feelings of others;

- they recognize when someone is upset and respond appropriately;

- they are able to read other's emotional cues (e.g., gestures, facial expressions, tone of voice) and react appropriately;

- they show concern when someone is treated unkindly or unfairly;

- they try to console others who are in pain, are sad, or are crying;

- they feel excited for others when something good happens to them;

- they tear up when they see someone crying; or

- they mirror the facial expressions of the person who is upset.

We can foster our children's empathy in many day-to-day ways. One of the most powerful ways is for us to emphasize with others in our own lives and to find ways of highlighting the empathy of others to our children. When we develop empathy, we are developing the building blocks that guide our moral behavior. We develop the ability to relate to others and the desire to help others for their own sake. Two important ways we feel empathy are by understanding how others feel and by being able to think of matters from another person's perspective.

PERSPECTIVE-TAKING

Perspective-taking is a critical foundational skill that we need in order to interact positively and effectively with those around us. *Perspective-taking* involves learning to notice others; it allows us to make sense of the behavior of those around us and to understand they may have different beliefs and knowledge about the world; it allows us to recognize that others have their own desires, feelings, and intentions; and it helps us understand how our behavior affects others. It requires the ability to "walk in someone else's shoes." An important part of understanding someone else's feelings, beliefs, and desires and responding empathetically to others is being able to understand another's perspective. Children who are able to take the perspective of others and empathize with them are more likely to understand the violation of trust that being dishonest creates.

Children's ability to take the perspective of others increases with age. Young children—around 3 to 4 years of age—first develop the ability to understand that others have "minds" that are different from theirs. They recognize that someone's feelings may be different from their own. Their ability to take the perspective of others increases throughout the elementary school years. By 6 years of age, they can see things from another person's point of view. Their ability to support and comfort others increases. With age, they gradually realize that they can view a situation in multiple ways, and they are able to imagine how their ideas appear to another person. By late childhood (10–12 years), children can extend empathy beyond those they personally know to include those they have never met. They can understand how different people may simultaneously have opposing or different viewpoints.

Understanding Perspective-Taking and Honesty

As discussed in Chapter 2, children's ability to understand that others have different thoughts, beliefs, and knowledge is instrumental in their emerging ability to lie. A lot of research has shown that children's early lying behavior in preschool and the early elementary school years is actually tied to their increased ability to understand others' knowledge or beliefs and then create false beliefs in others by lying. However, although this cognitive ability can enable lying and deception, as it develops, it can increase the ability of children and youths to walk in someone else's shoes and see how their behavior can negatively affect others or hurt them. The ability to take the perspective of others supports children's empathetic reactions and also appreciation of the consequences of their actions.

In one study, my colleagues and I found that early adolescents who have better perspective-taking skills were more likely to lie only occasionally, and when they did lie, the lies they told tended to be prosocial, politeness lies (Lavoie, Leduc, Arruda, et al., 2017). We found that in this older age group between 11 years and 14 years of age, those children who had very poor perspective-taking skills were more likely to tell more frequent lies, and those lies were largely self-serving to protect themselves or to blame others.

By fostering a child's perspective-taking skills, they are better able to reflect on how others feel and think about a situation, which helps the child sympathize and empathize with the other person and aids in their moral reasoning about how to act. The child is better able to predict others' response and actions as well as modify their own thoughts and behavior to engage in positive social interactions.

Developing Perspective-Taking

The following are ways in which parents can help their children develop perspective-taking.

Have Children Switch Roles
Switching roles allows children to feel the other side. If you are discussing a conflict between friends and siblings, ask your child to put themselves in the role of another (e.g., "What would the other person feel, say, and do?"). You can also act

out the conflict using dolls or puppets or by observing inter-actions between characters in books or on TV (e.g., "Why do you think Tom was so rude?" or "If you were Tom, how would you act?").

Encourage Children to Problem-Solve

Teach children that there is more than one way to solve a problem. Encourage them to brainstorm different solutions and recognize the needs of those involved. For example, you might say, "Anika and Ella are fighting over the building blocks. Is there a way they can both build without fighting?"

Ask Questions About How Fictional Characters Feel

Use books or TV to discuss what characters think, how they feel, and why they act the way they do. Give children a chance to reflect on the characters' feelings, beliefs, intentions, and desires as well as discuss how they influence how the characters behave.

Encourage Children to Walk in Someone Else's Shoes

Let your child imagine what it is like to be someone else. For instance, blindfold them and let them see what it is like to move around without sight. Let them reflect on how they perceive the world differently, what it is like to move from one place to another, and how their environment seems different or the same. Another way is to let them literally try on the shoes of another person and pretend they are that person.

Expose Children to Different Ideas and Perspectives

Take them to different community and cultural events where they are exposed to a variety of people and perspectives. Or, have them read articles about current issues in which the authors express different views about the topic. Encourage your child to discuss and reflect on the different perspectives and how those perspectives may affect the individual's actions.

Helping children to develop perspective-taking gives them an important tool to understand those around them, thus increasing their ability to engage in prosocial behavior. A child who is able to notice another child's need for help, who is able to deduce the feelings of others, and who can understand how what the other person thinks or believes is happening is better able to respond in a helpful manner.

SELF-CONTROL

Ask a child if it is okay to lie or steal, and they will likely say no. It's the same with adults. Yet, some may still do it. Certainly, people tell occasional lies. While empathy allows us to understand and feel the emotions of another, self-control helps us control our behavioral impulses so that the child does what they know is right.

Self-control involves being able to regulate yourself, resist distractions, handle emotions, inhibit impulses, delay gratification, and plan ahead. It is an internal mechanism to restrain our impulses and think before acting to do what we believe is right. We are less likely to make rash choices that may have negative outcomes. Self-control allows us to make safer and wiser choices, and because it is essential to moral behavior, it needs to be developed. It is important for developing virtues, such as kindness and generosity, because it enables the child to delay immediate gratification and to consult their conscience to do the right thing or to do something for someone else instead. Children who have greater self-control are less likely to be driven by their impulses and less likely to engage in transgressive behavior.

> When children develop greater self-control, they are more likely to be able to stop themselves from engaging in naughty or transgressive behavior, which, in turn, lessens their motivations to deceive.

Although there are individual differences in our ability to exercise self-control, it is definitely a skill that parents can help their children learn, and it is one of the most important skills we can teach our children. Children who have developed this skill are able to learn to suppress inappropriate, negative behaviors and are less likely to experience difficulties, such as aggressive behavior, anxiety, or depression. Children who struggle with self-control are more likely to have problems in school and issues involving their physical health (e.g., obesity, problems with drugs). The ability to exercise self-control develops through childhood, and the skill of self-control, if fostered and strengthened, increases dramatically in preschool and early school years as children get older.

A child who has strong self-control is able to calm themselves when they are upset or angry. They can save their money to buy a toy. They get their homework done first so they can go out to play later. They learn to wait patiently in line without pushing or cutting in. They learn to plan what they will do and follow through. They can put aside immediate gratification to do something for someone else, such as giving a cupcake to another child before eating one themselves.

Exploring Self-Control and Honesty

Greater self-control can lead to more honest behavior. I explain more in a minute. However, in younger children, we do find that for children who peek at a forbidden toy—that is, cheat—those who have greater self-control are more likely to lie about it. What does this mean? It means that for younger children, self-control can assist those who choose to lie because it helps them control their expressive behavior to try to be believable. To lie, a person needs to control both what they look like to avoid the telltale behavior that raises suspicions. Furthermore, they need to control what they say by checking they do not blurt out information that will undermine their lie. As a child's self-control ability improves, they can use that ability to be a better deceiver when they do choose to lie. As discussed in Chapter 2, this is an example of how children can use their developing cognitive abilities to become more effective at achieving their goals and deceiving effectively.

So why, then, am I suggesting that self-control is an important foundational behavior? When children develop greater self-control, they are more likely to be able to stop themselves from engaging in naughty or transgressive behavior, which, in turn, lessens their motivations to deceive. Self-control helps us control our impulsive behavior and can stop us from doing something that is tempting for selfish desires but may be against our moral standards of behavior. Studies have found that adults who have less self-control are more likely to behave dishonestly. For instance, in one study, adults who were low in self-control were more likely to lie about how many logic puzzles they answered correctly and to continue working past the stop time (Muraven et al., 2006). Adults who were unable to control their behavior were more likely to cheat to improve their score and lie about it to avoid detection.

As discussed later in Chapter 12, children who are impulsive may act in ways that get them in trouble and then lie to avoid the negative consequences. By fostering your child's self-control, they are more likely to be able to restrain their impulses and to do what they know is the morally right thing to do. Self-control helps the child to be in control of their actions and choices. In a situation in which a child is tempted to cheat or to lie, self-control allows them to think about the consequences of their choices and to control their emotions.

Developing Self-Control

What are some ways parents can help their children develop self-control? Some suggestions follow.

Remind Children of the Rules

Preschool children need consistent reminders. For example, a young child needs to be reminded repeatedly that they can't have cookies before dinner, whereas older children are more capable of remembering and need fewer reminders. However, some repetition is likely needed because even adults may forget the rules.

Teach Children to Stop and Reflect

One way to help children to control their impulses is to teach them to "stop" and then "think" about their situation and possible consequences of a wrong choice (e.g., "What would happen if I hit the boy for taking my toys?"). They may need to walk away for a moment from the frustrating situation to cool off and be able to think about the situation calmly. In middle childhood, children who understand the consequences and perspectives of others can benefit from being encouraged to stop and reflect on the outcomes of their behavior. Adults can help them think of different strategies to deal with the situation. Younger children may need help with thinking about what the consequences might be and then "act" right. This way, a child develops the skills to take responsibility for their actions.

Praise Children When They Make Efforts to Exercise Self-Control

Be specific in your praise—for example, "That was very patient of you! I know it was hard waiting so long in line, but you showed great self-control" or "You did a good job taking the time to get your homework done properly and not rushing it before going out to play. These answers are thorough and neat."

Emphasize Positive Consequences

Honor your promises. For example, if you tell your child that if they wait patiently while you are at the doctor's office, they will get a treat. Let them learn the benefits of delayed gratification but also the positive expectation that such behavior leads to positive consequences. You do not always need to reward self-control. Many situations have their own natural positive consequences for self-control. Emphasize those.

Play Games That Help Practice Self-Control

For younger children, try games like "Red Light, Green Light" to help them practice self-control. For older children, try games and sports that promote self-control, including digital ones like a popular obstacle game that involves changing colors.

Teach Children Strategies to Control Themselves

Children deal with different situations requiring that they exercise self-control, and you can coach them through these situations. For instance, you can teach them to take three deep breaths when they feel stressed or are in a frustrating situation.

Take a Break

Everyone needs a break. Moving from one boring task to another can be draining and deplete our cognitive resources, which leads to less self-control when faced with a temptation. (Perhaps that is why sweet treats can look even more enticing after a long morning of drudgery.) Taking a break between tasks and activities can help us rest and recharge our inner resources.

Model Self-Control

There will be times when your child does not show self-control or may have a meltdown and be unable emotionally to deal with a situation. When reacting to a child who is in meltdown or is acting impulsively, try to remain calm. Don't react with disapproval or dismiss their feelings. Acknowledge and talk about their feelings, show empathy, and discuss strategies to cope and deal with the situation.

Self-control is something we all have to exercise, and we are all bound to occasionally make unwise decisions. However, by fostering and strengthening this skill, we develop the ability to inhibit our impulses and reactions that may not lead to the best choices. We can regulate our emotions and think about what our choices are, and then act accordingly. One of the greatest gifts you can give your child is to help them develop this capacity. It is so important to our daily lives as well as to making good choices and living in a way that is positive for ourselves and others.

CONSCIENCE

Our conscience is the most important factor in determining whether moral principles are observed. Our conscience regulates our behavior. *Conscience* is a strong inner voice that helps us decide right from wrong. It is the ability to balance one's needs and desires with those of others and to behave in a way that is consistent with one's own moral standards—even when there is no one around to enforce those standards. It is expressed both by acting, such as giving one's bus seat to someone who looks tired, and by refraining from doing other actions, such as resisting taking a friend's desirable toy. A child acts in a way that is consistent with their conscience, even when their parents are not there to insist, correct, or intervene. Conscience reflects the ability to regulate behavior and comply with expectations.

Children begin developing their conscience when they are very young, and as they grow, they internalize these standards of behavior. Conscience development is also a strong predictor of children's moral behavior and development. We can have very bright, well regulated, and empathetic children. However, if they have not been taught moral principles and how to use these principles when deciding how to behave, they will not necessarily be honest. In fact, they may instead become very effective liars.

Exploring Conscience and Honesty

Conscience development draws on emotional development, perspective-taking, and self-control. In terms of emotional development, conscience development includes the ability to have empathy for others' concerns and welfare. It also includes self-focused emotions, such as feeling guilt (negative emotion) or pride (a positive emotion) when one's actions contradict or align with one's internal standards. A child who does something that violates an internalized moral principle, such as being honest, may feel guilt and remorse for lying. For instance, in Chapter 5, I spoke about Alysha, who lied about throwing out her lunch, which caused another person to be wrongly accused. When Alysha confessed to her mother, it was because she felt guilt for her lie and the harm it had caused. Her lie was a violation of her internal principles of what is good and right. When children feel guilt and remorse for breaking the rules, these negative emotions help them to learn to follow and internalize standards of behavior. The ability to empathize coupled with the ability to take another's perspective fosters an awareness of the effects of one's actions on the feelings of others and feeling concern for them, which can influence an individual's decisions on how to behave.

Another central component of conscience development is self-regulation. A child may have internalized standards of right and wrong, be able to empathize with others, take the perspective of how others think and feel, and perhaps feel guilt for any misbehavior but still act in a way that is discordant with these standards because of low self-control. Thus, a child may lie selfishly to get a desired toy for themselves, which may activate empathy and awareness that they have committed a violation, leading to self-censure through guilt.

Through the development of self-regulation, perspective-taking, and emotional development, children's behavioral control transitions from *external regulation*, in which an adult tells them what to do, to *internal regulation*, which is a growing sense of standards that govern their behavior. The child learns to behave and to act according to the learned moral principles, even when no one is looking.

Developing Conscience

Parents can help their child's conscience development by creating a strong, emotional bond and a warm relationship with the child. This means parents need to interact with their children from infancy and toddlerhood in a way that is responsive and sensitive to the child. Such interactions increase children's sense of security and trust, which, in turn, increases their confidence and willingness to comply with parents' requests.

Psychological research on children's conscience development has examined children's internalized conduct from toddler into early school age (Kochanska, 1997; Kochanska & Murray, 2000). This research has shown that when there a relationship characterized by mutual responsiveness and positive interactions with their mothers, it significantly fosters children's conscience development and their moral conduct. These relationships were described as having a high level of cooperative, reciprocal interactions that were infused with positive feelings between parent and child. When there was a high degree of warmth and cooperation between mother and child in toddlerhood and preschool, school-age children were found to have greater conscience development. When such a parent–child relationship is developed, the child embraces the parent's socialization messages and is more motivated to behave according to the parent's demands and expectations. This type of relationship helps fosters the child's perceptions of mutual responsibility to help other people and desire to respect moral rules and values at large.

While some children may be temperamentally better at regulating their behavior and controlling their impulses, other children may be more fearful or shy, which leads to greater negative emotions and greater guilt after a wrongdoing. Other children may have a harder time controlling their impulses. Parents can help their child by developing their abilities. For instance, parents can help a child who is fearful by using gentle, nonpunitive discipline strategies.

Throughout this book, we talk about practices that foster children's conscience. The same principles that apply to fostering honesty also apply to helping children to develop their conscience: setting a good example, sharing and teaching your own moral beliefs and standards, and expecting and demanding moral behaviors from your child.

Set Good Examples

Children need good role models. Seeing those whom they respect and love treat others with kindness, tolerance, respect, and honesty shows them clear examples of how to behave. Children observe how you react to everyday moral conflicts, and they will copy your behavior. This is especially true when children have a close bond with an adult. When there is a strong attachment and mutually respectful relationship, the adult's words and actions can greatly influence the child. The child is more likely to copy that person in their behavior and to adopt their moral beliefs. Of course, this requires spending quality time with your child to nurture that relationship and to ensure that you are your child's primary influence. Development of this strong bond at a young age can be nurtured even into adolescence, when your child may spend more time off in the world. Finding time to meaningfully connect and maintain that relationship means that you will continue to play a significant role in the child's life even as they engage more with the outside world.

Share and Teach Your Moral Beliefs and Standards of Behavior

We need to discuss and teach our children about what is right and wrong, what good behavior is, and how to behave. If you want your child to grow up to be a moral and ethical person, then emphasize these principles in your conversations as you discuss the world around you. You can discuss moral issues as they come up at school, in the media, or with their friends. Engage your children to think about these situations and ask questions: "Is this the right thing to do?" "How would you feel if someone treated you that way?" "If everyone acted like this, what would happen?" Ask your child or youth questions that let them reflect on the situation to understand the other's perspectives and understand the consequences of their behavior.

Expect and Demand Moral Behaviors From Your Child

Have firm expectations of how your child behaves, and uphold these standards. However, make sure they are reachable and clearly communicated. A child who understands the reason behind rules is more likely to adhere to them, especially in the context of a family home where they feel valued and loved as well as have a strong bond with a parent. However, be careful not to undermine your rules and expectations by being lax either in how you behave or in your application of those rules in the home.

Knowing What Can Undermine Conscience Development

Notably, physical punishment focuses the child's attention on the external sources of emotional discomfort and reasons for compliance, whereas discipline that teaches the reasons for moral behavior and the consequences of one's behavior fosters conscience development. With discipline, a child learns that lying is wrong because it takes advantage of others and hurts friendships. They are more likely to internalize this standard of behavior and to use it to guide their behavior when there is no external authority figure around to tell them how to behave or to sanction their behavior. In contrast, with physical punishment, the child learns that lying is wrong because it results in a spanking. To avoid punishment, they may just learn to avoid lying whenever an authority figure might catch them lying.

Using punishment can actually impede conscience development. It can result in immediate compliance, but it does not lead to internalization of the moral standards. The child stops because they are afraid of the punishment. However, that then becomes the only reason they stop. Punishment produces fear of authority, people-pleasing, and guilt, and it eventually may lead to rebellion when the child is older. The message that children learn is that something is right as long as you are not caught. They do not learn to take personal responsibility for their actions or to practice honesty, integrity, reliability, and other virtues.

A number of behaviors do not encourage conscience development. They include shaming the child and communicating worthlessness, using demeaning language, humiliating the child, engaging in sarcasm and cruel teasing, calling the child names or using negative labels, beating or hitting the child, and ignoring the child's efforts to improve.

CAPACITY-BUILDING WITHIN A FRAMEWORK ON MORALS AND VIRTUES

We are social beings who build strong relationship with others as a vital part of our own social and emotional well-being as well as to achieve our individual and collective goals. Honesty, trustworthiness, and integrity are an important part of successfully developing these relationships. Teaching your child about honesty helps them. But do not stop there. Honesty is not the only virtue we should teach our children. Kindness, compassion, courage, respect, fairness, and perseverance, among many others, are all virtues that create a framework to build a healthy, positive life. Teaching children to recognize, value, and behave according to these principles helps them interact with others in positive and prosocial ways. It helps them develop the inner tools to think, reason, act, and problem-solve difficulties. It helps them to find positive ways to achieve their own goals and maintain strong healthy relationships with others.

Going through this book, you will have noticed how in teaching children to be truthful, other virtues and abilities are also required to support open, honest communication. Teaching children to be prosocial moral individuals requires teaching and drawing attention to a range of virtues and behaviors. Parents who talk about such virtues or qualities and demonstrate them and show appreciation for them will have children who use these virtues or qualities in their day-to-day interactions. A framework of moral education or virtues training teaches and emphasizes a host of prosocial behavior and tools to handle life's challenges.

Here is an example. A parent emphasizes different virtues, including perseverance, to her children. She talks about what perseverance looks like in different situations, she labels when she sees it demonstrated by others, and she teaches her children to engage in perseverance. Her son has learned the value of perseverance, and it spurs him to not give up on trying to learn difficult math problems. He knows it is valued and appreciated in his family. When his performance on a math test is mediocre, this knowledge makes him less fearful of parental reaction. He knows that he did study hard and tried to do his best. The parent recognizes the child's effort. Equally, the parent demonstrates compassion as she empathizes with her son's disappointment at still not achieving a high mark, and she demonstrates helpfulness by finding ways to aid and support his learning. The child did not lie in this situation. There was no need to, no motivation, no value. He knew his hard work would be recognized and his truthful admittance of struggling and discouragement would be met with compassion, kindness, and help.

There are many ways to foster children's virtues and morals. This book deals with one in particular. However, the principles discussed here can be used more widely. Label, recognize, and appreciate these virtues in children and others: "I see you are being gentle with the books!" "I see you were patiently waiting for me" "I appreciate that you helped Sara get a bandage for her scraped knee, and you were caring in how you treated her." Teach them about these virtues, discuss them, and talk about what it looks like to practice them in different situations. Using this language can help guide, acknowledge, and correct behavior. It can also help them problem-solve and find solutions to their problems, as these examples illustrate:

- "How can you show patience with your baby brother?"

- "Was that kind to take Rita's pencil? Were you showing respect?"

- "How can you play fairly with those blocks?"

- "How can you say that with honesty and kindness?"

Children can learn to connect these virtues with their behavior and proactively think about how they will behave. This creates connections between the principles they have learned are important and their actions, which also can help them feel positive about themselves and others.

When you label their behaviors in these terms, it can help the children to see the "good" in themselves and feel that you see the "good" in them. Even children who behave badly exhibit some virtues, and that can be a good place to start helping them correct their behavior. When we label and recognize these behaviors, it can help their self-esteem and let them see themselves in a positive light rather than only in terms of being naughty or bad. It can help build from a place of strength to connect with them and to engage with them to work and correct other behavior.

> *Teaching children to recognize, value, and behave according to a range of principles helps them interact with others in positive and prosocial ways.*

You can teach and demonstrate different virtues to children in a number of ways. Throughout this book, I discuss how you can model these virtues in relation to honesty, but you can also apply this modeling to other virtues. This can be a family affair during which you engage in conversations, create family rules that uphold these principles, and have family gatherings and activities to promote such learning. For instance, parents can regularly gather the children, sit them down, and discuss different topics like how to be truthful, how to be kind, how to show respect, how to be caring, what tolerance means, what courtesy means and why is it important, and many others. Some people have virtue jars with a topic (e.g., courage, respect, caring) written on a slip of paper, and they select a topic. Others use stories or fables to initiate conversations and discussion. You can buy and use flash cards to aid discussion. When you do this and how regularly may depend on your family rhythms. However, early evening, when the daily affairs and chores are done and everyone is together, may be a good time for such discussions. Whatever way it is done, by having these discussions regularly, children become used to them, and as they grow, they increasingly engage in the discussions. They also look forward to special times with the focused attention of their parents. These can be opportunities to connect and to spend positive time together.

Such gatherings are not times to give lectures or chastise the child's behavior. They are shared moments during which the family discusses ideas and feelings together. Children may also have such instruction or discussions in other settings, too, like at school, or during other activities in their community, or through religious instruction. That is all part of a child's training and education. However, whether they engage in such discussions in other settings or not, it is an important part of the education they receive within the family as they grow and develop—whether that family be just one parent by themselves raising their children or an extended, blended family. The family is the first place children receive education, and it is their home base; it is a vital place for children to learn.

By incorporating recurring gatherings as part of your family practices and regularly engaging in conversations that emphasize honesty, perseverance, kindness, compassion, courage, respect, fairness, and many other values and behaviors, you are helping to build that framework of virtues. Your children can use that framework to guide them during other interactions and during those times when you may have to correct them or encourage them to find a better way to behave. It helps to focus their attention on ways of being and develop their own internal guidance to help them as they grow and make their own decisions on how to act and behave.

CONCLUSION

We have to learn to be honest and kind. We do not want children who are rude or brutal in their honesty. This means teaching children how to be honest in their interactions with others without being hurtful or without harming others. Children must be taught tact and to be kind with the words they choose. This requires teaching children about others' feelings and understanding the meaning of people's actions and intentions. Lying is often an easy and quick way to deal with socially awkward situations (e.g., receiving an unwanted gift, being invited to a party you do not want to go to). Being honest sometimes requires more thought to ensure one is not being rude or hurtful.

To teach honesty effectively and encourage children's truthfulness, we must deal with the underlying motives and abilities that help foster children's skill to act with honesty. This includes teaching children to understand how others feel and think, to have empathy and compassion for other's feelings, and to be able to have self-control over one's own behavior and impulsive desires. Honesty is embedded in the development of character. This means teaching children how to be truthful in different situation while also practicing kindness, respect, courtesy, and compassion. To truly foster honesty, we cannot ignore these other capacities and behaviors.

Finally, if we want our children to be truthful, to be kind, to be compassionate, to be caring, to have respect for others, to be courteous, and to engage in the world in ways that reflect the values we think are important, then we have to practice these virtues in our own lives and with our children. When we teach, demonstrate, and appreciate these values in our children, we create an environment that encourages and fosters in our children honesty that is compassionate, kind, and caring. Such a person is someone we want to be our friend, our family member, our colleague, our neighbors.

PART III

The Gray Zone

11

Secrets and Tattles

We can give clear messages that "honesty is the best policy," but sometimes the lines are blurred about what information is acceptable and harmless to talk about, and what information is bad and harmful to reveal. Navigating this terrain can be tricky for both adults and children. In particular, secrets and tattling can be confusing for children to understand. *Secrets* involve information that an individual keeps and is unknown to others; concealing the information is called *secret-keeping*. *Tattling* is when one reports another's wrongdoing or spreads gossip; such talk is a *tattle*. Adults often have difficulties with these concepts and therefore may give mixed messages about whether it is okay to keep something a secret or whether a child should report another's behavior. To further complicate matters, the concepts of secrets and tattling are related to honesty, which can lead to confusion about whether to report or disclose everything all of the time or whether to not repeat (i.e., gossip) some things or keep some things private.

In this chapter, I discuss secrets and tattles and how children develop an understanding of these concepts. I also address how parents can navigate teaching children about the nuances of when to disclose and when not to disclose information. This discussion requires us to consider the differences between harmless information and harmful information as well as what is private information and what is important information to share.

SECRETS

Secret-keeping is related to honesty. Often when we keep a secret, we may feel obligated to do so, or circumstances may require us to lie to conceal the secret. Secret-keeping can be for something good, such as a birthday party, a gift, or good news to be revealed later. Usually with these secrets, no one minds, and the secrets are innocuous. In other circumstances, we may keep minor transgressions a secret—for example, "Don't tell Mommy and Daddy we had this piece of cake before dinner" or "Don't tell Mommy that I spent this much money today."

The person with whom the truth is concealed may appreciate these secrets less. However, the secrets that are the most hazardous to the child are the those that put the child at risk and are threats to their safety. For instance, an adult may ask a child to keep secrets that conceal harmful actions that are putting the child or others in jeopardy, such as abuse. Parents want to know these "secrets." We do not want our children to "keep" these secrets. As discussed in Chapter 9, fostering a relationship of open communication can help children to feel comfortable to disclose uncomfortable information. It is important to talk to children about secret-keeping, including the different types of secrets and the importance of not keeping secrets from you.

Age Differences

In the preschool years, children learn that they can conceal information, and they are capable of keeping a secret by 5 years of age. Their ability to effectively keep secrets improves with age. One study my colleague and I conducted involved children between 4 and 11 years of age who were to make a craft as a surprise gift for their parent (Lavoie & Talwar, 2020). After making the craft, it was set aside to dry while the children did a series of other tasks. Later, each of the children went back into the room with their parent and was reminded not to tell about the surprise gift. The parent who had been briefed earlier asked their child three questions: "How was it? What did you do? What was the surprise?" To maintain the element of surprise, parents were told that there would be a surprise but not what it was.

While some children disclosed to the parents, excitedly telling them they had a gift, the majority of the children kept the secret by either deflecting the parent with statements, such as: "I don't want to tell you. It's a secret!" or not talking about it at all: "We did stuff." A third of the children lied to throw their parent off the scent: "The surprise was the Smarties [a brand of candy] the researcher gave me at the end," for example. Later, the children presented their fully dried craft to their parents. Younger children (4 to 7 years of age) were more likely to excitedly disclose the "surprise" to their parents. However, as children's cognitive abilities developed, they were more likely to try to avoid fully disclosing the secret. Thus, with age and cognitive abilities, children are more likely to keep a secret for prosocial purposes and to understand that the element of surprise requires withholding information until the big "reveal" moment.

As children grow and enter their teenage years, they may keep secrets about their own lives. In a longitudinal study, researchers asked adolescents about their secret-keeping in relation to their parents (Dykstra et al., 2020). They found that secret-keeping increased over time. As adolescents got older (the oldest adolescents at the end of the study were 16 years of age), they were more likely to keep secrets. This may reflect the adolescent's increasing desire to have autonomy over their activities and personal choices.

Frequency

How often do children keep secrets? In a study in which we interviewed children about keeping secrets and telling lies, my colleagues and I asked children what secrets they keep (Lavoie, Nagar, & Talwar, 2017). We also asked them to keep a diary over 3 days and record the secrets and lies they told. On average, our participants recorded telling two lies and keeping two secrets per day. When we interviewed them about the secrets they kept, the younger participants—in this study, children between 8 and 11 years of age—said they would tell secrets with good friends or keep mean gossip a secret. They also talked about kids who kept secrets to conceal misdeeds and avoid getting in trouble. Older youths between the ages of 12 and 15 years said they tended to keep secret personal information that they did not want to share with anyone because they felt it was embarrassing; they also said they would keep secrets to avoid hurting someone. Overall, participants felt that if a friend asked them to keep a secret, it was not okay to tell it to others, but they realized that it was okay to tell someone they trust secrets that concealed dangerous actions or when someone could get hurt.

For many of the youths in our study, especially the adolescents, they viewed their secrets as something that "belonged" to them and that they had the right to be in control of what information they shared. For them, keeping a secret was a way of maintaining personal peer relationships, perhaps partly because of the bond of trust formed when the secrets were kept. In this way, guarding secrets that a friend asks you to keep can be understood as a trust-building activity that contributes to social bonding and the maintenance of personal relationships. For the youths in our study, the secrets they kept were part of their desire for autonomy and to create or maintain closeness with others.

The reaction of the receiver of the "secret" information also affected the decision of the adolescents in our study to reveal or to keep a secret. For example, one youth explained that if she thought a parent would be angry about the information she was keeping a secret, she would conceal and not share it. However, if she thought the parent would not react negatively, she would be more inclined to share the secret. The anticipated reactions of parents or others affect an adolescent's decision to disclose or hide information. For instance, researchers who have examined adolescent secret-keeping have found that adolescents who perceive their parents will disagree with their choice of leisure activities are more likely to omit or conceal information about those activities than adolescents who believe their parents will not react negatively (Darling et al., 2006). Teens can keep secrets to prevent what they perceive as an invasion of their privacy.

What to Tell Very Young Children About Secrets

When children are preschool age and younger, it is better to discourage any secret-keeping—have a clear "no secrets" rule—because they may be unable to distinguish between when something involves harm or not. As children become older, you can discuss the differences between harmless secrets (e.g., keeping the identity of a gift secret until the birthday) and harmful secrets.

It is advisable that adults not ask children who are preschool age and younger to keep secrets and that adults not say things about another person that they do not wish their child to repeat. For instance, adults should avoid making personal comments about matters pertaining to themselves or about others within earshot of children at this age. Young children do not have the understanding to know why such personal comments should not be repeated in public.

> *When children are preschool age and younger, it is better to discourage any secret-keeping because they may be unable to distinguish between when something involves harm or not.*

What to Tell Older Children and Teenagers About Secrets

As children grow older, they develop a greater understanding that some secrets like a surprise birthday gift for a parent are okay to keep for a short duration. For children who are in middle childhood and adolescent years, it is important to explain the difference between harmless secrets and harmful secrets.

Harmless Secrets

Harmless secrets are those about someone's surprise birthday party or about what gift you got someone for their birthday. They can be secrets as part of a game. For instance, two children building a pillow fort make a "secret entrance" that only they know about—perhaps until the dog discovers it. I once came across children behaving furtively and guarding a corner of their playground. Eventually, they decided to let me in on the "secret": They showed me that they had made a little nest of leaves for a green inchworm they had found, and it was their "secret pet."

Another child I know has a "secret box" of treasures in which he stuffs things of interest to him. I was taken into his confidence, and he opened the box to reveal some crystals he had been given; smooth shiny rocks he had found; a couple of key rings of cute animals; a blue unicorn that pooped glittery poop when you squeezed it; some creatures the boy had created out of plastic modeling paste and pipe cleaners; and a toy plastic egg decorated with patterns he had made with a marker, and inside the egg was a lock of his mother's hair. These secrets are part of the world of child's play, of imagination, and of excitement.

Notably, harmless secrets are secrets that cause no harm to another and are kept for a limited time. You keep secret the gift you got your sibling until their birthday, when they find out the truth in a big and happy reveal. These secrets are not forever. These are not secrets about breaking rules, and they are not secrets that exclude others or involve saying bad things about others.

Harmful Secrets

Some secrets are harmful. Over the course of childhood and adolescence, parents have a number of opportunities to discuss *harmful secrets*, which are those about actions that can put others in jeopardy. Parents should initiate these conversations to ensure children understand the difference between harmless and harmful lies. Make sure children understand that they can always talk to you if they have been asked to keep a secret. Even if someone says the child should not tell the parent, you should emphasize that it's okay for them to tell you, and they will not be punished. Importantly, tell them if they are being touched in their private parts by another person, that should not be a secret, and they should tell you.

If the child is experiencing a problem, it should not be kept a secret. They should feel they can tell a trusted adult. Child predators may tell children, "This is a secret. Don't tell your parents." Or, a bully might threaten to a child that they "will get into big trouble" if the child tells anyone about the bullying. Parents should reassure children that they can tell their parents—that is okay to break a secret or promise that is related to unsafe touching or other harmful actions. However, children may fear their parent's reaction, so to alleviate the child's fears, let them know you will not punish them for telling the truth and revealing the secret.

Children also may fear that their parent's reaction will lead to negative consequences to themselves. For instance, teens who have experienced cyberbullying may fear that if they disclose that information, it will lead to restricted access to social media and to their smartphones. In such cases, parents need to keep their child's fears in mind and address those fears when speaking to the child by explaining the measures that need to be taken to help the child and find ways to protect the child while minimizing negative consequences. In the case of cyberbullying, parents can be proactive by talking about it before their child's potential exposure (children may witness cyberbullying without being the victim) and talk about ways to stop it, report it, and respond to it. They can also talk about what the child can do if they are a victim of cyberbullying. Educating children about such harms in advance can help children navigate these risks and also put into place a relationship in which these topics can be discussed frankly.

In other cases, the child may keep secrets that are harmful, and we can't prepare for every eventuality, nor do we want to instill fear in them about all the risks and harm imaginable. However, we can educate them about the most likely risks—like how to deal with negative social media content—and, most important, we can create a warm, strong relationship with our children that makes open and frank conversation possible. In the context of such a relationship, we can increase the likelihood that children will feel comfortable to come forward and talk with us when they need help.

Another type of secret that can be harmful to children involves one parent encouraging the child to keep a secret from the other parent. This type of secret, which is about behavior or facts, is different from fun "surprises," like a birthday gift. Having to conceal information from one parent puts a child in a difficult situation, and parents should generally avoid placing such a burden on a child. In the cases of conflict or divorce, asking children to keep secrets can further acerbate any emotional upset or conflicting feelings of loyalty and love for their parents. Asking children to keep these secrets can be harmful to the child's well-being.

Secrets Versus Privacy

While we want children to be careful about keeping harmful secrets, we also must teach them that they may keep some

When to Keep Secrets

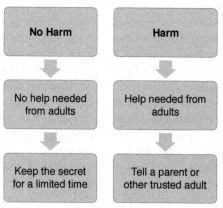

No Harm	Harm
No help needed from adults	Help needed from adults
Keep the secret for a limited time	Tell a parent or other trusted adult

things private. Toddlers and preschoolers do not understand the difference between safe and unsafe secrets. For these younger children, it is best that you do not say things you do not wish them to repeat. Toward the end of the preschool years and in the elementary school years, you can introduce the distinction between safe, surprise secrets and talk about unsafe secrets. You can also teach them about privacy.

Respecting privacy includes showing consideration for people's personal space as well as not repeating personal information, especially information that could be embarrassing. You can teach children that some family matters are private and not to be told in public. For instance, if one child is wetting the bed, they may not wish to have their sibling telling people about this problem. You can talk about respecting people's feelings as well as the right to privacy for personal matters that do not involve risk to the person's health or safety. You may wish to keep family affairs like financial problems private. You can explain to children that while those subjects can be talked about among family members and are not secrets, you want to keep the information private within the family.

Another example is if a family member is very ill. In one case, I know of a family that was caring for a grandmother who had experienced a stroke. The mother wished to keep private some of the details about the personal care that was necessary for the grandmother. She talked to her child about how the family was keeping these personal matters private out of respect for the dignity of the grandmother. Recognizing that the child might be upset or worried about her grandmother, the mother made sure to let the child know she could talk about these feelings with her parents or with a close family friend who knew of the grandmother's condition. It is important that children have outlets—where privacy can be maintained—to express their feelings and worries with a trusted adult. The mother also told the child it was okay to be honest with her friends about what was going on in her life and affecting her. She could tell them that she was sad or worried about her grandmother without having to give specific details.

Conversations about secrets may also require you to discuss sharing gossip and saying mean things about others. Again, parents should strive for consistency between the messages they give and the practices they engage in. If parents share lots of gossip about friends, family, and coworkers that they do not wish their children to repeat, they should reflect on what message they wish to give children about such information and how that message impacts the types of secrets they feel are acceptable for their children to keep. Younger children in preschool and early elementary school are less likely to understand the nuances of different types of information and behavior. Older children and teenage children are more likely to understand their family discusses some matters that may not be for public discussion. The most important part of the message that parents want to convey to children is that there are some things they should not keep secret and should tell their parents. Parents should be careful not to undermine this message.

TATTLING

Similar to secrets, tattling is another gray area in which it's not always best to share information. As discussed earlier about privacy, we can be honest without having to share everything. *Tattling* is when someone shares information when doing so is not necessary; the tattling is done just to get someone else in trouble or for personal gain. Being a tattletale is perceived as being "bad," can be viewed as aggressive, and is, at times, punished. However, at the same time, adults often appreciate when children report on others' behaviors so the adults can use that information to resolve sibling or peer conflicts, or to dole out consequences for transgressions. This reflects a wider difficulty we have with all-or-nothing rules about honesty: Honesty is important but not as a tool to "bludgeon others."

Some information is not necessary to share, or it can be shared maliciously. Adults, too, can run into difficulties about when it is considered acceptable to share information or not, as many whistleblowers can attest. For young children in preschool and early elementary school age, especially, it can be confusing when sharing information is acceptable and when it is not.

Age Differences

In research my colleagues and I conducted, we found that while children evaluated lies more negatively than truths, they rated truths that are considered tattles—in which the tattling harmed another—more negatively than confessions (Talwar, Williams, et al., 2016). However, this perception changed with age. Children 9 years and younger saw all truth-telling behavior as more positive and rewarded it. But 10- to 12-year-old children rated tattling less positively than other instances of truth-telling. In another study that observed preschoolers tattling behaviors (Ingram & Bering, 2010), the researchers found that pre-schoolers were most likely to report disputes arising from issues of property entitlement or physical aggression. They generally reported norm violations. The researchers also found that tattling was done more frequently by dominant children and was related to teacher reports of relational aggression. The most common response of the adult was to support the tattletale. In another study, researchers observed siblings in their home who were between 2 and 6 years of age. They found that tattling made up a large proportion of talk about the sibling's behavior (Ross & Den Bak-Lammers, 1998).

However, children's ability to distinguish between what behavior should be reported and other behavior that is not worthy of reporting increases with age. In one study, children between 6 and 11 years of age read vignettes in which the characters either reported tattling on a classmate who had committed a major transgression, such as pushing a classmate down, or more minor transgressions, such as when a classmate caused a small amount of another's juice box to spill (Loke et al., 2011). While younger children 6 to 7 years of age rated all truth-telling reports positively, children older than 8 years of age distinguished between reporting major and minor transgressions. The researchers also found cultural differences when they compared children in the United States and Japan. Children from Japan considered it more acceptable to report minor transgressions compared with their American counterparts.

Young children who are preschool age and early elementary school age are particularly interested in the enforcement of social rules and show considerable interest when they see others violate social rules. Young children are also aware that tattling sometimes results in positive alliances with authority figures. They may view tattling as an opportunity to demonstrate their awareness of social rules or align themselves with authority figures.

Children also receive feedback from peers about tattling, which can cause them to curb that behavior. For instance, research shows that adolescents liked less those peers whom they perceived as tattletales, and those they perceived as engaging in more tattling were more likely to be socially rejected by their peers (Friman et al., 2004). Furthermore, children who have increased social anxiety are more likely to report another person's transgression possibly because that particular transgression caused them more anxiety than other transgressions (Buta et al., 2015).

Thus, children, especially younger children, may tattle because they hope to please adults or recruit adults to help them. Some children may also be more anxious about social rules and more concerned about the violation of those rules, leading them to report frequently. However, with age, children tend to tattle less as they receive negative feedback from their peers and start to perceive the social cost of tattling on their peers for minor violations. The reactions and messages of adults around them can also encourage or discourage their reporting behavior.

What to Tell Children About Tattling

Children often share information as part of their impulse to relate what they see. In particular, they sometimes share information about something they saw and do not fully understand to see how an adult interprets what they saw. Children often tattle to help them resolve property disputes or in cases of physical aggression. In such instances, the children's goal is to get help for themselves or to get another child in trouble. Sometimes they tattle because they are concerned about violation of the rules, which they take seriously.

For instance, in their observational study of preschool children's tattling, researchers from Northern Ireland found that children frequently reported what they saw as norm violations, such as another child's taking more than their fair share of food from the snack table (Ingram & Bering, 2010). Often in such cases, the children already had plenty of food and drink for themselves. Another example they observed involved a child who reported that another child had collected all the dolls and put them under that child's chair. The child's reporting seemed to concern the principle of fairness: one child's having more than the others. Thus, children's reports can be motivated by a sense of social justice and a desire to enforce the rules. Adults should look beyond the statement to the motive behind the tattle. Other times children may report information because they perceive some wrong or rule violation has been done, such as: "He knocked over the tower!" "They're being loud," or "She said I stood on her foot on purpose! But I didn't!" In some cases, the researchers reported that the children were mollified when they felt that the adult had attended to them and that their concerns about another's behavior were acknowledged.

It is important to counsel children tenderly to divert them away from sharing every bit of information with adults. For instance, adults may deter children from reporting that another person is being punished or from sharing bad news like "Bobby failed his exam!" or "The teacher said Elisa was in trouble for talking all the time." Talk to your child about how being the bearer of bad news can make those involved feel bad. Discuss with your child how they would feel if that person were to share their own bad news with your child, and then your child naturally passed that bad news on to someone else. The person who had originally shared their bad news would be hurt and saddened. Parents can emphasize that it is important not to speak ill of others or find fault with them. This also means that adults need to exercise caution in their own behavior. They should not openly disparage others or backbite in the presence of their children.

Children who take rules seriously and are keen to follow them may report in earnest the misdemeanors of others, even when those transgressions are minor. These children may not mean harm by such reports; rather, they may think they are doing the correct thing by reporting. Parents can help their children to learn to when to report someone's behavior and when not to. This will take time as different situations arise. However, parents can help their children, starting in preschool, to start to distinguish between "tattling," which is reporting behavior that is not necessary for adults to resolve, and *telling*, which is when there is harm and adults may need to intervene. Parents can help children to differentiate among times when the situation is serious, when someone's safety is at stake, or when the child needs help to manage the situation or the behavior of other (e.g., another child keeps hitting or biting them). You need to give examples to your child for them to understand the difference. For instance, the statement "he took one of the blocks I wanted to use" does not suggest an unsafe situation, and the problem can be solved if the child learns to use their words to talk through it. However, the statement "he pushed the block tower on top of me" shows a potential for harm, and an adult is needed to make sure no one was hurt.

Children may also need help to solve minor problems with peers and to know how to express their feelings to others. For instance, if your child is upset because another child is not taking turns with the toys but, instead, is grabbing them, your child can be taught to assert themselves by saying, "It's my turn." You can teach them that if someone is about to be hurt, they should tell you. If no one is being hurt, they should try to work it out with the other child. You can encourage them to find ways to problem-solve and resolve conflicts with their peers. As they are developing these skills, they may need an adult to help them talk it through. You can ask them questions like: "What could you do to solve this?" "What could you say to them?" or "How do you think they will react if you do that?"

> *Adults should be patient and support children by gently reminding them of the difference between tattling and telling.*

Reporting on another to get them into trouble or reporting behavior that is an accident without any harm to others are examples of tattling. However, when someone does something that jeopardizes the safety of themselves or others, that is done on purpose to harm another or is dangerous, or that causes conflict that children cannot solve by themselves, these are examples of *telling*. Here are some examples of telling:

- "Rayna hit me."
- "Kian called me a name."
- "Jill threw a pen at me."
- "Toby pushed me down on the playground."
- "Enoch isn't getting in the line."

   Here are examples of tattling:

- "Sam is drawing instead of doing his work."
- "Ana looked at me funny."
- "Ira took my crayon."
- "Jane won't play with me at recess."
- "He isn't sharing with me!"

When Is it Tattling?

It takes a while for children to learn when it is and is not appropriate to report. Adults should be patient and support children by gently reminding them of the difference between tattling and telling. When your 5-year-old tattles, you can help them to start to develop this understanding by explaining that the perceived rule-breaking was not causing harm to anyone. Similarly, when the child reports something involving potential harm, the child can be praised for looking out for others.

As children age and enter the school-age years, their social skills and problem-solving skills also develop. Children 6 to 7 years of age often see tattling in a positive light. But, as researchers have shown, by 8 years of age and older, they see tattling in a less positive light. Their peers who may react negatively to tattling behavior also socialize children about tattling. Thus, most children start to avoid tattling. However, parents can occasionally remind their children about the distinction between tattling and telling. Also, importantly, children may need reminders that it is okay to report behavior when there is harm to ensure that the children report bullying behaviors. By their school years, children have often learned the negative connotations of tattling; thus, they may be reluctant to tell adults about bullying because they do not want to be called a tattletale. Adults should continue to give this message as children get older: Children should tell when they are being bullied or when they see others being bullied.

How You Can Respond to Tattling

When your child does tattle, you can reflect back to the child what they are saying without making a judgment or by asking further questions, such as: "Your sister isn't sharing with you, and you don't like that" or "He was standing on the chair and you wanted to let me know."

Young children do not easily distinguish between tattling and telling. All situations may seem important or equally worthy of telling. Parents need to patiently and gradually help their children develop the judgment to know when it is important to tell. A young child may report on their brother or sister about not picking up their toys because they think that is the responsible action, and they are observing the rules. If they are reporting on their older sibling who is doing something they do not like, they may also feel powerless and are using reporting as a strategy to recruit adult authority to restore the balance of power. Sometimes, the reason the child has chosen to report may not always be clear.

Children are constantly being corrected and told the rules. They also observe others being corrected and told the rules. Thus, they often think they are doing the right thing. They are concerned that others are not following the rules, and they are flagging that to the adult so that the adult knows the child needs correction. You can react by saying what you see, which acknowledges what the child has said and can help them figure it out. However, do not shame the child for coming to you. Even if the child is tattling to obtain the upper hand in a power struggle, the emphasis should be on gently encouraging the child to manage the problem for themselves. You might ask, for example, "Andy isn't picking up the toys, and you wanted me to know. Is there something you can do to help him?"

As children get older, you can help them develop the skills to deal with problems like when your child reports that their sibling will not share with them. You can assist them with problem-solving and how to communicate with others. For instance, you might say, "Your sister will not share with you, and you are not okay with it. Tell me what you can do to let her know you are not okay with that." Let your child try to think of something and make suggestions. However, especially for children in early childhood who are still learning these skills, the child may need some guidance and help with suggestions.

> Do not shame the child for coming to you. If they are tattling, gently encourage them to manage the problem for themselves.

You can have a conversation about telling versus tattling, but that is best done when the child isn't in the midst of the moment. Most importantly, in the conversation, talk about the times when it is important for your child to report to a parent or to a responsible adult. You can ask them to think of a time when they need a grown-up's help. You can talk to them about times when someone may be hurt or may feel unsafe, such as with bullying.

CONCLUSION

While "honesty is the best policy" is true in general, with secrets and tattling, we must appreciate the intentions of others and the harm caused when commenting or telling the truth. We keep a lot of ordinary secrets like surprises for loved ones that we hope will delight them or the childhood secrets of play. These secrets do not cause harm and, in some cases, create excitement and joy in the hearts of others. Similarly, a child may, at times, do something that causes no harm but that another child reports because that child perceives the action or behavior as a violation or because it is contrary to their own desires and goals.

At other times, though, it is imperative to report secrets or another person's behaviors. Children should not keep secret information when someone might be in harm's way. They should know that they can come forward and report another's bullying behavior without reprimand. Adults need to help children navigate these social situations and understand the nuances of telling the truth.

12

When Lies Are a Symptom of Other Problems

Very few children turn into chronic liars—that is, frequent, persistent liars—and most tell common lies to get out of trouble (like missing curfew or not doing homework). As discussed in previous chapters, people lie for a range of reasons. However, for the most part, people tell the truth most of the time; we lie, though, when we decide that a need overrides our tendency to be honest. Usually, these common lies are for self-preservation, such as avoidance of others' scorn or fear of punishment. We also may tell lies to preserve another's feelings or to be polite. Usually, these lies do not reflect maladaptive patterns of behavior, such as chronic lying or pathological lying.

Nevertheless, some lying may signal a deeper problem, such as a mental health issue or a tendency to manipulate others. Indeed, the problematic nature of lying is not only the act of deception itself but also its relationship to other, more serious antisocial behaviors. A lot of adolescent and adult antisocial and delinquent behavior can involve concealment or lying. Frequent, chronic lying can have a negative impact on the individual and hamper the development of important prosocial skills that aid in forming close and enduring relationships. Relationships are built on trust that cannot be built or can be eroded when an individual repeatedly violates that truth through lies. This chapter identifies warning signs that your child may have a deeper underlying problem.

If you think your child may have a deeper problem, talk to a mental health professional. Psychologists, school counselors, social workers, and other mental health professionals can help you determine whether your child needs additional help or whether their behaviors reflect a normal developmental process. If you need help finding a mental health professional, your child's physician should be able to refer you.

KEEPING THINGS IN PERSPECTIVE

It is important to remember a key point from earlier in this book: Most kids do not develop prolonged problematic lying behavior. Although, at times, a child may lie a little more frequently, usually they do so because of either developmental reasons or conditions in their life that make them rely on that strategy more. For instance, lying increases in early childhood as children learn to manage their own behavior and their relationships with others. As mentioned in Chapter 2, experimentation with lying is a common behavior with children as young as 4 years of age. Parents and teachers report that most children tell some lies. However, the majority do not engage in sustained patterns of frequent lying. For a small number of children, however, their lying may be of greater concern.

A relatively small percentage of children develop into chronic or problem liars. However, it is hard to get definitive rates of chronic lying because it is a difficult behavior to measure. The prevalence rate of frequent or chronic lying also can vary from as low as 3% to 23%, depending on who was doing the reporting: parents, teachers, or individuals remembering retrospectively their own behavior (Stouthamer-Loeber, 1986; Stouthamer-Loeber & Loeber, 1986). For instance, one study reported that approximately 13% of adults self-identify as being pathological liars—that is, they tell numerous lies habitually despite the distress it causes them and the harm to their social relations (Curtis & Hart, 2020). Others have reported that among juvenile offenders, the prevalence rate is close to 1% (Dike, 2008).

In a Canadian study in which researchers observed the prevalence of children's lying over a 3-year period, parents reported that their child told occasional or frequent lies more often than the teachers reported (Gervais et al., 2000). Overall, occasional lying by children (according to the parents and teachers in the study) was a normal and widespread behavior at school entry. However, the researchers also found that a majority of boys and girls were not rated as consistent liars from age 6 to 8 years—that is, they were not reported to occasionally or frequently lie both at home and in school. The study also examined the rate of persistent lying over the 3-consecutive-year period and found the prevalence was low at 4.9% for boys and 2.2% for girls. Importantly, findings showed that children who were more persistent liars over time were also reported as more disruptive—in other words, persistent liars were also more likely to be disobedient and engage in fighting, bullying, and destructive behavior. Interestingly, boys were reported to be more frequent liars than girls. However, it is unclear if this finding reflects a genuine difference between boys and girls or whether this is a bias toward believing girls are more truthful.

What has been found across studies, however, is that as children become older into high school age, persistent lying is related to other antisocial behaviors like stealing, truancy, drug use, or police contact. However, overall childhood lying is only at best moderately predictive of later maladjustment. For most children, other factors and people intervene, and lying does not become a persistent problem behavior over their lifetime.

DEFINING PATHOLOGICAL LYING

So when is lying more than a normal developmental behavior? When is it a sign of a deeper underlying problem? Often the terms "chronic," "prolific," "compulsive," "problematic" and "pathological" lying are used interchangeably, and no clear distinction is made among them. Even in the scientific literature, there is some murkiness in the use of these terms. Recently, psychologists defined *pathological lying* as

> a persistent, pervasive, and often compulsive pattern of excessive lying behavior that leads to clinically significant impairment of functioning in social, occupational, or other areas; causes marked distress; poses a risk to self or others; and occurs for longer than 6 months. (Curtis & Hart, 2020, p. 63)

According to this definition, pathological lying differs from prolific or chronic lying in terms of the distress the liar feels afterward regarding their behavior and the impact it has on the
individual's ability to function and relate to others.

Essentially, pathological liars lie repeatedly without even
knowing why they lie. They feel remorse and distress about their
lying afterward, but they are unable to stop, which leads to a
negative, escalating impact on their relationships that they try
to fix with more lying. They may lie out of habit or out of a com-
pulsion, regardless of context, and they cannot stop. Their lies
may be relatively harmless, but those lies still cause problems
with those around them who are alarmed by such behavior. They
lie frequently enough that their lies are often discovered by
those around them.

The habitual or pathological liar often tells believable lies
that may have truthful elements to them. For instance, the pathological liar may be sick with a flu or virus but tells others that they
have cancer or some other serious illness. Their lies are usually
motivated by internal reasons, such as being seen in a positive or sympathetic light, rather than for more external motiva-
tors, such as escaping punishment. However, other patterns
of problematic lying may exist. Some may lie as a means to
help them manage other mental health difficulties or threats to
their well-being.

CONSIDERING THE DIFFERENT CLINICAL CONDITIONS
ASSOCIATED WITH PROBLEMATIC LYING

A variety of syndromes and situations are associated with deception. Severe types of intentional deception, including chronic
lying, deliberate feigning, and false allegations, are of clinical
concern. These severe types of intentional deception are often
observed in youths who have conduct disorder (CD) and oppositional defiant disorder (ODD). Behaviors related to deceitfulness are a core component of both CD and ODD. In ODD
and CD, deception is related to either general defiance or other
antisocial behavior.

Because these two disorders are the ones most closely linked to problematic lying, I discuss each in turn first. Then, in the subsequent section, I describe other disorders and conditions that may, at times, be associated with problem lying in children and adolescents, such as attention-deficit/hyperactivity disorder (ADHD), malingering, and anxiety. After that, I briefly discuss clinical conditions that are often diagnosed in adults but can also be found in adolescents: personality disorders, eating disorders, and drug abuse and addiction. Because problem lying can also be associated with different social contexts that may lead an individual to lie more, such as child abuse and trauma, child custody, or association with a deviant peer group, the last sections address these conditions or situations.

Conduct Disorder

The most common clinical conditions associated with problem lying is *conduct disorder*, which is characterized by hostile and aggressive behavior as well as a disregard for others. Children with CD exhibit behaviors like pushing, hitting, and biting when they are young, and, as they get older, they often engage in bullying and they may hurt animals, pick fights, steal, vandalize, and commit arson. Part of this disorder is frequent lying and cheating. These are children and adolescents who may seem callous to the feelings and rights of others. They often seem to find aggression, deceit, and coercion—which creates a power differential in their favor—gratifying. Some can go on to have adult antisocial personality disorder (for a description, see the Personality Disorders section). However, with earlier treatment, the outlook is a better.

Because all children act out from time to time, however, parents should be cautious about ascribing the child's acting out behavior to CD. Conduct disorder is diagnosed only when the child exhibits a persistent pattern of this type of behavior.

To diagnose CD, several diagnostic criteria must be met. Deceitfulness is one criterion on that list. Also included is an assessment of limited prosocial emotions, including a lack of remorse and the presence of callousness. As a result, as part of a diagnosis for CD, the clinician needs to assess how the child thinks and feels about their deceptive behavior—and not only about the behaviors themselves. A professional makes the diagnosis of CD if that child exhibits a callous disregard for others and shows a sustained pattern of behaviors that fit into these general categories: aggression against people and animals, destruction of property, deceitfulness and theft, and serious violations of rules.

In general, children diagnosed with CD tend to have a higher than average rate of lying. For instance, some youths with CD may feign symptoms of ADHD to obtain medication. It has also been found that some youths with CD may fake or exaggerate physical complaints to avoid school and be able to do more desirable nonschool activities. However, caution should be exercised in jumping to the conclusion that all children who do not wish to go to school are *malingering*, that is, exaggerating or feigning illness to escape school. Clinicians report that only 7.8% of cases in which the child did not attend school were indicative of malingering (Kearney & Beasley, 1994). Furthermore, the children were not just feigning and lying to be "bad" in these cases; rather, they frequently were struggling and thus used maladaptive means to express themselves or to mitigate the consequences of their behaviors.

> *If you think your child may have a deeper problem, talk to a mental health professional.*

Treatment often involves psychotherapy and behavioral therapy for a sustained period as well as family support and parent management training to teach parents how to encourage desired behaviors and how to empathize and communicate with the child. In addition, for teenagers, therapy may involve other interactions with authority figures at school or in other settings. Because CD can often be diagnosed along with other conditions like ADHD, for example, medication can sometimes be part of the treatment plan.

Oppositional Defiant Disorder

Children with *oppositional defiant disorder*, which typically is diagnosed around early elementary school ages, have a pattern of behavioral problems that include being angry and irritable, frequently losing their temper, arguing with authority figures, refusing to follow rules, deliberately annoying people, blaming others for mistakes, and being vindictive. Unlike CD, in ODD, there is no explicit criterion associated with deception. However, in ODD, deception may appear as part of the child's attitudes toward authority figures.

While many children periodically exhibit some of the behaviors associated with ODD, in the case of children with ODD, these behaviors are greater in severity and sustained over time. For a diagnosis, a child will have exhibited extreme behavioral issues for at least 6 months. This disorder can take its toll on parents and can lead to frustration and stress. The parent–child relationship becomes strained. As a result, parents play a critical role in the treatment for ODD to help repair the relationship. With the help of a therapist, parents learn how to train their child's behavior through consistently setting clear expectations, praising kids when they follow through, and using effective consequences when they do not. Treatment may also include cognitive behavior therapy or social skills training to help children's peer relationships.

Attention-Deficit/Hyperactivity Disorder

Some parents report that children with *attention-deficit/hyperactivity disorder*, in which there is an ongoing pattern of inattention or hyperactivity-impulsivity, or both, that interferes with functioning, lie more frequently than children without ADHD. Lying is not part of the diagnosis of ADHD, and unlike CD and ODD, has not been reported to be strongly associated with ADHD. Not all children with ADHD tell frequent lies. Some may be impulsively honest, telling blunt truths without thinking. However, it may be that some children with ADHD use lying as a strategy to mitigate negative consequences of some of their symptoms or to appear in a more positive light to others. Anecdotally, lying in children with ADHD is common, especially for matters such as homework and to conceal anything that the child feels makes them look bad. In these cases, lying may stem from lack of self-control and delayed executive functioning development in children with ADHD.

In these cases, the children may be victims of their ADHD symptoms, resorting to lying to try to cover them up. Often the lies that these children tell are about everyday things like chores or work. For example, you might ask a child to put away their toys, and then, when the child has failed to do it, they may stubbornly insist you never told them to do it. This may not really be a lie; the child may actually have forgotten about your directive. Alternatively, they may have started cleaning up the toys, but because of difficulties staying on task, they may have become distracted and later lied to try to mitigate blame.

In another example, your child has difficulties getting their homework done and is unable to organize their time properly. Your child lies to you about getting the homework done because they feel bad about their inability to complete it. Later, their teacher sends a note home, but because your child is ashamed, they hide the note to avoid embarrassment and upset. It is important for the parent to realize that these lies spring from the child's inability to manage their ADHD symptoms and that the child may feel bad about their perceived shortcomings, so they try to conceal them. You need to talk to the child about honesty, and, depending on the circumstances, you may decide to discipline the child for lying, but you should also help the child manage the symptoms that caused them to lie.

A child who tells lies about doing their homework may do so impulsively and defensively to escape reprimand. This lying then could lead to a negative pattern with parents and teachers, who then become aware of these lies, leading to further frustration with the child, which only increases the intensity of the verbal reprimands and punishment. To stop the cycle, getting help to address the child's difficulties and ADHD symptoms help support the child and promote more positive parent–child and teacher–student interactions.

Malingering

One type of problem lying that has received some attention by researchers and clinicians is *malingering*, in which the person exaggerates or falsifies physical symptoms or illness. Lying is central to the clinical malingering of physical or psychiatric symptoms; the person uses deception for a secondary gain. Children may malinger for a number of reasons. For example, a child who pretends to be ill to avoid going to school may feel socially isolated or be a victim of bullying. Another child may lie about a parent dying because they feel neglected or are seeking attention. Yet another child may be coached by a parent to pretend to have a disability so they can receive disability benefits. A child may fake having a learning disorder to get more time on exams or pretend to have ADHD to gain access to medications. In these examples, children or adolescents lie to mitigate negative environmental factors or to receive some gain.

Researchers who have extensively studied malingering in adolescents and adults suggest that individuals malinger because they feel they have something to lose from self-disclosure or something to gain from malingering while simultaneously not perceiving a more effective means to achieve their desired goal (Rogers, 1990). Thus, a youth might decide to avoid punishment by pretending to be unfit to stand trial because of mental illness. Another might seek admission to a hospital to obtain a safe place with free room and board. Individuals are most likely to malinger when there is a perceived adversarial context, the personal stakes are high, and they perceive no other viable alternatives. Lying in these cases can have extremely negative outcomes for the individual and others involved.

Anxiety

Lying and concealment are sometimes associated with *anxiety*, that is, feelings of intense, excessive, and persistent worry or fear about everyday situations. However, in some cases, children with anxiety-related diagnoses may lie because they are worried about the consequences of telling the truth. Highly anxious children may be sensitive to what others may think of them and have a strong fear of negative evaluations by others. They may also fear criticism and failure. These worries and fears may, at times, motivate them to lie to appear in ways they think are more socially acceptable or to cover up failures or behaviors they fear others will criticize.

There is no evidence, though, that lying is a frequent behavior with individuals who have high anxiety. Because of their concern about social evaluations and criticism, they may adhere to the truth more often. In one study, my colleagues and I found that children who had higher internalizing (i.e., feelings of anxiety or depression) as measured by parent reports were less likely to lie or keep secrets (Lavoie et al., 2018). Feelings of anxiety at being caught and feelings of guilt may lead those with higher anxiety to tell the truth.

Personality Disorders

In some cases, lying may be an early symptom of personality disorders. Personality disorders are not usually diagnosed until adulthood or sometimes in later adolescence (Salekin et al., 2018). A *personality disorder* is an "enduring pattern of inner experience and behavior that deviates markedly from the expectations of the individual's culture" (American Psychiatric Association, 2013, p. 646). Individuals with personality disorders have problems maintaining healthy relationships. Deception is particularly associated with some personality disorders, such as a cluster of personality disorders characterized by emotional, dramatic, and erratic thinking or behavior (called Cluster B personality disorders). This category includes borderline, antisocial, histrionic, and narcissistic personality disorders. For instance, in *borderline personality disorder* in which the person has difficulty regulating emotion, lying may occur in the context of identity disturbance and feelings of not knowing who they are or what they believe in; lying also could be related to extreme impulsivity. Those with *narcissistic personality disorder*, which involves preoccupation with oneself and a need to be admired, and *histrionic personality disorder*, which involves emotionally overreacting to gain attention, may use deception to compensate for low self-esteem and to create a positive image to others or to create excitement.

In particular, deception has been associated with antisocial personality disorder and psychopathy in which individuals flagrantly disregard the truth and are deceitful as a means of manipulating others to further their own interests. Their behavior is not regulated by feelings of guilt and shame. They do not accept responsibility for actions, nor do they believe they are accountable for their actions. For instance, in *antisocial personality disorder*, in which a person shows consistent disregard for right and wrong, ignores the feelings of others, and exhibits callousness and no remorse for their behavior, lying and deception are common. The person usually tells lies to advance their own interests; this disorder is often associated with other criminal behavior. Antisocial personality disorder can be diagnosed at age18 years, but the diagnosis does require a record of problematic behaviors in childhood, such as a lack of empathy and a manipulation of others for personal gain. The diagnosis also requires a pattern of behavior, often associated with CD, since at least 15 years of age. In such individuals, lying has become a strategy used to manipulate their environment and to serve their own goals.

Lying is also thought to be a key part of *psychopathy*, a personality disorder in which manipulativeness and deceitfulness are often manifested along with a lack of empathy, guilt, or remorse. Psychopaths may lie more frequently and for a variety of reasons than others. In a study of Canadian juvenile offenders, researchers examined deception motivations in relation to psychopathic traits (Spidel et al., 2011). They found that juveniles with higher psychopathy were more likely to engage in deception for "duping delight"—that is, to manage others' impressions of them and to obtain material or psychological rewards (p. 343). Their lies were not merely a protective strategy to escape negative consequences and punishment but were more overtly aggressive in the pursuance of self-interest. These adolescents derived pleasure in conning a dupe. This duping delight may be a sensation-seeking strategy when the adolescent feels powerless or bored. It could also be a defense mechanism to boost their self-esteem.

Psychopaths like to dominate others, and this domination reinforces their self-perception of intellectual superiority by projecting inferiority onto the target. At the same time, psychopaths like to present themselves in a positive light to manipulate others. As a result, they tell lies to create the desired impression on another and create an image of themselves that they believe will help them get what they want. Psychopaths are always trying to take advantage of their environment for self-gain, and they tell lies to achieve these goals. In such cases, lying may actually be related to greater cognitive skills. The psychopath is often a skilled liar and can have a long career of effective lying. Their skill at lying may be a result of effective perspective-taking, self-control, memory, and flexibility of thought used for Machiavellian purposes.

On the whole, personality disorders are often diagnosed in adulthood. Overall, relatively little is known about lying in relation to personality disorders in children. Generally, it can be difficult to diagnose adolescents with personality disorders because the symptoms may be the result of a range of mental health issues, such as depression or anxiety. In some cases, a diagnosis is made in adolescence. A diagnosis like borderline personality disorder in adolescents under age 18 years must meet the formal criteria established by the *Diagnostic and Statistical Manual of Mental Disorders* (fifth ed; American Psychiatric Association, 2013), and symptoms must be pervasive, persistent, and occurring for more than a year as well not be limited a particular developmental stage.

Diagnosing personality disorders in children and adolescents remains controversial. Conduct disorder and ODD are more commonly diagnosed in children. However, it has been suggested that some children and adolescents may show symptoms of personality disorders that continue into adulthood. Yet, not all will necessarily develop personality disorders.

For instance, only 25% to 40% of youths with CD will develop antisocial personality disorder. In terms of lying, for most, it will not be a symptom of later problems, and for some, it may be a situation-specific behavior. Parents should note that it is a small percentage of individuals who develop personality disorders. In most cases, a child's lying behavior is not likely an indicator of personality disorder or even chronic lying.

Eating Disorders

Adolescents with *eating disorders*, behavioral conditions that involve disturbances in thoughts about or attitudes toward food, eating, and body image, can use deception to help them continue their obsessive behavior to control their weight and their perceptions of body image (Vitacco, 2018). They may use deception, such as hiding food to binge later, to maintain control of their eating behaviors and to deceive others into believing that treatment is working. To hide their behavior and avoid embarrassment, some may steal laxatives or diet supplements. They may lie about their weight to hide weight loss or to conceal excessive exercising, or they may wear clothing to hide weight loss or to make it look like they are gaining weight. In such cases, the lying is a tool to help the individual project an outward image to the world and to enable them to continue in their obsessive behavior. Here, it is important to deal with the underlying condition, which will consequentially lead to a reduction in concealment and lying.

Drug Abuse and Addiction

Deception is commonly associated with addictive behaviors. Those addicted to alcohol or drugs use deception to help them continue in their substance abuse behavior. In such cases, the individual may need to cover up what they are doing and provide explanations for where and what they were doing, which leads them to use deceptive cover stories. They also may steal to pay for drugs.

Other addictions besides substance abuse may lead an adolescent to deceive. Just as an adult with a gambling disorder may use deception to conceal their gambling activities, adolescents with internet gaming disorder may lie about the time they spend on the internet, or they may lie to avoid taking responsibility for their behavior.

In these situations, individuals use lying to conceal their addictive behaviors, mitigate the negative consequences, or actively enable them to continue in these destructive behaviors. Lying is a tool that helps support the underlying mental health issue. Thus, it is critical to deal with the underlying harmful behaviors.

Child Abuse and Trauma, Child Custody

Children who have been abused or traumatized may lie to conceal these experiences because of feelings of shame and embarrassment. They may also feel fear repercussions to themselves or loved ones if they tell the truth. In some cases, the child may have been threatened by the instigator of the abuse to keep the abuse a secret. Children who have experienced chronic neglect or abuse may manifest clinical problems as a result of the trauma they have sustained. In such cases, the child may have increased the use of lying and deception as an adaptive mechanism to protect themselves from harm and what the individual may perceive as dangerous social relationships. For instance, a child who has abusive parents may lie to prevent further punitive physical or verbal abuse. In such cases, deception may be a compensatory behavior that the child has developed to help cope with extreme abuse and abandonment. The child uses the lies as a tool for self-protection against victimization and serious threat.

When separation or divorce is occurring between parents, some children and adolescents may start lying more frequently. In some cases, the child may tell lies to achieve their own goals and manipulate their parents' lack of cooperation and communication to help them achieve their goals. They may also tell lies to get attention from parents who may be more involved in arguing between themselves. Or, they may tell lies to create a positive image of themselves to a parent because they fear the parent's abandonment or bad opinion. And, in custody cases, children may either lie of their own accord or through pressure from a parent. In such cases, a child may lie because they perceive a parent to be in trouble, or their goal may be to help a parent. Also, a parent may, at times, ask the child to lie to help conceal a fact or to make a false allegation. There is no evidence, however, that this sort of lying happens frequently in children whose families are going through separation and divorce or in a child custody case.

Deviant Peer Group

Sometimes, frequent lying may start to develop when an adolescent begins spending time with a peer group in which delinquent and antisocial behavior is happening within the group. A youth may lie for acceptance in a group or because of peer group pressure. Association with undesirable peers may lead to activities (e.g., shoplifting) that the teen may prefer to keep from their parents and may increase the necessity to lie. The group may also legitimize such behaviors as normal and acceptable, which may pressure the youth to conform.

Some research has shown that adolescents may be more inclined to lie to cover for a peer when in the presence of the peer or when they felt indebted to the peer. Youths may also lie to peers to conceal truths that they think their peers will consider unfavorable. However, lying becomes a significant problem when it is concealing serious harm to the individual or to others and when it is causing a negative impact on the individual's social relations. In such cases, lying may be a symptom of a larger problem with the youth's affiliation with a negative peer group, and there is a need to help the youth leave that peer group and find alternative friends.

GETTING HELP

Children are born with exceptional potential for social and emotional development, and it takes time for them to learn to behave "properly." Through gradual teaching, guidance, and example, parents can help their children acquire the skills needed to develop positive relationships and behave in pro-social ways. Children may, at times, be aggressive or oppositional to parents' commands, which is often part of normal development. It can be challenging for parents to know when children's behavior needs professional help. For instance, children's oppositional behaviors can arise out of a normal process of individualization and autonomy. There are developmental periods, such as the "terrible twos" or the teenage years, during which such behavior is a normal part of the child's development. Children between 3 and 8 years of age may tell lies more frequently as they learn to manage their own goals and their social relationships. For instance, it is common for young children to lie to get things they want, such as an extra slice of cake or to escape punishment. A few children, though, may fail to learn to recognize how to behave in socially acceptable ways and that lying is an unacceptable way to get what you want or to manipulate others. When these behaviors are excessive, they may merit seeing a professional.

If you see a repetitive and persistent pattern of aggressive, defiant, and antisocial behavior, there may be a deeper problem than developmentally typical behavior. You may need to seek professional help if your child engages in

- frequent lying without a clear cause and for no discernible reason;
- repeated unbelievable and fantastical lies;
- repeated lies that place the liar in a favorable light;
- frequent talk of grandiosity;
- lies to manipulate or control others;
- a pattern of lying that steadily gets worse;

- lies told along with other behaviors, such as intense rage, extreme mood swings, or lack of concern for others' feelings; or

- continuing to lie even when it is interfering with social relationships.

Even if a child shows some of these symptoms, it may not be a persistent problem. You can observe the child and note if there is any pattern. Have there been any recent changes in the child's environment (e.g., a change in family life) that correspond to the increase in lying behavior? Is it always related to a specific theme (e.g., going to school or avoiding a specific activity)? Is it only with parents or at school, or only with friends? Noting when lying occurs and what it is about may help you figure out what is happening that has led the child to start lying more often. If it is a persistent problem lasting over a long period—6 months to a year—then you may need to seek help. Furthermore, even if the lying is developmentally appropriate, it can be frustrating for parents to deal with and can lead to repeated escalating negative reactions. If *you* are having difficulty coping with your child's behavior, then you should feel comfortable about seeking help.

Parents who are concerned about their child's lying behavior can seek help from a therapist or ask a pediatrician for a referral. A professional who has experience working with children can help parents understand and determine whether the lying behavior is age-appropriate or symptomatic of a potential problem. Clinicians may use a variety of approaches to diagnose problems, such as CD, ODD, or other mental health problems, integrating information from behavioral observations, history of mental health, criminal activity (for adolescents), and objective psychological testing.

> If you are having difficulty coping with your child's behavior, then you should feel comfortable about seeking help.

Treatment may also include family therapy, parent training, and psychotherapy to give parents the skills and resources to help them parent their child or adolescent while also empowering the adolescent to cope with problems they face interacting at home and outside the home. Family therapy can help parents and children communicate better. The therapist can help the parent to understand what is happening with the child and to develop strategies for dealing with the lying behavior and other potential problems surrounding the lying behavior. Parents can learn strategies to reduce their child's desire and incentive to lie. Parent management training courses also can be beneficial. These training courses help parents to interact with their children, set clear expectations, recognize and reinforce desirable behaviors, and use effective consequences when necessary. A therapist may also work with the child individually to help them deal with problems and support them to develop more prosocially acceptable ways of interacting with others.

CONCLUSION

For most children, lying is an occasional behavior and not a persistent problem. Most children, like adults, will, from time to time because of specific circumstances and goals, be motivated to tell a lie. In most cases, seeking to understand the motivations behind the lie and the situations in which lying occurs can help adults to determine what is going on and to respond appropriately. However, when lying is a repeated, persistent pattern that children use consistently and frequently for a long period, then it may be a problem. In such cases, seeking professional assistance can help parents to determine if the lying is a problem and if it is related to other behaviors of concern.

Parents who find it hard to cope with their children's lying behavior should seek professional help. Therapists can provide support and strategies to help parents deal with the lies, improve parent–child interactions, and help the child to learn more appropriate behaviors. If lying behavior is having a significantly deleterious effect on your relationship with your child, then ask for help.

Final Thoughts

I started this book by talking about the importance of truthfulness, how vital it is to our relationships, and how we manage our lives and our communities. Presumably, if you have chosen to read this book, you think honesty is important and are concerned about its development in children. I hope that through your reading, you have been able to gain insight into what motivates dishonesty, what promotes honesty, and how we can teach children to be honest.

I would like to reiterate a few points. Adults *can* teach children to be honest. Parents are the first educators. Parents, as well as other significant adults in the child's life, provide examples of how to interact with others and furnish lessons on standards of behavior. If you want your children to grow up to be honest and truthful, you can begin early to emphasize such behavior by modeling honesty and talking about truthfulness as situations arise or as your children encounter examples involving telling the truth or lying. Parents make a significant difference in children's lives. What parents do, what parents say, and how parents act all influence the child and instruct the child about what is good and what is bad.

As parents, we should not take a passive or a reactive role to teach and influence our children to grow to be the adults we wish them to be. If honesty is an important behavior that we wish to inculcate into our children, then we *can* teach children to be honest and foster in them the capacities to help them choose, as they grow, to behave in ways that are prosocial and truthful.

Teaching children about honesty is an ongoing process. It is not a one-time conversation. As the child develops and grows, they will encounter new situations and dilemmas necessitating that they navigate maintaining positive personal relationships, pursue their own goals and desires, and take into consideration others' goals and well-being. You can help your child to understand and develop how to be truthful in these differing situations as they grow. What you teach becomes their foundation on which all other learning and experiences are built.

Yes, there will be bumps. We can't always "be good." Parents will make mistakes, and children will make mistakes. No parent is perfect, and no child is perfect. Life is not a smooth, easy road.

While we often notice dishonesty and focus on lying, most of the time, people are honest. We should be careful not to leap to moral outrage or indignation when we first detect our child is fibbing. People are truthful for the most part, yet we do occasionally lie because we deem it a more expedient thing to do or because our motivations and desires override that default to be truthful. Having that understanding can help us be mindful of our own behavior. Being a parent is an opportunity to reflect on ourselves and to put into practice those principles we feel should govern our life. It is a process, and we, as adults, also grow when we engage in the process. Much of parenting is a continuous learning process for both ourselves and our children, and recognizing that can help us to be compassionate and understanding of our own mistakes and other people's behavior. We have to have compassion for ourselves, and we must have compassion for children.

I hope that after reading this book, you have a much more nuanced understanding of why people tell lies and of how we can encourage in children the standards of honesty and the behavior of truthfulness in their social interactions. We also have to learn not to jump to hasty conclusions or react with moral outrage when we encounter our children's lies. Such reactions may prevent us from helping children to learn how to be truthful when they sometimes feel like lying is the easier, safer option. Having compassion and tolerance as a parent helps us overcome our own mistakes and correct our own behavior as well as remain calm so we can respond gently, firmly, and lovingly to our children.

Finally, savor your time with children. We need to find the positive in the day, to have shared moments of pleasure and love. Within the context of such a relationship, you can deal with all the many different challenges, upsets, and new situations that arise as a child grows and develops their own self-identity and autonomy. Listen when they talk, encourage them to problem-solve, and help them when they are having difficulties. Maintain a compassionate stance and nurture a loving relationship with the child so that within the context of that relationship, you can help teach and guide the child to be a caring, thoughtful, and truthful person.

References

Ahern, E. C., Lyon, T. D., & Quas, J. A. (2011). Young children's emerging ability to make false statements. *Developmental Psychology, 47*(1), 61–66. https://doi.org/10.1037/a0021272

American Psychiatric Association. (2013). *Diagnostic and statistical manual of mental disorders* (5th ed.). https://doi.org/10.1176/appi.books.9780890425596

Ashton, M. C., & Lee, K. (2016). Age trends in HEXACCO-PI-R self-reports. *Journal of Research in Personality, 64*, 102–111. https://doi.org/10.1016/j.jrp.2016.08.008

Barrett, K. C., Zahn-Waxler, C., & Cole, P. M. (1993). Avoiders vs. amenders: Implications for the investigation of guilt and shame during toddlerhood. *Cognition and Emotion, 7*(6), 481–505. https://doi.org/10.1080/02699939308409201

Bond, C. F., Jr., & DePaulo, B. M. (2006). Accuracy of deception judgments. *Personality and Social Psychology Review, 10*(3), 214–234. https://doi.org/10.1207%2Fs15327957pspr1003_2

Bookroo. (n.d.). *Top 10 lying books.* https://bookroo.com/explore/books/topics/lying

Bottoms, B. L., Goodman, G. S., Schwartz-Kenney, B. M., & Thomas, S. N. (2002). Understanding children's use of secrecy in the context of eyewitness reports. *Law and Human Behavior, 26*(3), 285–313. https://doi.org/10.1023/A:1015324304975

Broomfield, K. A., Robinson, E. J., & Robinson, W. P. (2002). Children's understanding about white lies. *British Journal of Developmental Psychology, 20*(1), 47–65. https://doi.org/10.1348/026151002166316

Brummelman, E., Nelemans, S. A., Thomaes, S., & Orobio de Castro, B. (2017). When parents' praise inflates, children's self-esteem deflates. *Child Development, 88*(6), 1799–1809. https://doi.org/10.1111/cdev.12936

Bryan, C. J., Master, A., & Walton, G. M. (2014). "Helping" versus "being a helper": Invoking the self to increase helping in young children. *Child Development, 85*(5), 1836–1842. https://doi.org/10.1111/cdev.12244

Bussey, K. (1992). Lying and truthfulness: Children's definitions, standards, and evaluative reactions. *Child Development, 63*(1), 129–137. https://doi.org/10.1111/j.1467-8624.1992.tb03601.x

Bussey, K. (1999). Children's categorization and evaluation of different types of lies and truths. *Child Development, 70*(6), 1338–1347. https://doi.org/10.1111/1467-8624.00098

Buta, M., Leva, D. S., & Visu-Petra, L. (2015). Who is the tattletale? Linking individual differences in socioemotional competence and anxiety to tattling behavior and attitudes in young children. *Early Education and Development, 26*(4), 496–519. https://doi.org/10.1080/10409289.2015.1000717

Byrne, R. W., & Whiten, A. (1992). Cognitive evolution in primates: Evidence from tactical deception. *Man, 27*(3), 609–627. https://doi.org/10.2307/2803931

Cargill, J. R., & Curtis, D. A. (2017). Parental deception: Perceived effects on parent–child relationships. *Journal of Relationships Research, 8*, Article E1. https://doi.org/10.1017/jrr.2017.1

Cumsille, P., Darling, N., Flaherty, B. P., & Loreto Martínez, M. (2006). Chilean adolescents' beliefs about the legitimacy of parental authority: Individual and age-related differences. *International Journal of Behavioral Development, 30*(2), 97–106. https://doi.org/10.1177/0165025406063554

Cumsille, P., Darling, N., & Loreto Martínez, M. (2010). Shading the truth: The patterning of adolescents' decisions to avoid issues, disclose, or lie to parents. *Journal of Adolescence, 33*(2), 285–296. https://doi.org/10.1016/j.adolescence.2009.10.008

Curtis, D. A., & Hart, C. L. (2020). Pathological lying: Theoretical and empirical support for a diagnostic entity. *Psychiatric Research & Clinical Practice, 2*(2), 62–69. https://doi.org/10.1176/appi.prcp.20190046

Darling, N., Cumsille, P., Caldwell, L. L., & Dowdy, B. (2006). Predictors of adolescents' disclosure to parents and perceived parental knowledge: Between- and within-person differences. *Journal of Youth and Adolescence, 35*(4), 659–670. https://doi.org/10.1007/s10964-006-9058-1

Debey, E., De Schryver, M., Logan, G. D., Suchotzki, K., & Verschuere, B. (2015). From junior to senior Pinocchio: A cross-sectional lifespan investigation of deception. *Acta Psychologica, 160*, 58–68. https://doi.org/10.1016/j.actpsy.2015.06.007

DePaulo, B. M., & Kashy, D. A. (1998). Everyday lies in close and casual relationships. *Journal of Personality and Social Psychology, 74*(1), 63–79. https://doi.org/10.1037/0022-3514.74.1.63

DePaulo, B. M., Kashy, D. A., Kirkendol, S. E., Wyer, M. M., & Epstein, J. A. (1996). Lying in everyday life. *Journal of Personality and Social Psychology, 70*(5), 979–995. https://doi.org/10.1037/0022-3514. 70.5.979

Dike, C. C. (2008, June 1). Pathological lying: Symptom or disease? Living with no permanent motive or benefit. *The Psychiatric Times, 25*(7), 67.

Ding, X. P., Omrin, D. S., Evans, A. D., Fu, G., Chen, G., & Lee, K. (2014). Elementary school children's cheating behavior and its cognitive correlates. *Journal of Experimental Child Psychology, 121,* 85–95. https://doi.org/10.1016/j.jecp.2013.12.005

Dykstra, V. W., Willoughby, T., & Evans, A. D. (2020). A longitudinal examination of the relation between lie-telling, secrecy, parent–child relationship quality, and depressive symptoms in late-childhood and adolescence. *Journal of Youth and Adolescence, 49*(2), 438–448. https://doi.org/10.1007/s10964-019-01183-z

Engarhos, P., Shohoudi, A., Crossman, A., & Talwar, V. (2020). Learning through observing: Effects of modeling truth- and lie-telling on children's honesty. *Developmental Science, 23*(1), Article e12883. https://doi.org/10.1111/desc.12883

Engels, R. C. M. E., Finkenauer, C., & van Kooten, D. (2006). Lying behavior, family functioning and adjustment in early adolescence. *Journal of Youth and Adolescence, 35,* 949–958. https://doi.org/10.1007/ s10964-006-9082-1

Evans, A. D., & Lee, K. (2010). Promising to tell the truth makes 8- to 16-year-olds more honest. *Behavioral Sciences & the Law, 28*(6), 801–811. https://doi.org/10.1002/bsl.960

Friman, P. C., Woods, D. W., Freeman, K. A., Gilman, R., Short, M., McGrath, A. M., & Handwerk, M. L. (2004). Relationships between tattling, likeability, and social classification: A preliminary investigation of adolescents in residential care. *Behavior Modification, 28*(3), 331–348. https://doi.org/10.1177/0145445503258985

Fu, G., Evans, A. D., Wang, L., & Lee, K. (2008). Lying in the name of the collective good: A developmental study. *Developmental Science, 11*(4), 495–503. https://doi.org/10.1111/j.1467-7687.2008.00695.x

Fu, G., Heyman, G. D., Qian, M., Guo, T., & Lee, K. (2016). Young children with a positive reputation to maintain are less likely to cheat. *Developmental Science, 19*(2), 275–283. https://doi.org/10.1111/desc.12304

Fu, G., Xu, F., Cameron, C. A., Heyman, G., & Lee, K. (2007). Cross-cultural differences in children's choices, categorizations, and evaluations of truths and lies. *Developmental Psychology, 43*(2), 278–293. https:// doi.org/10.1037/0012-1649.43.2.278

Ganis, G., & Keenan, J. P. (2009). The cognitive neuroscience of deception. *Social Neuroscience, 4*(6), 465–472. https://doi.org/10.1080/ 17470910802507660

Gershoff, E. T. (2002). Corporal punishment by parents and associated child behaviors and experiences: A meta-analytic and theoretical review. *Psychological Bulletin, 128*(4), 539–579. https://doi.org/10.1037/0033-2909.128.4.539

Gershoff, E. T. (2019, April 15). *Discipline shouldn't be punishing—for the child or the parent.* InfoAboutKids.org. https://infoaboutkids.org/blog/discipline-shouldnt-be-punishing-for-the-child-or-the-parent

Gervais, J., Tremblay, R. E., Desmarais-Gervais, L., & Vitaro, F. (2000). Children's persistent lying, gender differences, and disruptive behaviours: A longitudinal perspective. *International Journal of Behavioral Development, 24*(2), 213–221. https://doi.org/10.1080/016502500383340

Ghanem, C. M., & Mozahem, N. A. (2019). A study of cheating beliefs, engagement, and perception–The case of business and engineering students. *Journal of Academic Ethics, 17*(3), 291–312. https://doi.org/10.1007/s10805-019-9325-x

Gingo, M., Roded, A. D., & Turiel, E. (2017). Authority, autonomy, and deception: Evaluating the legitimacy of parental authority and adolescent deceit. *Journal of Research on Adolescence, 27*(4), 862–877. https://doi.org/10.1111/jora.12319

Grusec, J. E., & Redler, E. (1980). Attribution, reinforcement, and altruism: A developmental analysis. *Developmental Psychology, 16*(5), 525–534. https://doi.org/10.1037/0012-1649.16.5.525

Gunderson, E. A., Donnellan, M. B., Robins, R. W., & Trzesniewski, K. H. (2018). The specificity of parenting effects: Differential relations of parent praise and criticism to children's theories of intelligence and learning goals. *Journal of Experimental Child Psychology, 173*, 116–135. https://doi.org/10.1016/j.jecp.2018.03.015

Heyman, G. D., Hsu, A. S., Fu, G., & Lee, K. (2013). Instrumental lying by parents in the US and China. *International Journal of Psychology, 48*(6), 1176–1184. https://doi.org/10.1080/00207594.2012.746463

Heyman, G. D., Luu, D. H., & Lee, K. (2009). Parenting by lying. *Journal of Moral Education, 38*(3), 353–369. https://doi.org/10.1080/03057240903101630

Ingram, G. P., & Bering, J. M. (2010). Children's tattling: The reporting of everyday norm violations in preschool settings. *Child Development, 81*(3), 945–957. https://doi.org/10.1111/j.1467-8624.2010.01444.x

Jensen, L. A., Arnett, J. J., Feldman, S. S., & Cauffman, E. (2002). It's wrong, but everybody does it: Academic dishonesty among high school and college students. *Contemporary Educational Psychology, 27*(2), 209–228. https://doi.org/10.1006/ceps.2001.1088

Jolly, A. (1996). Primate communication, lies, and ideas. In A. Lock & C. R. Peters (Eds.), *Handbook of human symbolic evolution* (pp. 167–177). Clarendon Press.

Kanngiesser, P., Köymen, B., & Tomasello, M. (2017). Young children mostly keep, and expect others to keep, their promises. *Journal of Experimental Child Psychology, 159*, 140–158. https://doi.org/10.1016/j.jecp.2017.02.004

Kearney, C. A., & Beasley, J. F. (1994). The clinical treatment of school refusal behavior: A survey of referral and practice characteristics. *Psychology in the Schools, 31*(2), 128–132. https://doi.org/10.1002/1520-6807(199404)31:2<128::AID-PITS2310310207>3.0.CO;2-5

Kochanska, G. (1997). Mutually responsive orientation between mothers and their young children: Implications for early socialization. *Child Development, 68*(1), 94–112. https://doi.org/10.2307/1131928

Kochanska, G., & Aksan, N. (1995). Mother–child mutually positive affect, the quality of child compliance to requests and prohibitions, and maternal control as correlates of early internalization. *Child Development, 66*(1), 236–254. https://doi.org/10.2307/1131203

Kochanska, G., & Murray, K. T. (2000). Mother–child mutually responsive orientation and conscience development: From toddler to early school age. *Child Development, 71*(2), 417–431. https://doi.org/10.1111/1467-8624.00154

Lavoie, J., Leduc, K., Arruda, C., Crossman, A. M., & Talwar, V. (2017). Developmental profiles of children's spontaneous lie-telling behavior. *Cognitive Development, 41*, 33–45. https://doi.org/10.1016/j.cogdev.2016.12.002

Lavoie, J., Leduc, K., Crossman, A. M., & Talwar, V. (2016). Do as I say and not as I think: Parent socialisation of lie-telling behaviour. *Children & Society, 30*(4), 253–264. https://doi.org/10.1111/chso.12139

Lavoie, J., Nagar, P. M., & Talwar, V. (2017). From Kantian to Machiavellian deceivers: Development of children's reasoning and self-reported use of secrets and lies. *Childhood, 24*(2), 197–211. https://doi.org/10.1177/0907568216671179

Lavoie, J., & Talwar, V. (2020). Care to share? Children's cognitive skills and concealing responses to a parent. *Topics in Cognitive Science, 12*(2), 485–503. https://doi.org/10.1111/tops.12390

Lavoie, J., Wyman, J., Crossman, A. M., & Talwar, V. (2018). Lie-telling as a mode of antisocial action: Children's lies and behavior problems. *Journal of Moral Education, 47*(4), 432–450. https://doi.org/10.1080/03057240.2017.1405343

Leduc, K., Williams, S., Gomez-Garibello, C., & Talwar, V. (2017). The contributions of mental state understanding and executive functioning to preschool-aged children's lie-telling. *British Journal of Developmental Psychology, 35*(2), 288–302. https://doi.org/10.1111/bjdp.12163

Lee, K., Cameron, C. A., Xu, F., And, G. F., & Board, J. (1997). Chinese and Canadian children's evaluations of lying and truth telling: Similarities and differences in the context of pro-and antisocial behaviors. *Child*

Development, 68(5), 924–934. https://doi.org/10.1111/j.1467-8624.
1997.tb01971.x

Lee, K., Talwar, V., McCarthy, A., Ross, I., Evans, A., & Arruda, C. (2014).
Can classic moral stories promote honesty in children? *Psychological
Science, 25*(8), 1630–1636. https://doi.org/10.1177/0956797614536401

Levine, T. R. (2014). Truth-default theory (TDT): A theory of human deception
and deception detection. *Journal of Language and Social Psychology,
33*(4), 378–392. https://doi.org/10.1177/0261927X14535916

Levine, T. R., Serota, K. B., Carey, F., & Messer, D. (2013). Teenagers lie a
lot: A further investigation into the prevalence of lying. *Communication Research Reports, 30*(3), 211–220. https://doi.org/10.1080/
08824096.2013.806254

Lewis, M., Stanger, C., & Sullivan, M. W. (1989). Deception in 3-year-olds.
Developmental Psychology, 25(3), 439–443. https://doi.org/10.1037/
0012-1649.25.3.439

Loke, I. C., Heyman, G. D., Forgie, J., McCarthy, A., & Lee, K. (2011).
Children's moral evaluations of reporting the transgressions of peers:
Age differences in evaluations of tattling. *Developmental Psychology,
47*(6), 1757–1762. https://doi.org/10.1037/a0025357

Ma, F., Evans, A. D., Liu, Y., Luo, X., & Xu, F. (2015). To lie or not to lie?
The influence of parenting and theory-of-mind understanding on
three-year-old children's honesty. *Journal of Moral Education, 44*(2),
198–212. https://doi.org/10.1080/03057240.2015.1023182

Ma, F., Heyman, G. D., Jing, C., Fu, Y., Compton, B. J., Xu, F., & Lee, K.
(2018). Promoting honesty in young children through observational
learning. *Journal of Experimental Child Psychology, 167*, 234–245.
https://doi.org/10.1016/j.jecp.2017.11.003

Mazar, N., Amir, O., & Ariely, D. (2008). The dishonesty of honest people:
A theory of self-concept maintenance. *Journal of Marketing Research,
45*(6), 633–644. https://doi.org/10.1509/jmkr.45.6.633

Mills, R. S. L., & Grusec, J. E. (1989). Cognitive, affective, and behavioral
consequences of praising altruism. *Merrill-Palmer Quarterly, 35*(3),
299–326. http://www.jstor.org/stable/23086374

Muraven, M., Pogarsky, G., & Shmueli, D. (2006). Self-control depletion
and the general theory of crime. *Journal of Quantitative Criminology,
22*(3), 263–277. https://doi.org/10.1007/s10940-006-9011-1

Nagar, P. M., Caivano, O., & Talwar, V. (2020). The role of empathy in
children's costly prosocial lie-telling behaviour. *Infant and Child
Development, 29*(4), Article e2179. https://doi.org/10.1002/
icd.2179

Newton, P., Reddy, V., & Bull, R. (2000). Children's everyday deception
and performance on false-belief tasks. *British Journal of Developmental Psychology, 18*(2), 297–317. https://doi.org/10.1348/
026151000165706

Perkins, S. A., & Turiel, E. (2007). To lie or not to lie: To whom and under what circumstances. *Child Development, 78*(2), 609–621. https://doi.org/10.1111/j.1467-8624.2007.01017.x

Peskin, J. (1992). Ruse and representations: On children's ability to conceal information. *Developmental Psychology, 28*(1), 84–89. https://doi.org/10.1037/0012-1649.28.1.84

Pipe, M.-E., & Wilson, J. C. (1994). Cues and secrets: Influences on children's event reports. *Developmental Psychology, 30*(4), 515–525.

Popliger, M., Talwar, V., & Crossman, A. (2011). Predictors of children's prosocial lie-telling: Motivation, socialization variables, and moral understanding. *Journal of Experimental Child Psychology, 110*(3), 373–392. https://doi.org/10.1016/j.jecp.2011.05.003

Radcliffe, S. C. (2009). *Raise your kids without raising your voice.* Collins.

Rodriguez, J. (2017, April 27). *5 children's books that encourage honesty.* Scholastic. https://www.scholastic.com/parents/books-and-reading/raise-a-reader-blog/5-childrens-books-encourage-honesty.html

Rogers, R. (1990). Development of a new classificatory model of malingering. *The Bulletin of the American Academy of Psychiatry & the Law, 18*(3), 323–333.

Ross, H. S., & Den Bak-Lammers, I. M. (1998). Consistency and change in children's tattling on their siblings: Children's perspectives on the moral rules and procedures of family life. *Social Development, 7*(3), 275–300. https://doi.org/10.1111/1467-9507.00068

Rudy, D., & Grusec, J. E. (2020). Praise and prosocial behavior. In E. Brummelman (Ed.), *Psychological perspectives on praise* (pp. 103–110). Routledge. https://doi.org/10.4324/9780429327667

Salekin, R. T., Kubak, F. A., Lee, Z., Harrison, N., & Clark, A. P. (2018). Deception in children and adolescents. In R. Rogers & S. D. Bender (Eds.), *Clinical assessment of malingering and deception* (4th ed., pp. 475–496). Guilford Press.

Serota, K. B., & Levine, T. R. (2015). A few prolific liars: Variation in the prevalence of lying. *Journal of Language and Social Psychology, 34*(2), 138–157. https://doi.org/10.1177/0261927X14528804

Serota, K. B., Levine, T. R., & Boster, F. J. (2010). The prevalence of lying in America: Three studies of self-reported lies. *Human Communication Research, 36*(1), 2–25. https://doi.org/10.1111/j.1468-2958.2009.01366.x

Setoh, P., Zhao, S., Santos, R., Heyman, G. D., & Lee, K. (2020). Parenting by lying in childhood is associated with negative developmental outcomes in adulthood. *Journal of Experimental Child Psychology, 189*, Article 104680. https://doi.org/10.1016/j.jecp.2019.104680

Shohoudi Mojdehi, A., Shohoudi, A., & Talwar, V. (2021). Deception or not? Canadian and Persian children's moral evaluations of Taroof. *Current Psychology, 40*, 4372–4383. https://doi.org/10.1007/s12144-019-00341-7

Smetana, J. G., Villalobos, M., Tasopoulos-Chan, M., Gettman, D. C., & Campione-Barr, N. (2009). Early and middle adolescents' disclosure to parents about activities in different domains. *Journal of Adolescence, 32*(3), 693–713. https://doi.org/10.1016/j.adolescence.2008.06.010

Sodian, B., Taylor, C., Harris, P. L., & Perner, J. (1991). Early deception and the child's theory of mind: False trails and genuine markers. *Child Development, 62*(3), 468–483. https://doi.org/10.2307/1131124

Spidel, A., Hervé, H., Greaves, C., & Yuille, J. C. (2011). "Wasn't me!" A field study of the relationship between deceptive motivations and psychopathic traits in young offenders. *Legal and Criminological Psychology, 16*(2), 335–347. https://doi.org/10.1348/135532510X518722

Stern, C., & Stern, W. (1999). *Recollection, testimony, and lying in early childhood* (J. T. Lamiell, Trans.). American Psychological Association. https://doi.org/10.1037/10324-000

Stouthamer-Loeber, M. (1986). Lying as a problem behavior in children: A review. *Clinical Psychology Review, 6*(4), 267–289. https://doi.org/10.1016/0272-7358(86)90002-4

Stouthamer-Loeber, M., & Loeber, R. (1986). Boys who lie. *Journal of Abnormal Child Psychology, 14*(4), 551–564. https://doi.org/10.1007/BF01260523

Suissa, J. (2013). Tiger mothers and praise junkies: Children, praise and the reactive attitudes. *Journal of Philosophy of Education, 47*(1), 1–19. https://doi.org/10.1111/1467-9752.12016

Talwar, V., Arruda, C., & Yachison, S. (2015). The effects of punishment and appeals for honesty on children's truth-telling behavior. *Journal of Experimental Child Psychology, 130*, 209–217. https://doi.org/10.1016/j.jecp.2014.09.011

Talwar, V., & Crossman, A. (2011). From little white lies to filthy liars: The evolution of honesty and deception in young children. *Advances in Child Development and Behavior, 40*, 139–179. https://doi.org/10.1016/B978-0-12-386491-8.00004-9

Talwar, V., Crossman, A., & Wyman, J. (2017). The role of executive functioning and theory of mind in children's lies for another and for themselves. *Early Childhood Research Quarterly, 41*, 126–135. https://doi.org/10.1016/j.ecresq.2017.07.003

Talwar, V., Gordon, H. M., & Lee, K. (2007). Lying in the elementary school years: Verbal deception and its relation to second-order belief understanding. *Developmental Psychology, 43*(3), 804–810. https://doi.org/10.1037/0012-1649.43.3.804

Talwar, V., Lavoie, J., Gomez-Garibello, C., & Crossman, A. M. (2017). Influence of social factors on the relation between lie-telling and children's cognitive abilities. *Journal of Experimental Child Psychology, 159,* 185–198. https://doi.org/10.1016/j.jecp.2017.02.009

Talwar, V., & Lee, K. (2002a). Development of lying to conceal a transgression: Children's control of expressive behaviour during verbal deception. *International Journal of Behavioral Development, 26*(5), 436–444. https://doi.org/10.1080/01650250143000373

Talwar, V., & Lee, K. (2002b). Emergence of white-lie telling in children between 3 and 7 years of age. *Merrill-Palmer Quarterly, 48*(2), 160–181. https://doi.org/10.1353/mpq.2002.0009

Talwar, V., & Lee, K. (2008). Social and cognitive correlates of children's lying behavior. *Child Development, 79*(4), 866–881. https://doi.org/10.1111/j.1467-8624.2008.01164.x

Talwar, V., & Lee, K. (2011). A punitive environment fosters children's dishonesty: A natural experiment. *Child Development, 82*(6), 1751–1758. https://doi.org/10.1111/j.1467-8624.2011.01663.x

Talwar, V., Lee, K., Bala, N., & Lindsay, R. C. L. (2002). Children's conceptual knowledge of lying and its relation to their actual behaviors: Implications for court competence examinations. *Law and Human Behavior, 26*(4), 395–415. https://doi.org/10.1023/A:1016379104959

Talwar, V., Lee, K., Bala, N., & Lindsay, R. C. L. (2004). Children's lie-telling to conceal a parent's transgression: Legal implications. *Law and Human Behavior, 28*(4), 411–435. https://doi.org/10.1023/B:LAHU.0000039333.51399.f6

Talwar, V., Murphy, S. M., & Lee, K. (2007). White lie-telling in children for politeness purposes. *International Journal of Behavioral Development, 31*(1), 1–11. https://doi.org/10.1177/0165025406073530

Talwar, V., Williams, S. M., Renaud, S. J., Arruda, C., & Saykaly, C. (2016). Children's evaluations of tattles, confessions, prosocial and antisocial lies. *International Review of Pragmatics, 8*(2), 334–352. https://doi.org/10.1163/18773109-00802007

Turiel, E. (2002). *The culture of morality: Social development, context, and conflict.* Cambridge University Press.

Vitacco, M. J. (2018). Syndromes associated with deception. In R. Rogers & S. D. Bender (Eds.), *Clinical assessment of malingering and deception* (4th ed., pp. 83–97). The Guilford Press.

Wagland, P., & Bussey, K. (2005). Factors that facilitate and undermine children's beliefs about truth telling. *Law and Human Behavior, 29,* 639–655. https://doi.org/10.1007/s10979-005-7371-y

Warneken, F., & Orlins, E. (2015). Children tell white lies to make others feel better. *British Journal of Developmental Psychology, 33*(3), 259–270. https://doi.org/10.1111/bjdp.12083

Whiten, A., & Byrne, R. W. (1988). Tactical deception in primates. *Behavioral and Brain Sciences*, *11*(2), 233–244. https://doi.org/10.1017/S0140525X00049682

Williams, S., Moore, K., Crossman, A. M., & Talwar, V. (2016). The role of executive functions and theory of mind in children's prosocial lie-telling. *Journal of Experimental Child Psychology*, *141*, 256–266. https://doi.org/10.1016/j.jecp.2015.08.001

Xu, F., Bao, X., Fu, G., Talwar, V., & Lee, K. (2010). Lying and truth-telling in children: From concept to action. *Child Development*, *81*(2), 581–596. https://doi.org/10.1111/j.1467-8624.2009.01417.x

Index

About the Author

Victoria Talwar, PhD, is a professor and the chair of the Department of Educational & Counselling Psychology at McGill University. She is a recognized leading expert on children's deception. She has published numerous articles on children's honesty and lie-telling behaviors in leading peer-reviewed publications, including *Child Development*, *Developmental Review*, *Journal of Experimental Child Psychology*, and *Psychological Science*. Dr. Talwar has given workshops to parents, teachers, social workers, and legal professionals. Her research has been funded by the Social Sciences and Humanities Research Council, the Canadian Foundation for Excellence, the Natural Sciences and Engineering Research Council, the National Science Foundation, and Fonds de Recherche sur la Société et la Culture. Among others distinctions, she was awarded the Society for Research on Child Development Outstanding Early Career Contributions to Child Development Research award. She is a Fellow of the American Psychological Association (Division 7), a Fellow of the Association for Psychological Science, and a member of the College of the Royal Society of Canada.